GAIJIN

Nine Cautionary Tales of Life
in Japan's English Teaching Community

Peter Smith

BookLocker

St. Petersburg, Florida

Print ISBN: 978-1-64719-504-5

Epub ISBN: 978-1-64719-505-2

Mobi ISBN: 978-1-64719-506-9

Published by BookLocker.com, Inc., St. Petersburg, Florida.

Printed on acid-free paper.

The characters and events in this book are fictitious. Any similarity to real persons, living or dead, is coincidental and not intended by the author.

BookLocker.com, Inc.

2021

First Edition

Library of Congress Cataloguing in Publication Data

Smith, Peter

GAIJIN: Nine Cautionary Tales of Life in Japan's English

Teaching Community by Peter Smith

Library of Congress Control Number: 2021915699

ACKNOWLEDGEMENTS

I'd like to thank the many friends who patiently read through early drafts for their support and encouragement in pushing the whole project forward, among them Mike Rupp, Jeff Morrow, Neil McRobert, Kevin Axton, Masako Iyae, Tomoko Takahashi, Ayumi Sakagami and Chiaki Yamashita.

Special mention is reserved for Greg Meline, Martin Cameron, Robert Mortensen, Michael Smith, William Kervin, Katy Yoshida, Simon Longstaff, Holly Olsen, "Odie", Brendan Buckland, Jayne Ito, Donella Zakaria and Donald C. Gibson, for their comments, suggestions, corrections, and criticisms (plus help in tracking down the elusive Sam!). And extra special thanks to Paul de Vries for his invaluable help in pushing it over the line.

Finally, a big debt of gratitude to all the thousands of talented, inspiring and hard-working people here in Japan, both foreigners and Japanese, whose paths have crossed mine, many of whom appear fleetingly in the following pages, and who have helped to enrich beyond measure the life of this simple Gaijin.

Table of Contents

PART ONE: ARRIVAL

1) The First Gaijin

The question was: What would it do if it saw me?

Holding my breath and grasping the reedy branches of the rather flimsy tree I was precariously perched in, I stared down in wonder at the creature prowling barely twenty metres away oblivious of my existence - for now. The salty taste of the morning's chipmunk I'd killed with my hand-crafted sling lingered on my tongue.

I realized I was one of the only living humans to lay eyes on the fabled Ziqi-Jiang - "Terror of the Tundra". It was believed to have become extinct over a hundred years ago. It would appear that this was not the case.

The legends of this little-known carnivore had caught my imagination as a child - and the handful of accounts of unconfirmed sightings were what had inspired me to turn my back on a promising accounting career, pack it all in - ignoring the outraged (but all too predictable) wails and protests of my resolutely conservative family ("Are you out of your mind?") - and head out to the northern Steppes of Asia two years ago.

Images flashed through my mind of the time leading up to this moment: Fifteen months living amid the Sheragg people of Central Siberia had left me unrecognizable from the innocent boy I had been. What would my former colleagues' reaction be, were I to walk through the doors of the Bradford branch of Dorkson & Associates in my current state? Glancing down, I caught sight of the spectacular green and orange flames adorning my inner thigh. I remembered the searing pain of the tattoo. It's no disgrace to admit that I almost fainted. But now it was my badge of honour; the only Westerner ever to have been accepted by this rarely seen, semi-mythical group of nomads.

When they found me, dehydrated and delirious, I had been mere hours from death. My training as an accountant hadn't prepared me for the hardships of a sun-baked desert. I owed them my life and so much more. They had saved me, fed me and nursed me back from the brink. During my convalescence I had learned from them the knowledge which would allow me to survive this bleak and hostile land, knowledge which I arrogantly thought I already possessed. Resisting temperatures which plunged to minus 40 and below by coating yourself head to toe with grease from the tekipaki porcupine; How to stare down any roaming predator; How to draw precious liquid into the body by sucking the roots of the roaark plant, or licking the anus of the Siberian woolly hamster. How to carve a sling from the wood of a zabooki tree and then track and kill the rare sources of food on the plain. I was indebted to this proud people. What an incredible experience it had been, and it hadn't been without romance - how close I'd come to accepting their offer of matrimony to the feisty Jingha. Surely I would never come across the likes of her anywhere in my native West Yorkshire, nor probably even in Lancashire.

But I had never lost sight of my original goal and it was with a pain in my heart that I'd bid her - and her people - farewell, That final night we made love from sunset to sunrise - according to ancient tribal custom her two nubile sisters had to join in too - and since then I hadn't had any human contact at all. But I didn't need it. Confident now in my ability to live off the land, I'd kept pushing myself forward each day to the furthest horizons in my quest to catch a glimpse of the Ziqi-Jiang and now here it was, almost close enough to touch.

It stopped. It had sensed me. Slowly turning round and cocking its head up, I found myself staring into the burning eyes of this awesome creature. I gulped. I was on my own, my sling useless against such an adversary. I knew it could shake me out of the tree as easily as a ripe apricot. My chances of survival depended entirely on the hypnotizing technique passed down the generations of Sheragg. Had I mastered it? Would it work, or would that chipmunk be my last taste of earthly food?

Damn, wouldn't it be great to start a book like that?

Well, wouldn't it? That was always the way I imagined my future lay. Exploring some remote corner of the planet with adventures around every corner, dangers at every turn. Eye-popping natural marvels wherever I looked. But it didn't exactly turn out like that. The reality was somewhat tamer, notably lacking any tales of initiation rituals or sightings of rare endangered beasts.

You can only write the truth after all.

So my story is about the country I chose to move to in 1994.

After a standard British childhood spent playing far too much tennis and snooker while never managing to improve in either, largely in fact just killing time, waiting, itching to get old enough to catch the next train, plane or camel to far-off places, now that time had finally arrived: I was about to start my new life.

Asia was my destination, that much is true, but it would be far away from the savage lands peopled by the *Sheragg* tribes. Instead I'd be heading to one of the most technologically advanced, aggressively urban societies in the world: Japan.

So maybe no *Ziqi-Jiang* lurking among the trees awaiting me there, probably no need for hand crafted hunting tools, but surely there must be some different kind of thrills in store, possibly - you never know - even more exciting.

But what was the name of the location within Japan where my Asian adventure would start? Simple answer: Saitama. Hmm, it had a certain ring to it. I could imagine it on a map marking a desert, a recently discovered palace from some barely remembered civilization or a tiny emerald island in the South Pacific. No? At any rate it certainly sounded more alluring than most of the towns near my Yorkshire home. "Where would you like to spend the next year of your life, sir: Pontefract, Grimsby or Saitama?"

I mean, seriously, how was I supposed to know that it would turn out to be every bit as dull as the worst my beloved England had to offer?

Now I shouldn't complain. I will of course, but I really shouldn't. After all, the interview to land the job could hardly have been easier. I had no special training, no expert skills to offer. Just a desire to go and work somewhere interesting, different, maybe even a little exotic. Japan certainly offered that while also, rather conveniently, having an insatiable demand for English teachers.

Teaching English: That was something I had some experience in. And so I found myself in Swindon, waiting to be called in for my interview, bracing myself to come up with suitable answers to whatever questions I might be asked. Despite my lack of experience applying for jobs, I don't think I was sweating too profusely even before I sat down in the interview room and nothing over the following ten minutes sparked any increase in glandular activity. Let's be honest: "What's your name?" "Why do you want to go to Japan?" and "When can you start?" hardly add up to the most sweat-inducing questions a job applicant can face. The only potentially tricky one there was the second, to which the honest answer would have been something along the lines of: "Well, I've been to few countries, would like to go somewhere further afield and, hell, the salary you guys are offering is better than anywhere else in the world that I'm aware of."

I imagine that even if I'd said as much, I probably would have got the job, but obviously made an earnest attempt to answer as if my life depended on it, doubtless mentioning my admiration for Japanese culture (untrue), my desire to not only teach the language, but also to educate the Japanese about Britain and its multi-faceted culture (partially true). I think. By any standards it certainly didn't qualify as a rigorous interview. On the bus back home that evening, I congratulated myself on not having obviously screwed up. I was particularly confident in my answers to questions one and three. And when I received the letter a week or so later informing me of my having successfully passed the interview and that therefore I would be flying out to Japan the following month, I allowed myself a silent, triumphant whoop and then after a quick family celebration, I was able to turn my attention to the accompanying form. As well as the standard formula congratulating me on getting the job, I was invited to choose three places that I would prefer to live in upon my arrival in that distant country.

I spent far more time researching these potential destinations than I ever had preparing for the interview. With no real interest in Japan per se, my knowledge of the country was most definitely limited. In fact, off the top of my head I would probably have been able to name exactly three cities: Tokyo, Hiroshima and Nagasaki. None of these struck me as particularly desirable places to live. The biggest metropolis on earth? No thank you. The only two cities ever to suffer atomic bomb hits? Hmm, think I'll pass.

So where then? Well, that's what *Lonely Planet* is for! Copy purchased, I settled back to see where I'd fancy spending the next year of my life. The first place to grab my attention was Hokkaido. The northernmost of Japan's four main islands, Hokkaido was famous for its long, icy winters, fabulous skiing and mild summers. Sparsely populated, with a stunning volcanic landscape, it was an outdoor enthusiasts' dream. The only place in Japan where it would be possible to lose yourself in nature. Think the Scottish Highlands, just swap the haggis and kilts for sushi and kimonos. Very tempting. Or then again, what about Kyoto? The historic capital of the country, one of the few major cities in Japan spared extensive bombing at the end of World War II purely on account of its cultural legacy. Awe-inspiring shrines whichever way you looked, home of geisha, and the culinary capital of the country to boot. Surely that wouldn't be a bad choice either?

But the more I flicked through the pages, the more I became aware of the sheer amount of extremely attractive cities in Japan which I felt I'd be ready to move to in a heartbeat. How about Sendai, a large urban centre located midway between Hokkaido and Tokyo? Hiroshima turned out to be an attractive, thriving city, with ski slopes on its northern borders and Greek-like islands off its southern coastline. Other cities I'd never heard of: Fukuoka, Nagano, Niigata. Blimey! There were simply countless possibilities.

There was one city above all that jumped out at me: Kobe. Never heard of that place before, but apparently it was very popular with foreigners in Japan. Aside from boasting a great location less than an hour from Osaka or Kyoto, it was a good-sized city centre in its own right and beautiful mountains and a stunning coastline were both but a short drive away.

By now I was practically drooling. I had fun scribbling down the different Japanese cities. Sendai or Nagano? Hiroshima or Fukuoka? How to choose a top three from so many fabulous choices? I doubtless spent far too long shuffling all these names around before ending up with my definitive choice. Hokkaido and Kyoto were ultimately the most appealing places, but realizing that everyone else would reach the same conclusion, I decided to put Kobe top. Pretty smart there Pete, I thought, as I popped the letter in the post. A few days later, I received the reply.

And I was allocated Saitama.

And I wondered how far that was from Kobe. And I wondered why Saitama didn't feature too heavily in the guide book.

I wasn't unduly disappointed. Weren't all those other places I'd read about in *Lonely Planet* rather enticing? Maybe Japan was a country filled with hidden gems.

In a way, it was a sense of déjà-vu. Upon leaving high school, I'd worked as an assistant language teacher in France. I hadn't been given any choice as to my town of residence there and remember being rather shocked when I'd been assigned a school in Gers, simply because I'd never heard of the place. Of course! Why would I have? A cursory glance at any decent sized map of France would have been enough to reveal the depths of my ignorance regarding the general geography of the country. OK, so I considered myself a certified Francophile. I'd just enrolled on a B.A. of French and had developed a taste for the novels of Marcel Pagnol, Francois Mauriac and Henri Troyat; but how arrogant of me to think that a handful of trips to some of the more visited areas and a reading of maybe a dozen novels set in mostly fictional towns in provincial France could possibly have instilled in me anything but the vaguest appreciation of one of the most diverse countries in Europe. Toulouse and Bordeaux: OK. Anything in the hundreds of miles separating the two: Agen or Montauban? Auch or Moissac? Absolutely not.

Yet hadn't Gers turned out just fine? Surely Saitama would too.

It was probably not too surprising to discover that Saitama was actually nowhere near Kobe. Or Kyoto or Hokkaido, for that matter. It was located on Tokyo's northern border and it was mainly notable, it seemed, for its cluster of residential cities. No-one told me at this stage that its Japanese nick-name was "Dasai-tama", for which a reasonable translation might be "Shite-tama". Nobody in their right mind would actually choose to come and live in Saitama. Especially when there were so many other great places you could pick! All of this would be revealed to me in the fullness of time. But for now, blissfully ignorant of any shortcomings in the place which I would soon be calling home, I slept peacefully. There were two big plusses in any case. The first was that Saitama was only a short train ride from Tokyo, meaning it was easy to get to in the first place. The second, which I would not appreciate for another four months, was that Saitama was not Kobe.

On Jan 17 1995, at 5:46 am, Kobe was rocked by a massive earthquake, the biggest since the famous Tokyo quake 72 years earlier. The result: 6400 deaths and billions of dollars of damage. 400 miles away in Saitama, I would not be one of its victims. I may have been just starting to curse the application procedure which had left me in such an uninspiring place, but I had to later admit that possibly the company's policy of completely ignoring fresh applicants' requests of city of residence just might have saved my life.

So I was on the flight from Heathrow to Narita, Japan, my first trip to Asia. I was travelling with a small group of five Brits, all flying together to our new country of employment. At some unspecified point of the journey, unbeknownst to us, a painless and magical transformation had taken place. We didn't feel any different, but we were all (as of now) technically Gaijin. There was that delicious sensation of touching down in an unfamiliar land. What would await us here? Arrival in any new country is one of those times when time slows down. When you know this place will be your new home it almost seems to stop. Animal instincts kick in. Details which in everyday life barely register suddenly take on absurd levels of importance: The first glimpse of the country from the aeroplane window. The first breath of Asian air upon exiting the plane. The Chinese characters on every poster as you walk to Passport Control. The oriental smells wafting over on entering the airport lounge. The announcements in a language you don't understand. The airport workers' spotless uniforms.

And...the first Gaijin.

Still unaware of my own metamorphosis, I gawped. There was no shortage of Gaijin in Narita airport: Families, businessmen, tourists. But the only one of these that mattered was: A short, unattractive male New Zealander in his mid-thirties with a slight limp. He'd been sent from the company to meet and greet the latest group of recruits. There he was, easy to spot in his crumpled suit, holding up a company sign, ready to guide us from Narita to the main company branch in Shibuya. I don't recall his name. I remember that he seemed vaguely embarrassed in his role as shepherd - and he was right to be. All in all, one of the least impressive examples of the human species I'd come across in my 24 years on this planet. But nonetheless: My First Real Gaijin. The first example of a non-Japanese resident in this country - and I was fascinated by him. It was like laying eyes on a lion, spider monkey or alpaca for the first time. I would hazard that the lion we see in the local zoo probably isn't much of a lion. Back in the wild he'd be scoffed at, taunted by his friends.

"Call yourself a lion?" they'd say. "You ain't no REAL lion. Look at your brother, Zak. Now *there's* a real lion."

But at the zoo, those of us watching from outside the cage are unaware of the particular grades of lion, the shortcomings of the particular specimen in front of us. We've never met Zak, and we're happy acknowledging that the caged creature in front of us, pathetic though he may be to his peers, is no tabby, no Siamese cat. To us, he's a lion and that's enough. But that's where the metaphor ends. Because while I knew nothing of lions, I was no stranger to humans, and even with the limited depth of experience of my tender years, I could tell right away that this guy was a complete muppet.

"Nice to meet you," I offered.

"Yeah," he replied, avoiding eye contact. Did he fear my killer stare? He moved his weight from one foot to another, as if he needed to go to the toilet. The brown suit couldn't hide the fact that this was a scruffy dude. His constant weight-shifting drew attention to the scuffed shoes sticking out from beneath his creased brown trousers which were at least two sizes too long. His un-ironed shirt was unevenly stuffed down his belt and the whole impression was topped off by the untidy fringe hanging down over his forehead. It was fair to assume he was not the owner of a comb. You didn't need to get too close up to know there would be generous sprinklings of dandruff on his shoulders. One of those people you simply knew would have body odour.

So who exactly was this brother-of-Zak, and why was he the one sent to collect us? It was a company whose main selling point was that the entire teaching staff was composed of Real Gaijin. Native Japanese, I would discover, were used for all office duties, but Gaijin were essentially only ever used as teachers, one of the very few exceptions to this being meeting new recruits at the airport. But why had this task fallen to this individual, I wondered? Was he the one who had volunteered, thereby avoiding tiresome teaching time; or had he been specifically assigned for out-of-classroom duty out of

17

sympathy for the poor students? Whatever the truth, this slightly smelly, wholly mediocre character was my introduction to the world of occasionally eccentric misfits who'd chosen to make Japan their home.

The questions kept coming: Was this a typical Gaijin? Were Gaijin to be noticeably different from their cousins in their countries of origin; or were they a strange hybrid? Was there some strange behavioural quirk which marked them out as Gaijin, either before they landed in Japan, or through some mysterious process upon their arrival? More worryingly, would I end up like this if I stayed here long enough? Who knew? For now, suffice it to say he was a rather odd boy.

Genuinely curious about my new surroundings and momentarily stepping close enough to confirm both the B.O. and dandruff theories, I tried that ancient human art, the one that bonds us all - the very reason for our being here in the first place, no less: Conversation. And it was clear that our first impressions were not mistaken. He was, to be charitable, not entirely in his element meeting new people. I was full of queries about this country I'd just landed in, thousands of miles from anywhere I'd ever been on the planet before. But everything I tried to ask was met by a one word answer or a range of peculiar grunts, more usually associated with other species of primate - a bonobo perhaps? - and whose precise meaning was unclear. Aside from his inability to provide anything approaching satisfactory answers to our many questions, there was no curiosity on his part as to the new arrivals. No effort was made to give us any insights into what lay ahead. No anecdotes, no teasing, nothing. All his concentration was focused on making sure we got on the right train, and shortly after boarding the Narita-Shinjuku Express, we were happy to let him be, turning our attention instead to the sights flashing past the window. Once his flock had been safely delivered, he slipped away, both out of the room and out of our consciousness, and I never heard any mention of him again.

But his job was done. We had arrived in the country which some of us would call home for many years. And I was in Shite (tama).

I should probably add a few words about the company I'd joined. The name was Mega, or "Mega English Academy", and for two heady decades Mega was one of the most well-known brand names in Japan. Incredible in a country which could boast some of the most famous names in automobiles or electronics: Toyota, Nissan, Honda, Panasonic, Hitachi, Sony. Whether measured by profitability or recognizability on the street, Mega belonged to that rarified group. Having started out in the mid-1980s, Mega adopted a fast-food approach to teaching English and before long no city was complete without its Mega branch. A place where Japanese could go and meet a bunch of authentic foreigners. And learn English. A stunningly simple concept, and a stunningly successful one too. By the early 1990s, Mega was firmly entrenched in the two biggest urban areas, based around Tokyo and Osaka. Saitama, one of the 47 "prefectures" - counties - in Japan, had 30 schools. And it was aggressively expanding into every other prefecture.

The school I'd be working in was one of two branches in Omiya City, Saitama's administrative capital and probably the largest city I'd ever been in my life entirely devoid of interest. There was a huge station. There were lots of buildings, offices, shops and restaurants. There was a whole lot of something going on, like in any sizable urban centre. But what could you say? In spite of all the crowds, there didn't seem to be anything there. Omiya, the tenth largest city in Japan, didn't even warrant a mention in *Lonely Planet.*

A few months later, I would start speculating on whether the Mega schools around Japan might have been shaped by their locations. Was Hokkaido Mega filled with eager winter sports enthusiasts, disappearing every day off to hit the slopes and coming into the school with wonderful stories of unbeatable powder and off-piste courses to die for? Perhaps Kyoto's schools had a more scholarly feel, with conversations revolving around the countless shrines and temples. At weekends, maybe teachers and students would shoot off to search out the answers to questions which had surfaced during the previous week's lesson and each class might be a harmonious, joyous occasion in which each member would compete to pass on any nuggets they'd unearthed from the previous weekend's investigations.

It seemed unlikely. But it might conceivably explain the lack of spark which was immediately evident upon walking through the entrance of Omiya-Kita. Were the negative vibes I was receiving nothing to do with the company but merely a reflection of the uninspiring city of Omiya? Whatever the case may be, there was no denying this was not the happiest of working environments.

On my first day at my new workplace, a quick round of introductions to the dozen or so teachers in the room spectacularly failed to ignite any emotion to speak of. Everyone there notably had that palpable "Been here too long, met too many other new faces, don't need to know you" face and attitude. "Nice to meet you, now piss off." Hardly the friendliest bunch, on top of which my new teaching colleagues were not the types you'd take for teachers at all, which made complete sense as very few of them had come from any kind of teaching background.

There was Clive, an immaculately dressed, perfectly groomed, perfectly vacuous American who always hung his mobile phone on the doorknob at the start of every lesson - in 1994 mobiles were still an unusual sight - and made absolutely no secret of his boredom when his students were middle-aged businessmen rather than young twenty-something office ladies. Did he ever even say hello to me?

Dawn was another American who likewise had that unmistakable look of "Take me out of here pur-lease!"

"How long have you been here, Dawn?" I asked.

"Oh, God, almost like...nine months?" she answered. A barely imaginable length of time in this job, it seemed. I think it was our only conversation.

Dawn seemed to have the hots for Carl, a wannabe actor from Adelaide, who could be either funny or brutal depending on his mood. Carl radiated a certain charisma notably lacking in his colleagues and I tried to ingratiate myself with him.

"Get up to anything last weekend?" I chirpily asked, shortly after arriving.

"Errm, nothing much. Oh, wait, I got married." I can only assume he was practicing his deadpan comedy. Another time, I hoped to make him laugh by cheekily showing him the teachers' comments book and how badly his handwriting seemed to have deteriorated in less than a year on the job.

"What's your point, Peter?!" he thundered back at me, channelling his inner Samuel Jackson and scaring the bejeezes out of me.

Albert was a crew-cut native of Kentucky who had - as if we couldn't guess - spent some time in the army back home. Quickly promoted military style to assistant head teacher, it was very difficult for Albert to accept that the other staff, far from responding to the aura of respect and authority which he tried so desperately to exude, would be more likely to snigger instead, maybe occasionally raising a salute behind his back.

One of the few trained teachers there, Timothy - like me another brand new recruit from England - had had some Albert-esque mock-in-the-face-of-authority experience at his first middle school, which had been his downfall. He'd lasted precisely one year before jacking it in, slightly aghast at the reality of teaching in comprehensive schools in England and deciding that his future lay away - preferably very far away - from his home country.

Timothy had a knack of making life more complicated than it needed to be. He decided to take a trip to Laos with some of his new Mega teacher friends during the New Year holiday, only a matter of days after moving into his new flat in Kasukabe - another drab Saitama city a thirty minute train ride from Omiya. It was an incident-filled tour by all accounts, involving delayed planes, arguments over visas, plus healthy lashings of general culture shock, mostly to do with the almost complete lack of English speakers in Laos at the time. Relief upon returning to the country he'd called home for barely two months soon dissipated as he realized that he had no idea how to get to his flat; he couldn't even remember the name of the town. He spent his first night back in a hotel and the whole of the next day trying with increasing desperation to retrace the journey he'd only made a handful of times, the nightmare only ending when he fortuitously bumped into his flat-mate in a convenience store.

Then there was poor 22 year old New Yorker Shantel. Another new arrival, she seemed to look up to me, probably as I didn't ignore her like most of the other old-timers did. She also endeared herself to me early on by her somewhat naïve questions regarding her students' lack of grasp of basic matters of English grammar.

"Why don't they use 'the' and 'a'?" she would say.

"Well, that's kind of our job, Shantel," I told her. "Those words don't exist in Japanese, so we have to teach them how and when to use them."

"And sometimes," she continued, "I have to repeat the same question four or five times."

"Well, same thing, you know. It's not their native language which is kind of the whole point of us being here in the first place."

She looked at me, rather puzzled. Nice girl, Shantel, but a lot to learn. Now while all of us still stood out to a certain extent in a Japanese society where even in Tokyo remarkably few non-Japanese faces could be spotted, Shantel was immeasurably more exotic. She was an African-American · the only black member of staff · and there were virtually no black people living in Japan at that time. Inevitably, whenever Shantel walked down the street she drew stares. For most Japanese people, she would be one of the very first black people they had ever seen in the flesh. Some took a second glance. Some stared. Some gawped. And Shantel took it very badly indeed.

"Why does everybody gawk?" she complained. "Nobody seen a black girl before?" She soon took to sticking out her tongue at anyone who stared at her too long. She probably spent an unhealthy amount of time with her tongue outside her mouth. It wasn't long before she decided that she wasn't ready for Japan - or Japan wasn't ready for her and moved back to New York.

Omiya-Kita was a microcosm of the kind of characters I'd be meeting over the rest of my teaching life in Japan. Some pleasant people, most normal enough, but I couldn't help feeling that the concentration of slightly odd characters was rather denser than one might reasonably expect. And let's not forget the considerable few who were just downright weird. I mean seriously what was going on here? Christine had a manic intensity in her stare and smiled way too much, whereas Laura seemed constantly on the verge of tears, but nobody could tell why. Jake made a point of ignoring everyone, while Andy simply had to be related to the Kiwi at the airport, sharing the same issues of hygiene, fashion and conversation style even though he was from Ireland. It sometimes crossed my mind that a visitor to the staff room could be forgiven for thinking he had stumbled into the local mental institution.

The other school in Omiya was bigger and - if the rumours were true - even fuller of oddballs. I had no reason to doubt this, in fact every reason to avoid it as far as possible and I never reached out to this, or indeed any other of the dozens of Mega branches within a short train ride of Omiya. Of course! I hadn't come all this way to hang out with a bunch of foreigners. Japan and the Japanese were the main focus of my attention. If I'd inevitably be spending time working with other Gaijin then fair enough; but the mostly good folk of Omiya-Kita were plenty enough.

And of all these, special mention must go to Sam, whose story highlights many of the themes that I would become more familiar with further down the line. Sam was an American. A tall gawky American. A tall gawky American who loved playing the trombone. I tend to like gawky people. Not necessarily tall people, nor trombone players or Americans that much. But somehow it's always easier to make friends with people who are a little awkward in their physical movements than those who move around with confidence.

Sam liked to talk. He even talked in a kind of gawky way. He specialized in grievances. This is not to say that he didn't have an awful lot to moan about, but his complaints tended to be delivered in a gawky monotone drawl that left most listeners searching for an excuse to get away within seconds. I'm pretty sure that Dawn never gave Sam the time of day. I imagine also that Carl and Sam also never had too much to talk about, should they happen to be sharing a break together.

In a slightly embarrassing aside, one of the most interesting things about living in a foreign land and being around people from different countries, quite apart from the more obvious constant bombardment of new cultural experiences, is the random way you suddenly twig things that you really should have known many years ago, but didn't, for whatever reason. I have Sam to thank for my realization that "aeroplane" is a British only spelling. I remember well his confused look as I spelled out the last few letters during a teacher-student game of hangman. "We usually spell it 'airplane'," he said, scratching his neck, wondering what the heck they teach kids in schools in Britain. And the penny dropped. Those classic American comedy movies would, if made in Britain, simply have been called *Aeroplane*. Kind of disappointing, though I have no idea why.

Sam was never happier than when he was playing his trombone. He'd found a jazz club and he joined in the live shows once or twice a week, so a few of us including Sam's girlfriend, Miyako, felt duty bound to go along and support him occasionally. Actually, thinking about it, I went exactly one time. Jazz was never really my thing and even though I really wanted to support a friend doing something worthwhile and creative outside of teaching, well...let's just say that jazz isn't my thing.

Whatever your musical tastes, I don't think anybody would disagree that Sam was far more entertaining when he was simply drunk. And on most nights when he wasn't practicing trombone or hanging out with Miyako, he would join us in one of the numerous "Izakaya" restaurants or, even better, go and shoot some pool together. And almost every time Sam was drunk and holding a pool cue, there was a very good chance that something would get broken, or someone would be forced into taking sudden evasive action. His physical awkwardness increased with every beer, until at a certain point not too late in the evening suddenly something as simple as going to the toilet would become a huge challenge for him.

Any averagely tall foreigner in Japan requires constant vigilance to avoid bumping their head, but a simple duck is enough in most cases. Sam, standing around 6'4", had to stoop his whole body in a very ungainly manner that was entirely new to him since his arrival in the country. And while he was capable of this sober, performing two relatively simple movements · like bending down while moving his feet · seemed to be enormously difficult after a few drinks. So, a couple of minutes after disappearing into the gents toilet, suddenly Sam would come flying out, apparently all his brain focused on stooping low enough to avoid a painful bang on the head, and his legs - not receiving any signal as to how they should proceed - basically out of control. And in a bizarre headless-chicken-meets-newborn-pony kind of way, he'd emerge from the toilet, stagger across the room and crash into the wall on the opposite side. Most entertaining. I can only assume he always refrained from drinking when playing trombone in his jazz club. The mind boggles at the potential for damage.

Now this side story serves an important purpose, as we zoom in a little closer on Sam and what he was doing here in Japan. I have no memory at all of ever having had any knowledge of Dawn's, Carl's or Shantel's reasons for coming to Japan, but Sam had one. He'd met a Japanese girl while he was living in the US, and...they'd fallen in love. He'd followed her across the Pacific, having encountered no problems at the interview in America, presumably the format being the same as the one I'd sailed through in England. And - how convenient - his girlfriend lived in Saitama. I bet the Mega staff could hardly believe their eyes when they saw his request. "Hey, look at this, guys. Somebody actually *wants* to go to Saitama? What a dick!"

Things get a little hazy here, because I can't remember what his girlfriend's name was. It wasn't Miyako, because that was the name of his new girlfriend, the one he'd met after coming to Japan. This revelation, while slightly spoiling the end of the story, probably doesn't seem particularly shocking. Which is a shame: It should. Because even though it hasn't been explicitly stated, it might have been gleaned along the way that this tall, gawky, trombone-playing American had another important personality trait: He was very sincere. And while thousands upon thousands of long distance lovers may cross the world to meet up with their potential future spouses only to meet someone else and casually call the whole thing off, Sam was categorically not one of these. Sam was loyal. Sam was true. He's one of the very few people I have met that I can picture saying the marriage vows and absolutely never going back on them. For richer or for poorer, in sickness and in health, Sam would be there: Mr. Dependable.

And as *has* already been mentioned, Sam liked to talk. Boy did he like to talk. Injustice was his usual topic. The many bad things that had befallen him. How life had treated him unfairly, especially since he'd arrived in Japan. Once he started off complaining about life, it was nigh on impossible for him to stop. When this happened in his classes, as it frequently did, I was always impressed how few of the students complained. Many did; if the office staff were busy dealing with complaints from unsatisfied Mega students, it would be more likely than not that a Sam monologue was the cause. But most didn't even roll their eyes on leaving the room. Japanese hide their emotions well, I learned. (Additional note for a future lesson: Work on their "how to get someone to shut up" techniques.)

So just how did Sam manage to get so angry with the world? Let's rewind a few years and take a look.

Sam was born into a nice, rich American family. In their spacious California home, they had a huge garden with a beautiful outdoor swimming pool. Life was pretty much as good as it gets. Strife and struggle were not concepts young Sam ever had to worry about. Here I can only speculate, but maybe Sam Senior, exceedingly well off, occasionally wished that his son wasn't quite so awkward.

"How old are you now, son? 25 already? Still no girlfriend? And I wish you'd stop playing that damn trumpet or whatever the hell it is. That's no way to catch girls."

Well, maybe not California girls. But then one day at his jazz club, a young shy Japanese lady happened to stop by, and it may even have been because she liked jazz. And far from being put off by his height, his gawkiness and his playing style - that's not fair, I'll take that back, Sam played well - a few words were exchanged. Maybe a drink. Just the one, I hope, and suddenly Sam had himself an admirer. Over the following months, the relationship blossomed, the girl sitting in her regular chair at the club, occasionally ducking when Sam's trombone came a little too close for comfort...and counting down the weeks until the fateful day came.

"Sam, I have to go back to Japan. But I don't want to lose you. Lots of Americans come to Japan to teach English. Why don't you come, then we can be together. They have jazz clubs in Japan too. I think."

Doubtless, Sam was sorely tempted. Horribly prejudiced of me, I know, but I should probably add that on the basis of Miyako, I very much doubt Sam's original girlfriend was much to look at. But hey, when would Sam get another chance?

"Gee...Japan. That's a long way to go. I hear most people don't even have outdoor swimming pools."

But the idea was planted. How did it become a reality? Was he encouraged by his parents? "Go, Sam, she's the one for you." Forced? "For Christ's sake, son, you're doing nothing useful here, go out and make a life for yourself. And leave that trumpet here." Or quite possibly it was Sam, with his love for his shy admirer, who was the driving force. "Dad, Mom. You're not going to like this, but I've decided it's time for me to go. My girl is waiting for me. I love you, but don't try to stop me. It's my life."

One thing I know for sure is that it wasn't a sudden spontaneous decision to rush to the airport and board the next plane to Japan. There was, sadly, no scene where he surprised her as she emerged from her local sushi bar, barely able to stop herself choking up as she cast her mind back yet again to her American romance the previous summer. Then, suddenly aware of a tall figure in front of her, she slowly looks up.

"Sam? Is that you? Sam?! No, it can't be. Surely. Oh...my...God!! It's you, it really is you!!!" she shrieks, dropping her bag, bursting into tears there in the middle of the street as Sam slowly moves up, wipes the tears away with the corner of his lumberjack shirt and plants a kiss on her soy sauce-tinged luscious lips.

No, sorry, it wasn't like that.

He kept her updated with his job application. Then once he'd been accepted, he called her to let her know, then again to inform her of his arrival date and time, two months later. All very sensible, all very boring. Again, I apologise.

To be honest Sam didn't really know his girlfriend very well before he moved over. Beyond those few nights at the jazz club, could they even count a dozen dates? Sam felt certain it was love, but even so it was a huge call to leave his family and embark on this trip to the far reaches of Eastern Asia.

"How can I be sure she's The One?" he asked himself countless times. "I guess I just have to trust my instincts. Let's move over, be near her, pick up where we left off, take things slowly and see what happens."

And so Sam found himself at the airport, waving goodbye to his parents. A few hours later, I can see him shifting in his seat, trying to contemplate the implications of his decision to cross the Pacific. It hadn't been taken lightly. Loyal, sincere Sam was not dropping everything on a mere whim. But there was unquestionably an element of risk. I'm sure he envisaged a nervous first couple of weeks as they tried to relocate that spark in novel surroundings, saw themselves dating for a couple of years, playing the trombone as much as possible, working hard, gradually saving a little money for the future. He could probably already visualize himself then tying the knot. Wasn't that after all the logical conclusion of him sitting here now on the plane? But it didn't stop there, and Sam, staring out of the window - was he trying to catch his first sight of Japan, or was he peering inside the swirling mists obscuring his future self? - already realized that the really big decision would be the one he - they - would have to take about the same time as their marriage. Namely, would they settle down in Japan, or - more likely - would he bring his new wife back to make a new life together in his native California, hopefully not too near his parents?

But things didn't quite work out like he imagined.

The plane landed. Sam had arrived in his country of destiny. There was no odd limping Kiwi waiting for him. As he scanned the faces crowded around at the exit gate, one hand on his suitcase, the other on his beloved trombone, his first thought was: "I hope I can recognize my girlfriend."

Fortunately for him, Kasumi - yes, I think it's about time to give the poor girl some name - had a far easier job. Tall Americans stand out in Japan, even in airports. Tall gawky Americans carrying trombones are impossible to miss. No wild embrace for Sam and Kasumi though, just a quick hug. Kasumi's parents were there, after all, hanging slightly uneasily behind. The quick introductions were also slightly awkward. Kasumi's parents had never been introduced to either of her previous boyfriends. They had been wholly ignorant of her dating record, and were very happy to stay that way. But now this. And this was impossible to ignore. It had been a bit of a shock for Kasumi's Dad when he first learned that she was dating an American; but then he had come round surprisingly quickly. He was a generous man, a thoughtful loving father, not as conservative as many other Japanese, and if this was what his daughter wanted, then so be it. He'd be ready to help in any way. Even though Kasumi had told them not merely that Sam was tall, but his exact height, to be confronted by this giant in the flesh was slightly unnerving. There was something about Sam's gawky limbs that seemed to add a couple of inches to his height. But they were prepared. Super prepared.

The car journey back to Kasumi's house took just over two hours. The same distance in California would probably have been under an hour. But that's OK, thought Sam. He wasn't worried about slow moving traffic; he was genuinely excited to be reunited with his girl. But as a well brought up American boy, he knew how important it was to make a suitable impression on the couple who would very likely be his future parents-in-law. Sam had been spending some of his downtime in the US studying Japanese, and he had memorized a few phrases. Kasumi's parents were suitably impressed. "Wow, your Japanese is good," they said, Kasumi busy, not only translating her parents' compliments, but also helping to turn Sam's less successful attempts in her language into something understandable.

Sam was concentrating as hard as he ever had in his life before. He was only too aware that things often tended to break when he was around and that this was more than just coincidence. Various thoughts started churning around in his mind.

Important not to make any mistakes. Don't crash into things. Come across as pleasant. Smile, always smile. Don't do anything too embarrassing. Remember that book of cultural faux pas. What was that one about not blowing your nose, again? Don't bump my head on any of the doorways. Maybe better to refuse alcohol. Just let them see that I'm a good, honest, dependable type, and that I love their daughter. Yeah, probably should avoid alcohol, at least tonight. Maybe I can give them a trombone solo later if they like jazz? Actually, definitely avoid alcohol. Or is it rude to turn down a glass of wine? Oh and remember to take my shoes off before I go inside, I read that's a big no-no over here. Damn, I forgot to change my socks at the airport. Hope my feet don't stink too bad.

Kasumi had assured him he'd be able to stay at their house, but Sam certainly didn't like that idea. *Are you kidding?* he thought. On reflection he realized that actually it would help if the first day, maybe even two days, he had somewhere to stay, but then absolutely he would be out, move to a cheap hotel nearby for a week or so, however long it would take to find a suitable apartment where he could get himself set up.

He could imagine them telling him not to leave. "Stay here, there's space, we don't mind in the slightest." But Sam certainly did. The longer he stayed, the greater the chance of knocking over a priceless vase or treading on a toy poodle. If he could just negotiate the first day or two without committing some catastrophic error, without doing anything too shocking, he'd be safe. Even that would require a lot of effort. But then he'd be in the clear.

Besides, there was the question of propriety. This issue was becoming more and more important, the closer they got to the house. Was it really OK just to show up like this and stay in their home? Even in America, that would be a very grey area. He'd never been allowed to stay the night at any of his other girlfriends' houses. Well, actually he'd only had one real girlfriend before, and she'd never invited him over even for dinner, but there was no way he would have stayed there even if her parents had let him. Just not right. Way too forward, not to mention kind of creepy. Here, maybe there was an excuse as he was a foreigner, spending his first night in a brand new country, but surely part of making a good impression would be to insist on leaving just as soon as he could. Like the true gentleman he was. Actually that sounded grand. Far more preferable to be off to a hotel straight away, and not have to worry about all this cultural appropriate-ness stuff. Christ, all these ideas were starting to make him dizzy. He hadn't arrived yet, and he already couldn't wait to be out of there.

Two days.

That's all he asked, just two days. Surely he could survive a couple of nights.

Another problem popped into his head: Size. They probably lived in a tiny house, already full with just Kasumi, the parents and her younger sister. What would the arrangements be? Where would he sleep? Wait, Japanese people usually sleep on the floor, don't they? That's right, he'd read that somewhere. Hey, he'd be able to stretch out, not worry about kicking a hole in the wall. Maybe not as comfortable as his bed back home, but surely he'd be able to stand it for a couple of days. Ha, that's funny, to be able to stand lying down.

Then a horrific thought: How embarrassing if he was shown straight to Kasumi's room? They did have some very odd cultural habits in some countries that he'd read about. But wasn't that somewhere like Yemen? Where the hell was that?

Come on, Sam. Focus, man. You can do this. Show Kasumi's Mum and Dad you're a well brought up boy. And then get the hell out. What's so hard about that?

"We're here," announced Dad, as they drove into a small driveway. "It's just a small place," he added, proud that in fact it was rather spacious by Japanese standards. *You ain't kidding,* thought Sam. "It looks lovely," he lied, reminding himself that he'd only be there a couple of days. Maybe he could even make some excuse and leave the next day?

But for now, Sam was glad just to get out of the car. Even most American cars were never that comfortable given his huge lanky frame, but though he was far too polite to complain, the two hour drive with his legs wedged up against the seat in front had been a mild kind of torture. Now, how would his first night feel on the floor? Surely that's where he would be, maybe in the living room, possibly even in the kitchen? Well, at least it would be nice to be able to unfold, stretch out. The excitement of the long day was starting to get to him. His first ever long haul flight - in economy class, of course - and then all the stress of trying to make a favourable impression in a language he barely understood beyond a few phrases, while being anything but comfortable in a mid-size car. Well, for sure he was hungry and a bite to eat certainly would be very welcome - hope it's nothing too foreign, mind. Oh, and don't forget to pass on the beer. But to be honest more than anything he wanted to hit the sack, and suddenly, after all that worrying in the car, he was sure he'd be happy to sleep anywhere. Hell, even the garden would be fine...wait, had he seen anything resembling a garden on the approach to the house?

And now, as they stood next to the car, Sam trying to ignore the cramp in his left leg while breathing in the unfamiliar Japanese evening air, came the moment of truth.

He was guided past the main entrance with its modest porch, and towards a side entrance of what appeared to be a brand new extension.

"I hope you don't mind," said Kasumi, with a shy, half-expectant smile, "We've made a house. A home for you and me."

"I'm sorry?" said Sam. Maybe his hearing had gone to sleep in the car too.

Kasumi opened the door and watched as Sam entered the giant doorway, not even having to think about lowering his frame as he stepped inside. A brand spanking new house. That smell was unmistakable, whatever the country might be. A slight uneasy feeling came over him. What was the meaning of this? Here was the bedroom, with a double bed, longer even than the one he was used to in his California villa. Across the corridor, with its high, high ceiling was a bathroom. One of the biggest baths he'd ever seen in his life, with a toilet where he'd be able to stretch out his long, gangly legs without being able to touch the opposite wall. All through the house, there was not a chance of grazing his scalp, even if he stood on tiptoe. "Tailor made for lanky foreigners. Guaranteed, no head-bumping" screamed out from every corner.

As Sam moved from one room to another, the horror slowly started to settle in. His head started to thump. "Oh...my...God...they have actually built a house. They have gone out of their way, I mean, woh, way *way* out of their way, to build a giant house for me and Kasumi to live in. They have just met me for the first time. They expect me to come and live here right away with Kasumi?" The cramp was still there in his leg, and had turned to a tingling sensation which was spreading throughout his whole body. At that moment, Kasumi's Dad appeared with a twinkle in his eye, holding a bottle of ice cold Asahi Super Dry beer.

"Welcome to Japan," he said.

Sadly, Sam and I lost touch after I left Saitama. I still now occasionally remember his face as he related me the tale.

"Everything was so big," he said, shaking his head. "And new, too."

"Doesn't sound so bad," I offered. Indeed, in another set of circumstances it could have been the start of a perfect happily-ever-after story. Rarely has a future son-in-law been greeted in such style. But for poor Sam it was all a bit too much. He needed to do things in his own time, couldn't stand having things thrust on him. It's a huge shame of course, but I tend to agree with Sam on the whole. I don't know how long he stuck it out in his specially constructed giant extension - a week? Maybe two? - before abandoning his nearly betrothed and her far too generous parents and giving it all up for a small, cheap, cramped flat where he had to remember to stoop every time he went from the tiny kitchen to the living room where he slept on the floor every night, but where at least he had room to breathe. He got into his routine of working, complaining, playing his trombone at the club, where one day he started talking to a young lady who seemed to enjoy jazz and they started dating.

And where, I wonder, is Sam now? I suspect he and Miyako probably got married. I suspect he took her back to America, and they had three boys who play trombone, saxophone and double bass. I pray they got their coordination genes from their mother. Or if they are still in Japan, I hope he has a nice proper American size house so he doesn't have to pay constant attention to his four limbs on the odd occasion that he enjoys a beer or whiskey. I really hope that he, they, are all fine too, and I hope that he remembers me too occasionally, the English lad who couldn't spell properly, the games of pool we played and the beers we drank together. Here's to you, Sam!

2) The Amazing Mr. Peach

"Kumamoto boasts one of the most famous castles in Japan, one of its deadliest volcanoes as well of some of the best beaches in the Island of Kyushu."

That's what my trusty *Lonely Planet* said - and when had it been wrong about anything? Well, OK, it had failed to warn me about Saitama for one. But then I guess the lack of any information whatsoever pertaining to Omiya was strictly speaking an understandable omission rather than a mistake. Meanwhile a new branch of Mega had just opened in Kumamoto and I had been granted my request for a transfer away from Shite-tama. So if *Lonely Planet* gave this city in Southern Japan a resounding thumbs-up then bring it on, I say. I couldn't decide if the volcano was a selling point exactly, but then anything was sure to be an improvement on my first year.

It would be nice to say that my departure from Omiya was tinged with sadness, but it would be a lie. I couldn't wait to get the hell out. The Shinkansen whisking me away from Tokyo to Fukuoka was too fast to allow me to enjoy the scenery outside. I soon gave up, choosing instead to count all the reasons why I was glad not to be in Saitama anymore and well before I reached triple figures, I'd dozed off to sleep.

On the one hand my arrival, on time, in Kumamoto was a bit of a let-down. Some quick calculations had showed me that the distance I'd just covered was remarkably similar to my journey to Gers five years earlier. What a culture shock that had been. What did that small farming community in Southwest France have in common with London, where I'd boarded the train? I might as well have hopped into a time machine. But here in Kyushu - initially at least - everything was very similar to the city I'd left behind. Very Japanese. Very urban. Not at all unlike Omiya in fact. What's all that about? I thought this was supposed to be a tropical island? Yet there was not even the faintest whiff of the sea, nor the slightest sulphurous tang of toxic volcanic gases.

Had I come all this way for nothing?

Well at least there was an intuition - an indefinable, intangible sense hanging vaguely in the evening air - that this place held a promise of...something. And exiting the taxi and turning my head to the left, there, as if to confirm my hunch, all proudly lit up, stood the castle, hovering magically above the bustling tram street.

Any lingering fear that I was about to enter Saitama number two was firmly dispelled shortly after passing through the doors below the friendly Mega sign. Once inside everything looked oddly, uncomfortably familiar...the same sofas, tables, chairs, the same schedule listings hanging on the wall. But that was where the similarities ended.

"Welcome to Kumamoto," a beaming besuited Japanese man in his late twenties said, standing up from his desk. Giving my best crap Gaijin bow, I glanced around at the dozen or so faces all looking at me. There was the same mix of Japanese and foreigners - but what was this? All the Japanese staff looked genuinely pleased to meet me, and the Gaijin - the teachers - seemed...what was it that was so different about them...friendly? Yes. Cheerful? Again, yes. Everyone looked...just, well...fresh. Not a single jaded feature amongst them.

There were three Americans, Kenny, Charlie and Natasha; one Canadian guy, Steve; another Brit, Louise, and Sharon from Australia. "If there's anything you need, just ask," said Sharon.

Perfectly nice, normal folk. Maybe the Weird Gaijin was a phenomenon unique to Tokyo?

Rie, the manager, cheerfully gave me a quick tour of the school and introduced the sales staff, Motoko and Miwa, who seemed to be firm friends and loved nothing better than hitting the bars together after work. There was Yasu, a softly spoken guy it was impossible not to like and Taka, another friendly chap with a face of a manga geek but whose party piece, I was soon to learn, was to stick a lit cigarette between his butt cheeks, much to the delight of Rie. The welcome could hardly have been any different from the one I'd had back in Omiya. How many of the Japanese staff's faces could I still recall from that school, let alone names? It seemed like things were going to be different here.

Let's take a closer look at the Gaijin. Natasha was a rather prim and proper Chicagoan. Kenny, proudly hailing from Reno, Nevada, had a fleeting resemblance to Tom Cruise, while Steve was more of a Jim Carrey. Louise didn't have a Hollywood doppelganger but possessed a rather charming, lazily flirtatious manner coupled with a wicked sense of humour, while Sharon's severe appearance was deceiving, as she was possibly the silliest of everyone after a couple of beers.

But of all these resoundingly normal people, one would go on to become a legend within the Gaijin community. He stepped forward now. A slightly overweight, slightly ruddy-faced guy, baseball cap pulled down over his slightly curly, slightly blond hair. "Hi, I'm Charlie," he said, extending a slightly podgy hand.

"Nice to meet you," I replied.

Most people would probably agree Charlie was the least impressive of my new colleagues. Utterly unremarkable, you might say. He'd just arrived a few days before me, but he could as well have been there for months. There was nothing flamboyant about him, no hint of mystery. He was pleasant. Solid. Stodgy.

"Hi, I'm Charlie" was not only his greeting, it became his trademark catchphrase, delivered in a slightly high-pitched voice, slight smile creasing the corners of his mouth, hand outstretched. Charlie didn't discriminate on meeting someone for the first time. Wide-eyed bashful young lady, middle ranking nearly retired dull company man, or new travel-weary British colleague, all were met with exactly the same level of enthusiasm. Which is not to say it was either too enthusiastic or too unenthusiastic, merely that it was always the same.

I don't usually read too much into first impressions, but Charlie was different. I knew everything I needed to about him right there and then. He was clearly a plodder. And a plodder for me is just fine. They're similar to gawky people. It's easy to make friends with plodders. They have few expectations of others, just as we have few expectations of them, so with just a minimum of effort we can guarantee ourselves a friend. This friend will never go out of his way to help you. You're not going to make memories to last a lifetime. But if you just want someone to go out and share a drink with, he's your man.

I sensed all of this, crystal clear, the moment I met him and nothing that followed over the eight years of knowing him did anything to prove me wrong. In those eight years, as I imagine in the preceding eight, he stayed exactly the same. He seemed incapable of changing, even as events swirled around him. Events which would ultimately force him to leave, oust him against his will.

It was a great first meeting. Arriving the next morning for my first day at work, the previous day's positive impressions just seemed to amplify. Kenny really was a fun guy, always seemingly pumped full of adrenalin. Natasha - apparently a violinist back in Chicago - rolled her eyes and shook her head as he related some of the odd situations he'd found himself in since arriving.

"Oh my God, I met this gorgeous girl at the bar last night," he said. "She took me back to her flat, I thought it was a sure thing, but then she introduced me to her twin five year old daughters and switched on the karaoke machine and forced me to sing Disney songs for over an hour. Then she just kicked me out. I didn't even get a kiss!"

Yasu and Taka went out of their way to warn me about what to expect of some of my new students. "Hirotaka tends to talk too much about his job, bores the others senseless, so don't be afraid to cut him off. Yukiko can't stand China, don't get her started. Oh, and Kouki just got dumped by his girlfriend last month, he's really depressed so avoid any personal questions!" This kind of valuable personality advice was something I'd never experienced in Omiya. Rie was sweetness itself. Motoko and Miwa invited me to join them with Sharon and Louise for a few drinks that night. "Unless you want to go out with the men," chided Louise, fluttering her eyelashes. "I know some English boys are like that."

I suddenly didn't mind so much about the lack of volcanic activity beyond the doors. This place was smoking. Why hadn't I put Kumamoto down as my first choice when applying for Mega?

So my new life started on a very positive note and over the next few weeks things just got better and better. Kumamoto Mega was everything Omiya wasn't. In a word: Fun. And that went doubly for the city, which was a great place, no question. *Lonely Planet* jumped back up again in my estimation, all past errors instantly forgiven, forgotten. The castle was fantastic, the surrounding parks filled with little alleys and barely visited historic buildings in which to get lost for hours. Mountains rose up in every direction beyond the city limits, in stark contrast to the flat horizons I'd become used to in Saitama. The main shopping streets were filled with wonderful restaurants of every kind.

Every night was a new adventure with my new colleagues. We were all in a kind of wonderland, enjoying living in this delightful city with its warm and friendly people, but probably nobody was enjoying himself more than Kenny. I'm not sure which Kenny took more pleasure in - his nocturnal escapades, or relating details of those capers the next day. There were no secrets with Kenny. Everything was deemed worthy of repeating to as many people as possible, whether it concerned his girlfriend, his room-mates or himself. He was one of those people at whom you just felt like shouting, "Enough, Kenny! Too much information already." No, I didn't know you had to shave your pubic hair when the doctor examined you. And no, I'd rather not look, if you don't mind. No, I'm not really interested in your new girlfriend's lack of enthusiasm during your love-making. What? No, Kenny, I really don't need to know about all the condoms in the garbage. Your room-mate's? Well, that's kind of personal shit. Shut up!

The weeks passed. Charlie was always there, on the fringes. He smiled at Kenny's stories. He came out to all the parties. There was no outrageous behaviour from Charlie · was this really the future legend? It's quite rare, but rather reassuring to meet someone so...neutral. If you asked a hundred people what they thought of Kenny, you'd be likely to get a range of answers from "incredibly nice guy" or "hilarious", down to "annoying" or "immature", ending up with the inevitable: "He's a dick." But with Charlie, I'd imagine he'd make exactly the same impression on almost everyone. Either: "I can't stand him. Such a plodder." Or: "I like him. Sure, he's a bit of a plodder, but he's OK."

Steve was the enigmatic member of the team. You could sense a certain mystery lurking behind the smile, a decision not to impart any personal information of any kind. It made for a rather frictional relationship with Kenny. Whereas Kenny was like a puppy whose tail would never stop wagging, and had compiled his list of hottest girls in Mega, Steve tried to conduct himself in a far more dignified manner. Fat lot of good it did him. On one occasion a female student in her thirties invited him out to see a movie, to which Steve innocently agreed. He was horrified when she came into class the next week bragging about her "new Canadian boyfriend". He was the type who plays by the rules but ends up in shit; the one whose secrets always spill out. It was his hard luck that he was Kenny's roommate. Steve soon acquired another girlfriend who he swore to secrecy · Mega was strict about its "no-socializing with students" rule · but Kenny delighted in keeping us updated on their latest news, condoms and all, rendering useless any attempt at discretion.

Charlie listened to all the gossip. It was hard to tell if he was interested in it. Steve had a girlfriend? A student? No reaction.

"What about you then Charlie, meet anyone special yet?"

"No," he shrugged.

He didn't seem marked down for greatness.

And so things continued for a few months: Party months. Motoko and Miwa were the ringleaders, trying to entice everyone into their web. And it wasn't like they had to try hard.

"Let's play the *O-sama* game!" announced Motoko, mid-way through a party one night after work at a crowded Izakaya.

"What's that?" I asked innocently.

"Well, we write numbers on chopsticks, then one person is the king - the *O-sama* - and he or she has to choose two numbers and give out a challenge."

"Oh, like a kind of dare game, I see." The others seemed familiar with it, but it was my first time and I was given the honour to start - the first *O-sama*. I had no idea what a typical challenge might be, or what the limits of the game were. Rie nodded encouragingly and so I said, "5 and 8 take off your bras."

Could you believe it? 5 and 8 turned out to be Rie and Motoko, the best looking girls, who wasted no time in fiddling around under their shirts and then suddenly two bras appeared on the table. I was gob-smacked. Further dares involved Natasha caressing Yasu's ears and Steve kissing Miwa's toes. That evening in karaoke was the first time Taka did his smoking bottom routine. This, incidentally, was nothing to do with any chopstick game. It was just what he apparently did most evenings.

Sharon and Louise seemed entirely at home in this environment but Natasha was a little less sure. I'm sure she frowned upon such games, but equally she never missed a party. She was a good sport, but you felt that probably ear fondling was her limit. She sometimes spoke of her boyfriend waiting for her back in Chicago. You sensed that it was not the most passionate of relationships; that if the Gods were to throw somebody her way in Japan she might break the whole thing off without shedding too many tears. But at the same time you felt that this was unlikely to happen. There was a touch of Rose in Titanic. You could see her playing her violin as the ship sank. Would a Japanese Jack come along to deliver her from her fate?

One important way Kumamoto Mega was mercifully different from Omiya was in its lack of a head teacher. This, I think it's safe to say, was precisely why it was such a fun place. There was nobody to lay down the law. Teachers, staff and students, we were all friends.

Something of a veteran now, I realized that back in Saitama, the staff's main job had been zookeepers, making sure all the Gaijin were kept in line, did their job and stayed away from potentially damaging scandals. This was the big risk in the company whose main selling point was hiring young Westerners to teach English in a country where Gaijin were still considered exotic creatures. The perils were not hard to spot. After all, what was foremost on the minds of many of the young Japanese students? Exactly the same as was on the minds of most of the teachers. I imagine that right at the top of the manager's "things-to-do" list was: Avoid Scandals. That could only really work if there was a full time manager. The regional manager, Fletcher, based two hours away in Fukuoka, was a man with eyes like burning coals. He came down once a month, nominally checking that the lessons were all being taught smoothly, but fooling absolutely nobody that he was in fact keeping abreast of the latest complaints regarding flouting the company no-socializing policy. Everyone was instantly on their best behaviour on those monthly visits, smiling sweetly, trying to avoid those hellish eyes in case flames should come flying out. Fletcher back in Fukuoka, a quick sigh of relief and as you were. Cigarettes inserted back between buttocks. It's OK, we said, this rule is just CYA. It was a minor miracle how Mega had become so successful, but its position was precarious. The company bosses were only too aware of the constant potential for scandal. And scandal could bring down the whole school crashing down.

These were matters Charlie didn't need to worry about. He plodded along. We talked a lot in the flat, at the school, at the parties, but I have no memory of what we ever talked about. Nothing bad about the guy, he just wasn't given to excessive verbosity and he wasn't angry with the world. Actually, maybe that was the reason for his occasionally infuriating unflappability: He was just happy enough with everything without ever being bowled over, nor indeed ever really seeking anything which would bowl him over. You sometimes got the impression that even if he found something to truly bowl him over, he wouldn't, in fact, be bowled over. So there was no point searching in the first place.

"How was it, Charlie?" would invariably be answered by a slight smile accompanied with a slight shrug. "It was good." Possibly with an additional "I guess." Whether the question was referring to his last lesson, the movie he watched, his trip to the beach or the night drinking with his buddies, the answer never changed. I realized as I got to know him better that this was a man with limited expectations of the world, or indeed of himself. A man who didn't get too excited when everyone else was throwing themselves into a frenzy and equally a man who didn't get unduly agitated in situations of mind-numbing boredom. This was someone who accepted things as they were because he knew that they could easily be a lot worse. A plodder. It's the perfect word.

And so, you must be asking, what was so exceptional about him that he is still breathed of when other more memorable, more dynamic visitors to the country have long since been forgotten? The answer is very simple: Because of his name and because of what happened to him while he was here.

His name was Peach. Charlie Peach. I'd never met anyone with that name before. I have no idea how common it is in the US. I'd hazard a guess: More common than you'd expect, but still not overly common. Probably guaranteed to raise an eyebrow or two on most introductions. But by happy coincidence, "peach" just happens to be a legendary name in Japan. One of Japan's most famous folk tales is the saga of *Momo-taro* - literally "Peach Boy". The story, as familiar to Japanese as *Snow White* or *Cinderella*, is of an old childless couple who've long since given up hope of having their own baby. One day a peach comes floating down the river as she's washing clothes, but hidden inside the peach is a tiny boy, sent from the Gods. The delighted couple raise the child who, once grown, embarks on a never-ending fight against demons invading the land, supported by a cast of friendly monkeys, dogs and - why not? - pheasants.

This was manna from heaven for Charlie. Whereas I had my own luck of sharing my name with such well-known characters as *Peter Rabbit* or *Peter Pan,* a connection I usually tried to use as sparingly as possible, only really in emergencies to be honest and in any case with no relation to anything Japanese, Charlie had been gifted a chance to deflect attention away from his resolutely middle-of-the-road character and onto the happy coincidence of his surname. Memories of him therefore tended to become memories of the association with his name.

"Do you know Charlie?"

"Oh, yeah! Momo-taro! Peach Boy! Amazing name!"

Charlie was no dullard. He realized just what a God-given opportunity his name was and he never tired of it. Sometimes a person he'd just been introduced to might fail to spot the connection, in which case he'd be sure to wait patiently for the penny to drop, providing a few hints when necessary.

"And so," he would declare, a slight smile forming on his face as he adopted a suitably dramatic pose, both hands pointing toward his chest, one foot slightly in front of the other: "I am...Peach Boy!" It was worth the dozens of lukewarm reactions just to get the occasional guffaw and it became part of the standard introduction - the second stage, after the "Hi, I'm Charlie." Strange thinking back how "I am Peach Boy" never became quite as much of a trademark as the notionally much less impressive "Hi, I'm Charlie." Maybe ultimately he just wasn't quite exciting enough to fulfill all the promise suggested by "I am Peach Boy." It was clear there was nothing dynamic there, no superhero lying beneath the surface. "Hi, I'm Charlie" really did sum him up perfectly. Years of friendship later, we really hadn't moved on beyond that opening sentence. Anyone joining us for a beer at that point hadn't missed out on anything.

But you know what, I liked him. He may not have been cool but hey, neither was I, and most importantly Charlie was not a bad guy. He worked. He drank. He smoked. He shrugged. He smiled. He shrugged. (He did a lot of shrugging.) He talked. He never did any form of exercise. In fact Charlie managed to make life look remarkably simple. With Steve nervously twitching around, Kenny constantly in search of another buzz and others of us maybe starting to ask existential questions or merely missing home, Charlie just got on with things. On his second night in the city, he'd gone on a walk around the block looking for something to eat. He found a vaguely American looking sign. *Rock Bar* it said, in English. He went in, ordered a beer, the master rustled up some tasty dish and he got talking to the five or six regular customers who were there, curious by the sudden arrival of this foreigner in their midst. And bingo, that become part of his weekly routine for the whole time he lived there. Remarkable!

Charlie, Natasha and I shared an apartment. It was an interesting mix. Memories of all the people I'd shared with in my life came flooding back. Music blaring out late at night before exam day; unwashed dishes, un-vacuumed floors; arguments about money - buying toilet rolls, gas bills. Thank God all that was behind me. I felt Charlie was a perfect room-mate, but Natasha definitely didn't share my opinion. Charlie just rubbed her up absolutely the wrong way. They were two different brands of Americans that would never have hit it off before leaving for a new life abroad and made no effort to do so here. Quite funny how two people can ignore each other so completely while not only living, but also working together. No hellos, goodbyes, nothing. The moment they met, they instantly saw a certain stereotype of a kind of American they'd automatically avoid back in the US and decided there was no reason to act any differently here. I was the slightly exotic Englishman. I was safe.

"I really like that CD, what is it?" Natasha asked me one morning.

"Smashing Pumpkins," I said, not telling her I'd recorded it from Charlie the week before. Anything connected with the guy was somehow contaminated, instinctively making her recoil. Fascinating to observe!

I had to admit that Charlie was a real cartoon caricature of an American in so many ways. He always wore a baseball cap outside the school and somehow he didn't look right without it. He loved Coca-Cola. The fridge was permanently stocked with it.

"I don't know how he can drink that stuff," shuddered Natasha. I'd like to bet she'd got through her fair share back in America, but she would probably never buy another can in her life, tainted as it was now by association with Charlie. And he loved his cigarettes, Marlboro naturally, and · with what was probably his only earnest effort at being health-conscious · they were always Super Lights. Much cheaper than in America and as a further bonus, cigarette packets in Japan were free from all the cheerful health warnings of cancer and horrible death adorning the packet, detracting from the enjoyment of a quick puff between lessons.

And that, in a nutshell, was Charlie's life. Work. Sleep. Smoke. Drink Coca-Cola. Pop round the corner to his local. What could be easier?

At work, Charlie was an employer's dream. Always reliable, always cheerful. Never breaking the rules, never complaining, never being complained about. He did what was asked of him, following all the lesson points religiously. A standard lesson started with a few minutes of general chit-chat, followed by grammar drills and new vocabulary. The teacher would then read the conversation, practice more drills, do some pronunciation exercises and end with a role-play loosely based on the lesson's central grammar point. It was dumbed down as far as possible so if each step was followed, teachers who had never taught before - i.e. the majority of the staff - would be able to produce a passable lesson. Genius, you might say. The downside was that most teachers would inevitably start squirming at the relentless monotony of the lessons we had to serve up, some after only a week, others after a few months. It happened to Kenny, Steve and Sharon. It happened to me - it happened to everyone. Everyone that is except Charlie. There was never a snide comment about how dumb a particular lesson was from him. No rolling his eyes as he had three low level lessons back to back. He just got on with it. Every time. Hangover or no hangover: "Hi, I'm Charlie. Let's do Lesson 25." Amazing!

Over the months, Charlie did pick up a few ideas of his own that he deemed to be of some value and incorporated them into his lessons. These were delivered with a glee rarely shared by his students and offered a certain sadistic pleasure to anybody watching. The most famous of these, which became his second trademark, was *The Hokey-Pokey.* This is doubtless a wonderful little song for large groups of kids, but I would argue of a more limited educational value to a pair of 40-something housewives, not to mention the frequent cause of entirely justified embarrassment.

"Do you know *The Hokey-Pokey?*" Charlie was getting started.

Silence.

"No? You don't know *The Hokey-Pokey?*" he would ask in mock horror, basking a little in this bemused reaction as the students scanned the page in front of them unable to find the relevant point of the lesson.

"Right, stand up," he said, also, I felt, savouring a little too much the undeniable pleasure teachers can enjoy of watching their students obediently follow commands. And so the spectacle unfurled.

"You put your left hand in," he said wisely, encouraging his still bemused students to copy him. "You put your left hand out." Pause. "In, out, in, out, and shake it all about," happy that the command-obey lag was shortening, even if the mild puzzlement stayed the same. And now his favourite bit, also coincidentally but unarguably the least educationally-important part: "You do the Hokey-Pokey," allowing himself a broad smile now as he performed some odd shaking movement. "That's what it's all about!" - almost triumphant now, having reached the end of the chorus. Once the foot, head and bottom verses were over, the students were finally allowed to sit down, not in fact having any idea what it was all about and frankly relieved to get back to the textbook. I can still see Natasha fidgeting away every time she had to witness this. She probably still suffers nightmares about it, safely back in Chicago though I assume she is.

And so Charlie, with his life totally under control, shifted his focus to what would become his major obsession: Money. Already he probably couldn't believe his lucky stars. From what I gathered, he'd worked mostly as a mechanic back in Nebraska. Now here he was on the other side of the world, earning a very reasonable salary for sitting down, reading the same page over and over and throwing in the occasional silly dance, with no need to get all dirty and greasy.

Not only that, it was easy to pick up extra lessons. Kumamoto was a cosy, friendly kind of town, but decidedly provincial, with limited opportunities to meet Westerners. The arrival of Mega meant a sudden influx of exotic foreigners in their midst and for many, a weekly lesson wasn't enough. Some of the more forward students occasionally approached us outside the school, not unlike drug dealers, asking surreptitiously if we could teach them privately. Many teachers ran away screaming. They had already reached their limit, couldn't contemplate doing the same thing in their free time. But for some, like me, a few extra hours were of enormous help financing those sometimes expensive weekend trips away which I tried to cram in. For the truly greedy, there was almost unlimited potential here. You could easily end up making more outside the school than your original Mega salary. And some did just that, taking a deep breath and focusing on stacking the yen up, ready to sacrifice a year or two of their lives to give themselves a head start in the next stage of their career once they'd returned home. And of all of these, Charlie was king. He started to pick up a few lessons on his days off and then a few more before and after his workdays. He soon became legendary as the teacher who never refused.

"Do you know anyone who gives lessons at 11p.m. on Saturday?"

"Well, there is one person."

One of the reliefs of embarking on private lessons was that you were free to break away from the rigid format imposed on us by the company and do your own thing. It was a breath of fresh air just to be able to teach in your own style.

But the truly staggering thing was that Charlie always used the Mega textbook. It had become his bible. He knew every stage of each lesson by heart. He would just pick up the book and teach, occasionally throwing in *The Hokey-Pokey* for good measure. And soon Charlie was pulling in seriously big money. Before long he was pretty much at his limit. He'd reached a point where his schedule was so full that he simply couldn't squeeze in any more lessons. Unable to further increase his monthly income, he started experimenting to see just how much of that money he could save. Untroubled by the need for other stimulation like travel, entertainment, or expensive dinner dates, he had virtually no expenses. But the possibilities of how to spend even less started to roll around. We'd seen the signs of this over the months. Saving money gradually became his passion, his raison d'être. Coca-Cola had already been degraded to some budget variety cola which apparently caused no lasting harm to his health or happiness. The beer in the fridge had also at some point likewise suddenly morphed into some barely recognizable, barely drinkable brew. But by far the single biggest item of expenditure was the one he turned his full attention to now: Rent.

It would be fair to say that Mega was, if not ripping us off, then definitely over-charging us for a simple room in a three person share flat, and once Charlie realized this he started to search around for his own place. It wasn't hard to find somewhere he could be alone with a room that could be used for teaching and still pay less than he was now. The new game was to see just how much money he was able to slash off his monthly bills and I was willing to bet Charlie would find the cheapest place in the city. Natasha was just praying that it wouldn't take long. She'd probably have happily contributed a few dollars if he'd asked her, but there was no need.

"I move out at the end of the week," he announced one evening. "I'll have a house-warming party on Sunday night." I think he actually invited Natasha but she did well not to come. When we arrived, it already felt like he'd been living there for years. It had Charlie's personality stamped all over it. It had probably taken him one afternoon to set it up exactly how he wanted it, and little or nothing would change over the years. Any house over thirty years old in Japan becomes almost worthless. This was $250 a month, less than half what he'd been paying in the shared flat and it had everything he needed. The whole house seemed to say "Hi, I'm Charlie's house." Looking at his pinkish complexion, I was suddenly reminded of the story of *The Three Little Pigs*. This house was his house of sticks and it was all he needed. Charlie Peach was set.

Fast forward 12 months. Things never stayed the same for long in Mega. The staff had been shuffled around, Rie being the main casualty. She'd been sent off to Tokyo for retraining. Too friendly to the teachers, it seemed. Not treating us like the animals we were. The mood in the office changed. Sharon was the first Gaijin to leave. She was a model teacher in the classroom and a legendary drinker outside it. How did she manage to look so...sober every morning? But you could tell she was bored with the system, there was no fulfillment for her and so she returned to Australia. Natasha followed next. Her Jack never turned up. She stuck it out for a year and that satisfied her. No compelling reason ever materialized to extend her stay and delay the inevitable marriage. Louise simply disappeared. Steve moved to another city with his girlfriend, mostly to avoid Kenny. But soon Kenny had also gone, first from Mega and then somewhat surprisingly out of Gaijin folklore. He came, he partied, he tried his best to wreak havoc, but ultimately he failed to leave a major imprint. Maybe he just tried too hard. Or maybe he was a bit too normal. Charlie would be the one they'd still be talking about for years to come.

"So what about girls, Charlie? Found yourself anyone yet?" we asked one Friday night. Or more accurately, we asked him the same question every Friday night. We'd started an end-of-week tradition of going to the local cheap Izakaya. We had three hard-core members: Charlie, myself and one of the new faces, Murray, a fellow Brit, plus a host of others who came and went. Murray was completely bald in spite of being just thirty years old, possessed a healthy sense of humour and an equally healthy sexual appetite rarely troubled by such trivialities as looks. Among his growing list of girls was "The Dog", his own nickname for a lady of indiscernible age who was a regular sight at the dance club we always ended up in. She had not aged gracefully, had probably never been a pretty girl and certainly didn't care at all. She loved dancing, but seemed aware enough of her lack of natural beauty to permanently wear a hat and wide-rimmed sunglasses. Only at home with the door safely closed did she reveal what lay beneath. "She's really ugly," confirmed Murray, shaking his head at the memory. That didn't stop him being one of a handful of Gaijin who would take turns escorting her home.

And then there was "The Stalker", a student who'd gone out on a couple of dates with Murray, become smitten and would be waiting outside his house most Fridays or Saturdays when he rolled up at two or three in the morning.

"Must be a nightmare," I said.

"Oh God, yeah. She just doesn't go away. She was there again last Saturday."

"So what did you do then?"

He looked at me and shrugged. "I shagged her," he said. Nothing if not practical, our Murray.

It would then be my turn to relate my own far less exciting adventures. Fun to embellish of course, but the truth was I'd found my girl, the relationship was getting serious, what is good for your emotional well-being is sadly not conducive to cracking jokes with mates over a late night beer.

"How about you, Charlie?"

Unusually among the Gaijin community, Charlie spent the first couple of years unattached. "It's been a looong time," he said, enjoying emphasizing the "long" when asked about his last girlfriend. Not that it seemed to bother him in the slightest. It didn't. Before you knew it we were back onto his favourite topic: Money.

"Passed a million, yet?"

"Still working on it," said Charlie. And he wasn't really joking. I think in his mind it was maybe starting to become a realistic target.

"And where do you keep it all anyway? Doesn't the bank get suspicious with all the deposits you make?"

"Oh, I don't put it in the bank. There's like zero interest there anyway. I keep it in my drawer."

"In the drawer? Seriously? Isn't that kind of dangerous? I know there's not a lot of crime in Japan, but your house is not exactly Fort

Knox." The image of the little pigs' house returned, this time with the wolf outside trying to blow it down.

"It's fine. I enjoy counting it."

I think the only time Charlie got genuinely excited was in October, when an American country music festival was held in the mountains outside the city. The largest of its kind outside the States, apparently. "You should come," he said to me and Murray.

"Erm, don't think so Charlie." If there was one type of music I could categorically claim to have zero interest in, it was country music. "We don't listen to that in England, Charlie. Anything else, sure, but country? No way."

"Suit yourselves," shrugged Charlie. He certainly wasn't one to waste too much energy enforcing his will on others. "It's great though," he added. Rare praise indeed.

In my mind, I could see hundreds of Charlie look-alikes, all drinking Budweiser or Coca-Cola, wearing baseball caps or cowboy hats, while saying "yee-ha!" a few too many times. A slightly queasy moment. The closest I ever came to entering Natasha's brain. One Charlie was fine, but a whole stadium full of them?

And for Charlie here was another reason never to leave Kumamoto. All the other original teachers had left. I was planning my own departure soon. But Charlie was truly set, deeper and deeper with each passing week. Earning money by the bucket-load, with his own pad, even an American music festival to look forward to once a year. The only missing piece of the puzzle, surely, was the girlfriend. Then he would become immoveable.

Any slight effort on his part would have been rewarded. He had the full house of qualities sought after by potential partners: Still young at 29; a full head of curly hair; not bad-looking; rich, steady, dependable.

"In fact Charlie, how the hell have you managed to stay single all this time?"

"Unlucky I guess," he shrugged.

And when she came along, it was a surprise to everyone, possibly Charlie most of all, that it was in the very shapely form of Maki. She'd started hanging around of late, can't quite recall the original connection. Definitely after some Gaijin boyfriend, that one! Maybe her sights were set slightly higher than Charlie, we said, for Maki was indeed a pretty girl. But the lucky boy would be none other than our Charlie.

"Three times. That's my rule," he told us when relating how he'd secured his first Japanese catch. They were standing outside the house, him asking if she wanted to come in. "Gotta ask 'em three times. Even if they say no twice, they'll say yes on the third time." Not quite sure where this piece of wisdom came from. It wasn't as if it had been a tried and tested technique until now, but it certainly seemed tailor-made for Charlie's personal use: A minimum of effort, unless you count repeating the same question three times "an effort". This was no problem for Charlie, for whom repeating the same lesson maybe ten times a week was merely part of his routine.

Sadly Maki would be little more than a footnote in the history of Charlie. I guess she most probably wasn't overly disappointed when they drifted apart after only a few months together. Probably one of the less exciting, less fulfilling relationships she'd enjoyed. It could

61

never have worked out anyway because Maki turned out to be something of a shopping addict, with a particular weakness for shoes. Maybe she needed someone like Charlie so she could pursue her passion to her heart's content, but there was no way Charlie would ever tolerate it. It was the worst imaginable sin. For Charlie the perfect girlfriend would be someone who was happy with one budget cola a day. Two would be pushing it. It'd be more likely to see Natasha and Charlie hooking up than him sanctioning a girl who bought two new pairs of shoes a week. Or Charlie and Murray, for that matter. No, Maki was out. A perfect mutually beneficial break-up.

But if we thought his brief romance might usher in a new era of "Charlie the Playboy", we were mistaken. Whatever it was that had briefly stirred within Charlie was not a monster awakening, it was just a hiccup. A yawn. It was back asleep again. Friday conversation reverted to Charlie's vast fortune hiding under his underpants and Murray's stalker who still hadn't given up. Murray certainly wasn't happy, but continued to treat it rather like a cold: A minor nuisance you can't really do anything about. Time ticked. Charlie's drawer swelled with crisp Japanese notes. I left Kumamoto. Took my girlfriend and went off to live in New Zealand for two years. Came back. I think they just about noticed I'd been gone. Don't think I'd missed much. Or been missed much. And then shortly after came a rumour that Charlie had got himself a new girlfriend.

"Is it true?" we asked.

"Yeah, I guess," he shrugged. He really did an awful lot of shrugging; it was an integral part of Charlie. He was neither coy nor boastful.

"I met her at a party. She came back and cooked for me."

"Three times?" I asked, remembering his golden rule.

"No, only once," answered Charlie looking at me as if I was nuts.

"No, I mean your rule. Always ask them three times, remember?"

Charlie apparently didn't remember too clearly. "No, actually I didn't ask her at all," he said, happily realizing just how little effort had been involved on his part. The usual questions followed: How many pairs of shoes did she have? Did she have any psychotic tendencies?

"No, no. She's just a normal girl."

"Cute?"

"I guess," with a shrug.

"What's her name?"

"Yumi."

Thanks to Yumi, our boring conversations about money and what Charlie would do with it when he went back to the US, how he would smuggle it all back · maybe he'd like to put some of it in our banks, we'd be happy to shield him from any tax expenses, etc. · were put on hold for a while. There would be much more to talk about with Yumi every week than there ever had been with Maki.

"Did you see her again then, Charlie?"

"Yeah, actually she came round again last Sunday. She was there outside when I got back from all my lessons." I shook my head, remembering that Charlie had a full schedule of private students on his day off. No such thing as the luxury of a weekend for Charlie. Time is money. Murray was on a different train of thought. "Oh, you got yourself a stalker, Charlie!"

"Don't be stupid," I said. "Waiting outside his house once doesn't make someone a stalker. She probably doesn't have your number, right Charlie? So then what happened?"

"She came in and cooked dinner again."

"Hmm, sounds like she's auditioning for something. Careful Charlie, your single days may be over. Hope she's a good cook, at least."

"Yeah, she's good, I guess." Then a pause. "She's a little strange," he added.

This was a very un-Charlie like thing to say. There had never seemed to be a "strange" category in his mental filing system before.

"How do you mean?"

"I don't know. She's just...a little strange."

"Keep your distance Charlie," warned Murray. "Mark my words; she's one to stay away from." And of course, Murray, with his long and maybe not always painful experience of stalkers, had hit the nail on the head right away.

The next week Charlie was less hesitant in his appraisal of Yumi.

"She's weird, man" he said, obviously now starting to feel a little concerned about this unwelcome intrusion into his weekly routine, aware that maybe forces beyond his control were starting to gather for the first time since his arrival in the country.

"She was waiting for me again. I said I was tired, told her to go home."

"You charmer, Charlie. That's no way to treat your girlfriend."

"She's not my girlfriend!" If Charlie had been a different person, these words would have been hissed out, but that wasn't Charlie's style. "We've only been out a few times, not even real dates. I never invited her to my house either."

The evening progressed and with a few more beers inside him, Charlie seemed to relax more, He wasn't one to revel, but I think he enjoyed the fact that he had an interesting story. Maybe even a little prouder to have a stalker rather than a mere girlfriend.

And I too began to look forward to our Friday evenings in a much more proactive way than I ever had before. Over the next few weeks, it became clear that Charlie had indeed got himself a stalker.

"Yours still waiting every Friday, Murray?"

"Yup."

"How do you deal with it?"

"It's a nightmare. It never stops."

But for Murray nothing had changed over the years. It had developed into exactly the same odd pattern almost every week. He would arrive home to find her waiting outside his door, argue with her for a while before giving up, realizing only too well the futility of trying to chase her away and aware that it was far simpler just to let her in. Impressively, it hadn't interfered with other girlfriends he'd managed to juggle around.

"What's she actually like?" I asked, realizing that I knew hardly anything about this girl's character. Was there much variability in stalkers' personalities?

"God, she's mental. A complete lunatic." Murray rolled his eyes around for extra effect.

In a way I was starting to feel a little left out. Why didn't I have a stalker? It wasn't fair.

Murray's situation at least seemed...stable? stagnant? stalemate? What's the correct word for a stalker situation which doesn't worsen? He had reached the stage where he was resigned to his predicament, where even if he didn't like it at least he knew what to expect. Charlie was different. He was still trying to work out the implications of this wholly unexpected disruption in his life and the possible ways things might evolve. He was desperately trying to find a way to get rid of her, get quickly back to the simple routine he'd enjoyed for years now. But what to do? How to proceed? Was there any simple solution?

"Why don't you try *The Hokey-Pokey?*" I suggested helpfully. "That should chase her away."

"She's really strange, man," Charlie started the following week. "She came round on Sunday evening. I told her to go away, but she didn't say anything, just stood there. Then she started ringing the doorbell. She didn't stop for, like, twenty minutes. I opened the door, told her to cut it out but she didn't even look at me. She just continued pressing the damn thing for another hour."

The next Sunday she was back, ringing the bell again. Charlie disconnected it but undeterred, she simply stayed put and knocked on the door. It was no longer confined to Sundays now either. She came round any night of the week, sometimes staying outside all night long. Occasionally she would simply stand in the street, shouting his name out for hours on end.

"Why don't you go to the police?" I asked.

"Oh, that doesn't work," Murray, with all his experience, chimed in. "They can't do anything unless there's some damage."

"She's a psycho," said Charlie the following week. Murray and I had long since reached the same conclusion. The man was shaken. His simple life of gathering money had been rocked.

"She smashed the plant pots in the entrance."

Oh. The next level had been reached.

"So that means you can go to the police now."

Yes, he had been already in fact and they had said it was not a police matter, just a little domestic spat. No help forthcoming there, so Charlie had enrolled one of his friends from *Rock Bar* to come and help. Maybe she'd listen to a voice of reason in Japanese? No, apparently not. Not interested.

The next week she broke the headlights on his moped. Scratched it for good measure too. And the week after that she threw a stone and broke his kitchen window.

"I think it's time to send in Murray," I suggested. The time for *Hokey Pokey* had clearly been and gone. Murray looked interested for a few seconds, before deciding that probably one stalker was plenty. There was no mistaking the clear escalation of Yumi's actions, nor the effect it was having on Charlie, who had gone from annoyed to ruffled to bewildered in a very short space of time. All of these emotions were new to him, at least in his time in Japan, and now he was moving up to the next, entirely unfamiliar zone: Genuinely scared.

It was hard to believe how useless the police were. Charlie had been to ask their help again, but was told politely they couldn't do anything unless the nature of the offences got serious. Charlie shook his head in disbelief. Broken windows, smashed pots. These were hardly everyday occurrences in Japan. Maybe if the police were focusing their resources on a murder epidemic or drug gang warfare, they could be forgiven for choosing to pass on such trivial issues as stalkers. But this was Japan, one of the most crime-free countries in the world. What did the police actually do? They were always unfailingly happy to give directions to tourists or help senile 80-somethings find their way home, but apparently their mandate didn't stretch to protecting victims of vandalization and destruction of property. Maybe that was covered by the tax office? Very strange.

So it seemed like Charlie was on his own. And things didn't look good. What were the options? There was the temptation to become aggressive, threaten to do her some harm, but on further thought Yumi was clearly beyond rational thinking and you suspected that may be akin to going down the path of Mutually Assured Destruction. The sad truth was that whatever he did or didn't do it was hard to imagine the situation not getting worse. I'd completely decided by now that I was entirely happy without a stalker.

The following Friday, Charlie somewhat unexpectedly asked if he could come and stay at my house for one night, maybe two. "You know, I just need a good night's sleep. I'm starting to go crazy."

"Sure man, any time" I said, smiling. "What are friends for?" A moment's reflection followed. "Provided you can guarantee that Yumi won't be tailing you," I added nervously. I wasn't even really joking.

Two days later I was waiting for him, having just returned from an afternoon drive to a local hot spring. He had told me that his last lesson finished at six o'clock, slightly earlier than usual, and he planned to come over straight from his student's house already having dropped off an overnight bag the previous day. While I was getting ready for our guest, my eye caught a vaguely familiar house on the local TV news, with flames and smoke pouring out of the top.

"Asami," I called to my girlfriend. "Take a look at this. Charlie's house is on fire!" We stood in front of the TV for a few moments, watching. It was surreal in a way how unsurprised we were.

"I wonder if he knows?" she asked.

"Let's ask him." I picked up the phone and dialed. There was that unmistakable high tone, "Hi!"

"Hey, Charlie, do you know your house is on fire?" I felt like I was asking him if he knew his socks were on the wrong way round.

"Really? No, I didn't know that. Well see you at 6:30 then."

"Sure." Then, turning to Asami: "Erm, no he didn't know."

By the time Charlie arrived fifteen minutes later, the live news report had changed. But I assumed the house was still burning.

"And," I said, sitting down on the sofa and passing him a cup of coffee, "it was definitely your house. No mistake."

We chatted for a while. He finished his coffee and stood up. "Well I guess I'd better go and take a look. See if there's anything left."

"OK. Good luck," I said. As soon as he'd gone, I commented how only Charlie could take the news of his house burning down so well. That was the Charlie I knew. Barely turning a hair in the face of horrific news. Then I suddenly remembered about the money-filled drawer. Oh shit. That's gonna hurt. Surely even Charlie couldn't stay impervious to that. No insurance there. I imagined all those paper bills curling up, turning first to flames, then ashes and blowing up, up into the air and away on the wind. *I'll huff and I'll puff and I'll blow all your money away.* I felt like crying just thinking about it.

Two hours later, Charlie was back. We went out on to the balcony for a smoke.

"How did it go?" I asked.

"It was good," he shrugged. "I guess."

This was either a stunning show of putting on a brave face in adversity, or the man had clearly lost it already. Too many sleepless nights can do that.

"Sorry about the money. Shit, Charlie. The house too of course, I guess, that kind of sucks too, but the money. Your money. Your precious money. How much did you have in there?"

Without answering, Charlie took a drag, then reached his hand into his bag and pulled out a wad of money. And then another. And another. I stared, somewhat speechless.

"The firefighters let me in," he explained calmly. "There's not much left of the house. Not much left of the top drawer or the middle drawer, but the bottom drawer was OK. A bit soggy, what with all the water they sprayed, but it's all there."

And for the first time, I laid my eyes on the money that had so often been the topic of our weekly conversations. The legendary pile of money in Charlie's bottom drawer, hiding under the underpants. Soggy. But intact. The fire had burnt down everything but the one thing he really cared about.

"Mind if I keep it on the balcony, let it dry out?"

"As long as you want, Charlie." Who was I to refuse?

And so the story has a happy ending. The piggy came to his friend's house of bricks. He was safe. That night doubtless Charlie slept with a slight smile on his face, dreaming of his safe stash, relieved also no doubt because the police now would surely have to act. And they did, not before time. Yumi was arrested, didn't even try to deny anything. She went to court and from there was sent to a mental institution. The wolf drowned in a pot of boiling water. Not only that, but in true Japanese style, her family came around, bowed, apologized profusely for their daughter's terrible actions and offered serious amounts of money by way of compensation. Rosier and rosier. It almost began to feel like Charlie had planned the whole thing from the start.

But something had in fact changed inside Charlie. Imperceptible at first, his life had started to unravel. His routine was out of whack. Now without a house, Mega found him an empty room in a flat, where he became a room-mate with a couple of the newer faces. It was hard for him to get used to it.

"It doesn't matter Charlie," we said. "Just look around and you can find another house, piece of cake. Maybe you can find one even cheaper than the last one."

"Yeah," he said, but you could see that he wasn't quite himself. The shock of seeing his rock solid existence crumble away had in fact, despite initial appearances, shaken him at some deeper level. He was more than just a money-making robot after all.

Yumi the wolf had blown down the house, and effectively by so doing had called his time in Japan. We'd teased him about it many times before. "What are you going to do when you go back to US anyway? You're gonna hate it." But it was just a question of time.

"You know, I'm thinking about leaving," he said one day. "Going back to the US, maybe buying a house in Arizona. I have some family just outside Phoenix."

And another three months later he was gone.

Funnily enough, just a month before his departure he came to the Izakaya with a girl. This was something that had never happened before. I don't remember her name, but she seemed pleasant. Normal. Maybe even a reason for changing his mind?

"She's nice," he said simply, without a hint of a shrug. This, coming from Charlie, was a ringing endorsement. Maybe if she'd just come along a couple of months earlier he might even have considered staying, but the process of leaving had started. He'd already mentally said farewell to the country which had been his home for so long. Eight years spent working hard, building a life for himself only to see his house burn down. We held a small party for him at the Izakaya. They even stretched to a small cake in recognition of his years of custom. It was not a madly emotional occasion, but it was something. I hope he appreciated it. It was kind of hard to tell.

He was not the type who was ever going to make much of an effort to stay in touch, but we got a few messages, just enough to know what happened over the next couple of months. Me and Murray had a bet on how long he'd stay in America. I'd only give him six months, I said. "Three months," said Murray. Murray won. Next thing, we heard he'd found a new job. He was already in China. China: The new Japan, now the new world centre of the insatiable demand for native English teachers. I imagined him starting all over again. He was probably rich enough to retire already, but I pictured him in a modest house with a fridge full of Chinese brand Cola, introducing himself to everyone. "Hi, I'm Charlie!" Did they have any legends in China relating to peaches, I wondered? Were the houses made of bricks?

I only ever met him one more time. It was a few years later, when my daughter was just speaking her first sentences. I got a phone call, picked up and heard a familiar high-pitched "Hi".

"Charlie? Is that you?"

"Yeah, I'm back in Kumamoto," he said. "Do you mind if I stay at your place a couple of nights?"

"What, did your hotel burn down?"

Actually, he hadn't made a special visit to see me. I would have been astounded if he had. Apparently he had stayed in touch with the girl he'd met just before he left Japan. Maybe romance hadn't blossomed in China and he'd decided to part with some of his precious cash to come back to meet her. But something had gone awry in their plans and they didn't meet up - she changed her mind at the last minute? - and so I was a fall-back. We went to the bar that night. I introduced him to a few people. "Oh, you're the guy whose house was burnt down by a stalker? I heard about you. What's your name again? Peach, that's right! Wow! Amazing story."

The next day, I introduced him to my daughter, who'd been born just a year after Charlie had left. "Hi, I'm Charlie," he said. She looked suspiciously at the pink, podgy hand stretched out in her direction. "It's OK," I said. "Charlie and I used to be good friends." A broad smile lit up her face when I told her his unusual surname.

And now, over a decade later, we often come across old photos of her father in his single days, sometimes with a slightly chubby guy in a baseball cap standing to one side and I tell her, "That's one of Papa's old friends. His name is Charlie." And she cocks her head, then there's a flash of recognition.

"Oh...that's Mr. Peach?" She only ever met him once. But she remembers him.

3) Jim Takes a Boat Ride.

Here's the thing about Japan: It's a nice, easy place to live. Things work here. A train running late is not even an issue. Sure, we get the occasional earthquake, but even that tends to be interesting rather than scary. Most of the time, that is.

There's a real toy-town quality to every city, with the small, clean trucks buzzing around the streets, delivering things. The garbage collectors efficiently run around in their spotless uniforms, rain or shine. Road workers are unfailingly polite. There's never a bum crack to be seen. Oh, and they take really short coffee breaks.

There really is a fraction of the numbers of homeless, beggars, criminals to be found in most countries. Not only that, you can consider yourself unlucky if the wallet you left on the train or in the bar doesn't eventually find its way back to you.

It's different from back home. Lots of dangers we just assumed we had to accept simply don't exist here. If you need any more proof, there is the common sight of 14 or 15 year old girls cycling home alone from cram school at 10:30 pm, parents unconcerned. It really is a safe place. It's not hard to see why many Gaijin end up staying here.

"How long have you been here?" I asked an Australian guy I bumped into while I was hiking a few months ago.

"Oooh, a long time," he said in that kind of semi-embarrassed way people adopt when admitting to some act of idiocy committed while drunk. Same batch as me, I thought. Came over in his mid-twenties, got married, had a couple of kids, possibly once thought about going back home, didn't do anything about it, then one day realized he'd been away too long and he was too old to start up again. And life's pretty good here anyway. Comfortable. More years pass and going home becomes ever more unlikely. And then you have to remind yourself: This is now home.

Yes, it's easy to see why people stay. But why do they come in the first place? What is the attraction of Japan? That's a trickier one to answer. For a few, it might be some casual or even occasionally deep-seated interest in a point of Japanese culture - martial arts, say, or even manga. But this surely only applies to a small minority. Then there are those who come for reasons of romance or business opportunities. But I think it's safe to say that the majority just arrive as travellers, curious to explore a new country while earning a decent income. And for many, short term plans morph seamlessly into long term stays.

So when you meet other Gaijin in Japan, the question of why they came here in the first place is rarely interesting. There is a pretty even split between those who feel attracted to joining the Gaijin community - the birds of a feather types - and those who will avoid it like the plague, choosing either to shun other humans completely or else to immerse themselves in Japanese culture, increasingly hostile towards others who see their Gaijin features and assume they are interested in striking up casual (English) conversation. Those who prefer to avoid other Gaijin as far as possible can hardly be blamed. As well as a sprinkling of genuinely nice folk, there are lots of Gaijin you meet on an almost daily basis where you sometimes can't help thinking, "How did this guy ever get a job here?" Then you remember that it's easy, that's how you got your teaching post in the first place. And you start wishing that it was a little harder to get a job. You wish that you could count yourself among the chosen few, one of those who were selected to work in this country for their superior intelligence and ability.

But we are not.

"At least they should surely set the quality level a little higher," you find yourself muttering under your breath. "They really should make more of an effort to keep some of the dross out."

You see the guy whose social skills are so limited that he exhausts himself just saying hello, and you can't stop thinking, "What on earth would this person be doing back in his home country?" before realizing that this is precisely the reason why he's here.

Oh yes, make no mistake it's an easy place to get a teaching job. Used to be, at any rate. It's definitely disappointing that I can't provide an interesting anecdote when I'm asked about why I came to Japan or how I got the job.

"How I got the job?" I want to repeat. "I gave them my name and told them when I wanted to start! Ha! How about that for boring!"

Jim's tale provides the ultimate proof that anyone can get a job in Japan. But at the same time, his story is undoubtedly far more interesting than mine. In fact I doubt if there is anyone in the whole country with a more amazing story of how they ended up here. If there is, I sure would love to hear it. Spoiler alert: There's no tragic ending, no crazed angry lover, no life slipping out of control.

Oh wait…actually there is. But all this comes at the beginning.

So let's go back to Kumamoto Mega. A new teacher was coming. It was rather exciting. We didn't know anything about him, except that it was a him. He was to be the first addition to our staff since my arrival, four months earlier. What would he be like, we wondered?

Had he come directly from his country, probably a fresh university graduate? Would he be a Virgin Gaijin or had he been transferred from elsewhere, maybe having already lived in Japan for a year or two? We were hoping for the former. It's always nice to have a linguistic and cultural beginner to take under your wing and show them the way. From my year in Saitama where new arrivals were almost a weekly occurrence, I remembered enjoying the feeling of being looked up to by some new face, impressed (however briefly) that I was able to communicate effectively in this foreign language. And eat raw fish without grimacing. Not that it really mattered. The most important thing would be to have a like-minded person, someone who was ready to embrace the whole experience for what it was. Conform? Click? Whatever the right word is, basically not rock the boat.

It was a memorable day when Jim Parker walked into the school for the first time. All eyes were on our newest teacher. With his broad smile he didn't seem short on positivity, which was a good start. But it was easy to spot that there was something different about him.

"Nice to meet you my name is Jim," he said without pausing, revealing a heavy South African accent I'd only ever heard before on TV. But the main difference had been spotted even before he opened his mouth. It was unmistakable there in his balding scalp, his greying beard. His blue eyes may have been twinkling, but there were no two ways about it: Jim was, definitely and unequivocally, old. The guy must have been double my age. Now that came as a total surprise. In the little world we'd created over the last few months, there was a real university vibe. It was almost as if we'd had so much fun at college that we'd entered into a pact to recreate those good times once more before sadly saying farewell and, with a huge sigh, finally entering the real world of work, where we would be allowed to start to get old. But that wasn't going to happen for a while longer if we could help it.

Until now, our nearest definition of "old" was Charlie, who was rapidly closing in on thirty. Thirty!!! Maybe that went some way to explaining his insatiable desire for cash? The Japanese staff were of a similar age, mid to late twenties. There was a rumour that Rie, the manager, in spite of her adolescent appearance and shy smile, was actually (gasp) in her mid-thirties, although I couldn't quite believe it and there was no way of possibly corroborating this. But Jim, standing there with his patently Santa Claus / Colonel Sanders facial features backed up by his considerable girth, just seemed like he'd wondered into the wrong office. "Sorry, didn't you see the 'no over 40s' sign on the door? The invisible one?"

So there we were, suddenly and rudely confronted with this entirely unwelcome vision of what was waiting for all of us within a couple of decades. Who the hell was this guy? Assuming there wasn't some bureaucratic error, what on earth was this old dude doing, starting a job as a teacher in Mega? Was he a failed businessman? Forced abroad by his wife to send money home? Mid-life crisis, wanting to make a fresh start? Was there a samurai hidden within that ample frame that simply refused to wait any longer to come out? Well you couldn't rule anything out, but I guessed it was more than likely that he'd already done a bit of time in Japan. I was not alone in having worked in another Mega branch before my happy arrival here in Kumamoto. Maybe Jim too had worked in another town or two? Looking at those wrinkles, you couldn't help thinking maybe he'd done a year in every city in the country. At the very least, surely this wasn't his first stop in Japan?

"How long have you been in Japan then, Jim?"

"Oh, about two weeks."

Bang goes another theory.

"I see, so you're new here. First job?"

"That's right."

Yes, he was a Virgin and I certainly was NOT expecting that at all.

We'd wait a little before finding out the details of his pre-Japan life, because for now the most important thing was to see if he would fit in to our world. A world in which we spent an unhealthy amount of time drinking together. The Japanese staff, Rie, Motoko and Miwa, Yasu and Taka, plus a new arrival, Daisuke, were regulars. Sharon was sure to be there. Kenny would be out most nights as long as it didn't clash with other social engagements, but Steve was disappearing fast, retreating into his shell. Charlie had just moved into his house of sticks, while Natasha had a new spring in her step, the prospect of having to face Charlie before breakfast no longer something she needed to worry about.

There was a kind of apprehension among us. Our antics were frequently rather immature. Should we change our behaviour in deference to this senior citizen? Would he even want to come out with us in the first place? Maybe he would be reluctant - either out of fear, disgust or simple lack of interest - to revisit the world of the young that he had once presumably inhabited?

Again, completely wrong. Over the next few weeks, Jim threw himself into our little party scene with a gusto beyond even that which Kenny could muster. He approached life with an energy that put most of us "youngies" to shame. He never missed a night out.

"So, where are we going tonight?" he'd ask, eyes gleaming.

"Not tonight Jim," I'd groan. "I need a break," marvelling at the ability of this guy to recover from the previous night's damage so easily. You'd sometimes be forgiven for thinking he hadn't seen the inside of a bar for years.

I have to confess here a certain prejudice I have always had towards older people. Where exactly this comes from, I will never know, but at certain points in my life it has caused problems. At university, something grated when professors "hung out" with their students. It just didn't seem right. There was a structure for things. Young people go to bars; professors should be home working on their latest theses or having meetings with colleagues behind closed college doors, not socializing with their students, pretending to be cool. I watched with a certain mystery when some of my friends were able to carry on their conversations, switching between fellow students and teachers with no apparent unease. Did they forget that the professor was *over fifty*?

Then in an office job in France, I shared a desk with a certain Barry Titley, who, if he didn't have any grandkids, was certainly old enough to have done so. I'd managed not to make any jokes whatsoever about his name, and after he'd assured me of his "young" credentials, going as far as to invite me to his house to watch some porno movies together, apparently under the impression that was how us young ones spent our time · or at least showing that he wasn't some stuck·up puritanical sort · I'd gone on to forge an easy·going relationship, admittedly with a few misgivings, until one day I uncharacteristically briefly forgot his age and made a slightly sarcastic comment to something he said. Maybe something about creaking bones or middle aged beer bellies, in the same way that I might have teased one of my younger friends for bum-fluff on his upper lip - and Barry virtually exploded. A stream of vitriol followed about young people lacking respect, etc, etc. It was something so slight yet the reaction was so enormous; and it confirmed me in my long held belief that older people should be treated at all times with politeness, occasionally with respect, but they were not to be befriended.

Arriving in Saitama, as well as the teachers fresh out of college, there were a few who were more advanced in years and I tried to avoid them as far as politely possible. Who wanted to socialize with someone old and boring like that? What were they doing here anyway? Didn't fit in? Couldn't find a place back in society? They should be appreciative that Mega was willing to take them on. Thankful that Mega was such a successful company that they couldn't satisfy the demand for teachers by employing only recent graduates. These oldies should be bloody grateful!

Anyway, Jim did more than anyone in my life to cure me of this strange bias. Only a week passed before any apprehensions about his age subsided. We were out having a few drinks, sitting around the table, joking around. A few teasers to start with - "I wonder who the oldest person here today is? Who could it possibly be?" - which didn't seem to offend him in the slightest, and before long we felt no real need to hold back. Anything became fair game, from vague ageist jokes, to more specific references to receding hair, colour thereof, or his ever expanding bulk. Soon I forgot that I'd ever been concerned about causing offence and became comfortable teasing him as much as anyone. In fact, once the green light had been given, we were pretty merciless, and Jim took it all in the best of spirits.

It was a revelation of sorts. Wow, I thought. It is possible to go out and take the piss and have a laugh with people even in their mid-forties. And with my dumb age prejudice quickly evaporating, I had to admit that the guy was ridiculously good company.

"That beer tasted exactly like another one," he would say every night, shortly after sitting down in our chosen Izakaya, having already downed the first ice cold beer of the evening and thrusting a few fingers in the direction of the waiter, who hurriedly brought the next round.

Jim loved telling stories. Theoretically speaking, that is. He rarely got to the end of them, distracted by one thought or another, or shot down in the telling. But even if he got to the end of the story, it didn't matter what the punch line was. Probably there was no punch line or he got lost in the crucial final phase: Jim was no natural wit, but it was the way it was delivered that was important.

"And she had all the personality of a bag of Portland cement!" he said, banging his glass of beer down, splashing half of us. Or: "I told her to take off her clothes and she did!" staring around at us, challenging us to contradict him. The sheer enthusiasm of the guy rendered the inherent interest of the story irrelevant. Of course! We were too busy laughing at him, this big fat man reliving his youth, untroubled by any notions of PC.

Jim had moved into Kenny's apartment, another room-mate for the luckless Steve, another unwelcome presence.

"Oh my God, he's hilarious," Kenny would say on an almost daily basis. Talking to himself, walking into Kenny's (or Steve's) room any time of day or night a propos nothing, crashing into things, farting, making all kinds of inappropriate comments (for someone of his age), snoring at barely believable decibel levels, wandering around naked after a shower. This was fertile material for Kenny, far better than snooping around after Steve.

Jim's conversations were peppered with his favourite expressions, repeated constantly with the same delight as if he was pronouncing them for the first time. "She's got all the personality of a bag of Portland Cement," he announced yet again when asked about his new student. Spoken as if he'd just invented the phrase. I thought he had a number of times, unsure whether a particular saying was from a bygone generation, restricted to South Africa or made up by the man himself. "I wouldn't go in there for a while, it smells like something died," he would announce proudly after emerging from the toilet. Hmm, thanks for the warning, Jim.

So what exactly had Jim been doing before he came to Japan? Well, it wasn't the easiest thing to discern. Jim's style of talking was random, to put it mildly, often the end of any given sentence having little in common with the beginning. There were references aplenty to sports. Rugby especially seemed to have been a big part of his young life. Lots of mentions of girlfriends, wives. Some stuff about England, boats, life at sea. Had he travelled with his English parents to South Africa in a boat when he was a boy? If so there was no trace of a British accent when he spoke. He seemed to identify himself absolutely with South Africa. He spoke with great respect of Mandela. That was a relief - not one of those white supremacists then. That could have been another reason why he'd come here: Disgust for the new regime, nostalgia for the good old days of apartheid. But no, Jim was no racist. He'd proudly joined demonstrations in support of Mandela; the guy was one of his heroes.

How about family then? There seemed to be a daughter. "She has no tits at all," he declared without being asked, shaking his head at the injustice of it. There was at least one marriage in there somewhere, but who knew if that had any relation to his daughter? "Sheila" was a name frequently mentioned. "Called Sheila last night. She's started a diet!" again with those staring eyes, a demand for some reaction, even though we were clueless who Sheila was and why he suddenly talked about her, and it was pointless asking because he'd be back on a totally different subject.

There was the constant danger that without interruption Jim would start rambling unchecked for the whole evening. Memories of his life in South Africa suddenly turned to Hong Kong for no apparent reason. Then a few other countries would be randomly dropped in.

"There's Grandpa going on about the war again," said Murray. Eyes rolled. He's off again. We teased him, but he didn't take the slightest offence, kept ploughing on. But if half the stuff he talked about was true then he certainly seemed to have lived quite a life. "If you don't enjoy yourself, then someone else will do it for you" was his often repeated mantra.

Some of the more mature students were delighted by Jim's arrival. They assumed he would be better informed on world issues than us "kids" and looked forward to more challenging topics for discussion. They viewed him as one of them, and approached him with offers of friendship, imagining he might be more receptive to their invitations for a coffee and chat about politics.

They were wrong.

"I never hang out with old people. They're so boring!" he announced, again with that pause and glare defying someone to challenge him, his South African accent hovering over the table. Well, I wasn't going to argue with him, was I? On the contrary, I was surprised to hear my own opinions so closely echoed, delighted someone shared my prejudice, not to say thrilled by the not so delicate way he'd phrased it.

"Old people are boring."

Yes, I couldn't agree more. But how were we to define old? What was the point at which people became boring? How come Jim managed to conveniently exclude himself from his definition of "old"?

On a simple level, Jim was just looking for an excuse to hang out with younger girls. But there was something interesting at a cultural level that I think Jim inadvertently put his podgy finger on · a certain paradox, by which Japanese people age on the outside far more slowly than your average Westerner and yet crustiness, for want of a better word, sets in on the inside far earlier.

"Young people."

I wasn't sure if I was allowed to fit into that category specifically any more. It was a real shock when I realized, celebrating my 25th birthday, that I would be in the older half of revellers enjoying a *Club 18-30* vacation. The term "young people" as I had understood it most of my life seemed to apply to those up to university age. That ruled me out by three years and counting, but I didn't feel I'd changed at all on the inside. The suit and tie felt like a façade. I loved my job and the challenges of teaching all different ages and abilities, but in terms of bonding on a personal level, it was only really in my classes with college students when I felt on the same wavelength. The bond weakened rapidly as the students' age increased. In Japan, the transition from university to working man is rather abrupt, and I was frequently struck by how suddenly a Japanese 22 year old who gloried in stories of his own stupidity and immaturity would adopt a middle-aged outlook on life only months after gaining honest employment. If you wanted to equate maturity with being boring, Jim certainly had a point. There was many a guy in his early thirties who could already be classified as "super crusty." You couldn't help feel it was rather odd seeing Jim dismiss someone ten years younger as old and dull, but it was hard not to disagree with his reasoning. I for one could understand exactly where he was coming from.

My own maturity, or lack thereof, was of a far more Western variety. When I excused myself in the middle of a lesson one time to go and relieve myself, I congratulated myself on electing not to explain that I'd been drinking until the early hours of the morning, much less that I'd just been vomiting up last night's tequila. "How's that for professionalism?" I wanted to say. Not particularly impressive, but I think it's fair to say that I hadn't become crusty quite yet.

Jim conducted himself very unlike any other middle-aged man I'd ever met. But for Christ's sake the guy was not so far away from fifty, and this fact only stuck out even more in this land where people always seemed to act their age. Surely there was at least a hint of crustiness in there?

It's frequently commented upon by Japanese and Gaijin alike - probably because it's true - how little Japanese tend to change physically as they age. Let's take a look in Jim's classroom now and try an experiment. He's sitting with a group of four students and a caption underneath invites us to pick the only person in there under fifty years of age. The only reason anybody might have for picking the Gaijin is by assuming it's a trick question: The oldest-looking person must be the youngest, otherwise what's the point of the question? And you can see that by any normal criteria - hair (lack of), facial hair (colour of), nose (reddishness) or stomach (bulk thereof) - Jim looks far older even than 64 year old Mr. Hirayama. Experiment over.

But wait! Let's have another look at that test group and see if we can't try and measure what's on the inside, see how closely their biological age corresponds with how they comport themselves. How can we proceed? Maybe a short survey?

Do they spend more of their time on social media or in the garden? What makes them laugh: Fart jokes or political satire? What makes them happy: A new pair of socks or game software? Which will they click on: The latest Miley Cyrus gossip or the Tom Hanks new release info?

Or maybe we could use some computer trickery to get rid of those outward signs of ageing and see if our test group's behaviour suits their new young bodies?

Ultimately it is of course a futile exercise. All you could say was that at the end of the day when Mr. Hirayama looked in the mirror, he was merely happy that his wrinkles were not too severe. But when Jim looked in the mirror he saw his twenty-year-old self staring back and couldn't understand why other people wouldn't too. He believed in himself absolutely as a young man. He had faith. Portland bags full of it.

His faith in his desirability was truly remarkable, the cause of endless head scratching among the rest of us. He still saw himself as attractive to the younger members of the fairer sex, when even my forty year old single female students sniggered disparagingly when I mentioned the fact that Jim was "available."

So in spite of being double our age and looking even older than that, his words and his actions were frequently strangely adolescent. The question was: Should we be embarrassed about it? Should we slap him on the head and tell him to grow up?

There he was sitting next to young Akari, being way more attentive than was strictly called for, nodding his head vigorously at her most banal comments, covering his eyes in mock horror, raising his eyebrows exaggeratedly, simply trying way too hard to make an impression. Kind of creepy Jim, tone it down! Act your age, man!

"Do you think she likes me?" he asked, when Akari had excused herself from his clutches. His refusal to see himself as any different from us twenty something's was truly heroic. But we had to be honest.

"Yes Jim, I'm sure she likes you, but if you're asking me if I think she is attracted to you then unless she has a thing for over-age, sweaty bald men with body odour and a huge paunch, I think it's safe to say: No."

Jim inevitably got used to being turned down so many times that it really should have started to gnaw at his self-belief. But of course it didn't. The man was impervious. He genuinely saw himself as still "on the market". There didn't seem to be any doubts at all that girls half his age might run off screaming after one look at his middle-aged features. Any worries that he had seemed to lay in other directions.

"You see, I'm quite big," he said after explaining, well, something. Thanks for that Jim.

And his sheer bloody refusal to accept his age seemed to work miraculously. He arrived one night with what appeared to be his girlfriend.

"This is Satoko," he said, face bursting with pride.

"So you two are a couple then?" I asked Satoko, a plain, slightly nervous girl who seemed to be around my age.

"Ooooooh no," she blurted out, while Jim sat next to her, arm draped around her shoulders, beaming away. Satoko did her best to deny any romance for the rest of the evening, but was last seen heading out after a suitable pause in the general direction of Jim's apartment. The old devil.

But clumsy efforts to flirt with girls half his age aside, his lust for life did him credit. Office life in Japan frequently revolves around karaoke. This is a fact. I was torn on the whole karaoke debate. It was one of those things that you had to do sparingly if it was to remain enjoyable. The more often you went, the more tiresome it would become, and I could feel my karaoke tolerance diminish month by month. But there was no denying it was useful to bond with our Japanese staff members. The shyest member, Daisuke, simply *had* to do his *Pachinko Man*, we wouldn't let him not sing it. And Rie and Miwa would show off their incredible voices, with stunning versions of Dreams Come True or Utada Hikaru. What is it about Japan that turns out such great singers? Well, spending so many hours in a karaoke box, for a start.

If Jim was anything to go by, South African rugby didn't have any vocal tradition like say the Welsh do, but he was no worse than the rest of us Gaijin. But really, wasn't he past it to get anything out of the latest hits of SMAP, or Amuro Namie's *Body Feels Exit*, let alone some of the newer teeny J-pop efforts? Well, apparently no he wasn't. For a man with a tendency towards classical music and opera (entirely appropriate), he was remarkably open to music of different cultures and younger generations. In Jim's book, a night out singing the latest J-pop hits in karaoke was something to be relished rather than merely endured. "That really hit the mark," he announced approvingly - and somewhat surprisingly - after a rendition of all-girl pop group Morning Musume's new hit brought another three hour session of karaoke to a close.

"They're out to kill me," said Jim one evening, staring at me as if I might have some clue what he was on about.

"Who's that, Jim? Are you talking about boring old men whose daughters you tried to seduce?" Actually, no. Don't worry, I'll explain.

Jim looked in many ways like he was one of the more sedentary staff among us, but this was another gross misreading. He was in fact the most restless of everyone, putting us to shame in his relentless exploration of the area.

To be honest, we were a pretty lazy bunch when it came to learning more about Kumamoto's local history or geography. Entirely in keeping with our university vibe, you could say. To Charlie's credit, he made time from his teaching-every-waking-minute schedule to join the local September festival, when horses are paraded noisily through the town in memory of a glorious military campaign in Korea 400 years ago. Sounds like an unmissable event, aside from one crucial factor: The festival gets underway at 4 am. "Think I'll pass," I said, every year. Jim made it, heroically rousing himself after a few hours of beauty sleep that you'd think he needed more than anyone else.

For most of us, free time spent not drinking was probably just free time recovering from previous time drinking. In other words, trying not to make sudden, unnecessary movements or decisions. The illusion that we were still in college was helped by the fact that nobody owned a car. Why would we? None of us had any plans to be living here beyond the short term. And in any case, it wasn't that hard to get around. This may not have been Tokyo, but public transport was reasonable. It was possible, with a minimum of effort, to get out and explore.

"Let's go and spend the day in Nagasaki, check out the A-bomb museum," you might suggest. It was only a two hour ride from here after all. But even with the best intentions, there was always that tendency to wake up just a little later than you were planning, thereby missing the train you were thinking about catching. Add to that the fact that it was just slightly hotter than comfortable for sightseeing and figure in the traces of alcohol still in the blood and it was much more likely you'd be spending your day off well within walking distance of your air-conditioned bedroom.

Not Jim. He was the first of us to get wheels. Two of them, to be precise. Was this just a cynical ploy to whisk some easily impressed young lady off to the countryside? Well actually, one look said no. His "motorbike" was no Harley Davidson and the sight of portly Jim astride his scooter was probably even more laughable than watching his chat-up routine at the bar. But who cares? Certainly not Jim. His only concern was the danger he faced on the roads.

The people who were out to kill him were the motorists he had to share the narrow lanes with. Fair enough; my limited experience of cycling in and around the city had quickly taught me that I probably would be better off staying home if I wanted to reach the ripe old age that Jim had somehow managed to attain. Jim was made of sterner stuff though, his readiness to brave the dangers in spite of his misgivings reaping the rich rewards of the intrepid traveller.

Soon he was coming back with tales of paddling around in secret pools fed by gushing waterfalls only thirty minutes outside the city, chancing upon a shrine with a huge six metre long phallus statue, or soaking in a barely visited hot spring with unbeatable ocean sunsets. I searched my *Lonely Planet* in vain: These local treasures were well beyond its scope.

Back in the more familiar environment of our regular nocturnal haunts, we still hadn't got completely used to the bizarre left-field comments Jim so effortlessly excelled in. You certainly never knew what you would get next. One humid July night, we were at a *yakitori* bar, enjoying their delectable never-ending themes of chicken-on-a-stick while talking about another new teacher, Paul, who'd arrived a week earlier and who didn't seem interested in socializing with the rest of us, choosing instead to head back home each evening.

"The baboon doesn't see its forehead," Jim suddenly announced, staring around at us with something which might have been construed as the wisdom of a man who had seen life and understood it. We assumed this was an opening statement to be followed up by at least something - but no, Jim was back to his thoughts, slurping down another swig of beer before burping loudly and grinning inanely at poor Motoko, sitting next to him.

Another sultry night, we were trying to cool off in the roof-top beer garden and Kenny was moaning about Rie's slightly curious mood swings of late. Jim declared:

"Oooh, I can't stand Kiwis. They have no sense of humour!"

Definitely less ambiguous this time, but I was similarly clueless as to what the hell he was referring to. And again, nothing more forthcoming.

There's nothing like a suddenly pronounced statement, with no apparent relation to anything previously touched on, to totally destroy the flow of conversation - and Jim was the undisputed master of this. Had Rie been talking privately to Jim? Were her moods connected to some ill-fated romance to a New Zealander that we were unaware of? We'd never know, as Jim elaborated no further.

Six months later and Jim was showing no signs of slowing down.

"Coming out tonight, Jim?" I'd ask.

"Does the Pope have hairy armpits?" came the answer. Spoken with the usual flourish. Spoken as if he didn't use the same expression every single day.

Once at the bar, two minutes after the first beer arrived he would say, "That beer tasted exactly like another one," slamming the empty glass down on the table and thrusting a finger in the air towards the waiter.

"So, what did you think of the new teacher, Hannah?"

"She's got as much personality as a bag of Portland cement!"

"Heard anything from Sheila recently?"

"The diet's going really well. Says she's already lost five kilos."

"So you're not going to join her then? Maybe a bit of exercise would be good for you too? You must have put on at least ten kilos since you came here. Why don't you skip the beer for a month? Might improve your chances with the ladies."

"As much chance of that as meeting a friendly Kiwi. More chance of becoming a monk than giving up drinking." Certainly no chance of becoming a monk, I thought. And just what was it about Kiwis that got his goat up?

There was only one time when I managed to touch a nerve, just when I was finally convinced that any topic was fair game. Jim and I shared a love of books and both of us were pretty avid readers. I was into a series of titles on evolution by the likes of Steven Pinker and Richard Dawkins. I was absorbed in one by Daniel Dennett · *Darwin's Dangerous Idea* · with some memorable chapters, one of which particularly tickled me, relating to the author's frustration pursuing a logical argument with a religious believer. How come you are allowed to say whatever you want? he lamented. You can't have a scientific debate about evolution unless you leave your entirely illogical faith out of it. I might as well say God is a ham sandwich wrapped in tin foil.

I quoted this passage to Jim, assuming he'd share my enjoyment of this inventive take-down of the irrationality of religion. And Jim paused, and pulled back.

"You know Pete, my faith is very important to me," he said. Wow. I was stunned. Jim was religious? A real and total surprise, that one! "God loves Kiwis too," I wanted to say to him.

So over the course of twelve eventful months, I got to know Jim, laughed at his eccentricities, got carried away by his enthusiasm for everything, snickered when he did his shy teenager routine on a young lady at the bar, saw plenty of rugby, soccer and cricket games together, and piece by piece put together the life that he had had before that day he entered the Mega office, the newest, oldest, member of our school. The more I learned, the more remarkable it seemed to me.

"You should write a story of your life," I told him on occasion. "It would make a great read." And he muttered something unintelligible about never trusting a Kiwi, and as far as I know never got round to it. There were far too many other things to do for Jim. Life was for living, not for writing about.

And so this, with apologies both to Jim for my many errors and equally to the wonderful people of New Zealand for their blameless demonization in the story, is my version of the tale of how Jim Parker came to be a teacher in Kumamoto Mega, Japan.

Jim was just 13 years old when Parker Sr. made the fateful decision to leave England and move his family over to South Africa. Teenage Jim was none too pleased to be uprooted from his school and friends and even less pleased when he was targeted by some of the bullies for his posh British accent. But Jim was not a small boy and he wasn't afraid of standing up for himself, not averse to throwing the odd punch. Fortunately most of his energy was soon channelled into rugby. A typically active sports-mad lad in England, playing rugby in South Africa was something of an eye-opening experience for young Jim. Here, it was more than just a sport - it was something closer to a religion. The more Jim played rugby, the more he felt at home in his adopted country, and the less he stood out as a Pom.

Before long his impressive physique started winning him some female admirers and chasing women soon became his new favourite pastime. Moving from high school to college, Jim's twin loves of rugby and women continued. Make no mistake, Jim was a ladies' man in his heyday. Upon graduating from college he threw himself into the world of work. Always generous, always smiling, always patient, he quickly became a regular face in all the trendiest spots in the city. He knew all the places to go and quickly picked up all the techniques to pick up the choicest girls. He was never one to stay for long in the same job; he was always looking for a new opportunity, a higher salary, a prettier girlfriend. He played the game and he was good at it. Did a round of the jobs in banks, insurance companies, acquired all the knowledge necessary to set himself up as a private investment adviser.

"It was tough. Took a long time to make it."

But make it he did. He bought himself a nice house in one of the wealthier Cape Town suburbs, added a smart Mercedes in the driveway. Years of hard work and harder womanizing ensued until he met The One: The girl that would become his wife. He just knew it the moment he laid eyes on her. A sweet, sweet angel. Not the usual performance for this one. Time to listen to the word of God for once. Not an easy bit on the side, this treasure, this diamond. *Gotta take your time*, he told himself. *Play the old-fashioned dating game*. And he did. He showered her with presents, waited an almost indecent amount of time before asking her out on a first date. Resisted every molecule in his body screaming out to take her to some hotel. He treated her with respect, played the perfect, honorable Gentleman. A first real kiss on the lips to celebrate when she accepted his proposal, and he was almost at the point of his dream, the dream he'd cherished all his short adult life: To have a virgin wife.

"I stopped seeing almost all my other girlfriends," he said, amazed at himself in this frank recollection of how good he'd been in the run up to his wedding.

And then on the Big Day, after the modest reception party, it was time to take his new wife to the bridal bed. The moment when the fruits of all that self-imposed near celibacy would be rewarded in the sweetest night of his life. What would it feel like to make love to your wife?

"She just lay there, might as well have been dead!"

No ecstasy. No tearful clinging to her man for making her a woman. No reaction at all in fact. Nothing. Oops. A few more weeks of this and Jim quickly reached the conclusion that this was not merely beginner's shyness; the girl was simply not interested in sex. He'd wasted his time. Jim's patience soon evaporated and it wasn't long before he was back to his old haunts, his old ways, his old girlfriends - plus a few new ones for good measure. And then the reaction came - in the form of a divorce paper. House, car, everything to her.

"Bitch."

Back to square one for Jim. But he still had a healthy appetite for work and hadn't lost his flair for networking. Before long he'd changed his job and was soon making more money than ever working as a consultant, advising businesses how to maximize their profits. He'd go around to companies telling them how to be cost-effective. "Lay off a quarter of your employees," he'd say, receiving a handsome check for his advice, as the employees received their notice of termination. A matter of years and he'd already bought another house.

"Worst job I ever had. But it paid well. You just have to leave your conscience at the door."

Then at a party at the house of a friend with a swimming pool, he laid eyes on his next celestial vision.

"Her tits were bursting out of her swimming costume," he said, shaking his head at the memory, emptying the remaining half of beer in one hearty swig. No virgin bride this time for Jim; his second marriage was based on pure lust.

"I knew it was a mistake to marry her all along."

But at least it was a fun mistake. Until the divorce papers came through a second time, that is. And here was his moment of destiny. His good looks were rapidly going the way of middle age. His once proud rugby playing physique was not so proud any more. Those muscles had become simple layers of flab. The hair was starting to go.

"What's the point of the whole thing? Work your bollocks off, and then the bitch just takes everything, I have nothing to show for it. No, in fact I'm not going to do it. The bitch thinks she can just come along, take everything and drop me in the gutter. Ha, I'll show her."

And he showed her.

He sold his house, his car, bought a boat, transferred the rest of the money into a Swiss bank account and sailed out of Cape Town Harbour with a middle finger salute in the general direction of his second ex-wife. Whose name I very much doubt was Sheila.

Up the coast of Africa sailed Jim, further and further from life as he'd known it, slowly getting to grips with this new life aboard a boat.

It wasn't easy, but Jim was in no rush. Months later he arrived in the Mediterranean. Time to stop for a while, join the millionaire yacht owners, play around. Champagne parties on the boat every night. A chance to make up for lost time. Not that Jim had ever wasted much time when it came to chasing girls · the few months before his first wedding notwithstanding · but now there was nothing like work to distract him from pursuing a purely hedonistic lifestyle. "Want to board my yacht? Fancy a trip over to Malta? I could use a pair of hands, especially when they come attached to a long slender body."

He may not have been a movie star, but he had the boat, he had the twinkle in his eye, he had all the lines. And so the girls came and went, the money frittered away, until one day Jim simply got bored.

It was time for a change of scene. Wasn't that why he'd bought the boat in the first place? There were plenty of other places to explore after all.

Next, it was off through the Pillars of Hercules, across the Atlantic to the Caribbean: The Bahamas. And that was even better. And cheaper! This was the way to go. Months more partying followed, but there was always a nervous eye cast towards his savings. His bank balance was still healthy but it was sinking fast. He wasn't going to be able to do this forever. What to do then? Well, how about Asia? With his experience in the financial world, maybe he'd be able to land some work in Hong Kong. There were bound to be all kinds of business opportunities for someone like Jim over there, besides which he'd always been interested in exploring that part of the world. He was a big fan of James Clavell, so what could be better than seeing some of those legendary ports with his own eyes: Singapore, Macau, Shanghai.

And so that became his next plan. He stocked up for the long trip, sailed all the way back to South Africa, stopping only to add more supplies, check in on his daughter, and then around the famous Cape Horn and a first sight of The Indian Ocean. Almost a year after leaving the Caribbean, he arrived in Hong Kong. That's some voyage, but with people nervously eyeing the handover to China, it was not quite the Mecca he'd imagined after all. By now cash was starting to run seriously low, but if he'd imagined stepping off his yacht and into some high-powered job, he was wrong. He'd gained a few more years, a few more pounds around his stomach, that could have been the reason · or maybe he'd simply been away from the world long enough to have become irrelevant. No joy. It was fun at least to spend a few weeks here. With no work prospects, he found himself taking part in a rowing regatta someone had organized between groups of ex-pats. This was basically a social occasion, where drinking was more important than winning. Except for one team: New Zealand. Those dastardly Kiwis took things rather seriously and went on to claim top prize, while refusing to socialize with the other teams.

"Bunch of humourless wankers."

And he was off again, following the coast up to North East Asia. Jim was by now a seasoned sailor. From nervous beginnings, he'd taught himself everything he needed to know, mastered all the necessary skills and over three years had sailed all around the world, mostly by himself. For short legs here and there he'd had the occasional (long-legged) companion, but that was more often for social reasons than for any need of another experienced pair of hands. He was comfortable with the rhythms of the oceans, happy in his own company, often seeing nothing but the sea and sky for weeks at a time.

He'd got used to spending days without bothering to get dressed. Just him, the boat, the sea and the wind. Day after day after day.

The supplies he picked up in port could be easily supplemented by fish. Here was something else that had become second nature: Catching and gutting fish. He often didn't bother cooking it. Quite delicious fresh from the sea and raw. Money, it was true, would be a problem a few months down the line, but here at sea there was no real need to worry about that. Maybe he had partied a little too hard, but no; life was for living, and something would turn up. Regrets were for cowards. Hadn't he had experiences few other people would ever enjoy? All thanks to his boat. Perhaps it would be impossible to ever go back to a normal job on dry land? Or even if he did, surely it would be just to try and put together as much cash as possible so he could get back on his boat and continue his adventure on the seas. This was the life! Why hadn't he started sailing earlier? What was the petty politics of banking compared to this wonderful, total freedom sailing around the world?

Jim spent most of his time now formulating a plan which would allow him to stay on his beloved boat as long as possible. He suddenly hit on it: Australia! Yes, that was the logical next destination. They speak English; the culture is broadly similar to back home in South Africa. Plus didn't they hate the Kiwis?

Yes, Australia was calling him; he could already see himself dropping anchor there and looking for work. What did it matter what the job was? Even manual farm labour paid well. He wondered where the most lucrative fruit-picking opportunities were in Australia? Surely not too hard to find. Then it would be just a matter of working hard and saving. Next, with a bit of cash back in the bank, there'd be the biggest adventure of all awaiting him: Sail across the Pacific! Circumnavigate the globe!

That sounded grand. That sounded wonderful. And he knew it was within his capabilities. "But for now," he decided, "let's follow the currents, sail on northwards to Taiwan and Japan." Maybe he could spend a few weeks in each country, get a taste of whatever delights, female or otherwise, were on offer there before setting sail again back down to the Southern Hemisphere.

The seas held no fear for him now. He was entirely comfortable living on his boat. Maybe Jim had gotten a little too confident in his abilities, because October in the seas around China and Japan is a dangerous time to be sailing: Typhoon season. And maybe Jim prayed to the Lord to send any typhoons out of his path. And maybe the Lord didn't listen because the Lord was busy listening to lots of other unreasonable requests from other people, or possibly He didn't listen because, just possibly, He is in fact a ham sandwich wrapped in tin foil. Whatever the truth, Jim realized that a large typhoon was indeed heading his way, about the same time that he realized that he was too far from any port to take shelter.

There's only so much you can do when sailing into the path of a typhoon. Take everything down that can be taken down, tie everything down that can be tied down, and that's about it. Once he'd done everything possible, it was just a case of sitting there and watching the huge waves crash over the boat, wondering with each lurch whether this was the one than would capsize it.

"Must have been terrifying," I said, barely able to imagine being entirely alone on a raging sea.

"I thought I was fish food, more than once." This, delivered in a far quieter tone than usual.

But Jim didn't become fish food. His prayers were in fact answered, the stormy seas slowly started to calm down, the waves became slightly less horrific and Jim started to dare to hope that he might actually make it after all. Once the typhoon had passed, his boat was still floating. He was still there. But damage had been done, severe damage which required urgent repair. He needed to find a harbour. The typhoon had blown him to the south west of Japan, Kyushu Island, so the nearest port was Nagasaki.

Jim's first sight of the country that would become his home came as a relief. A sight he thought he might never see again. It wasn't a glorious arrival, limping in on his battered boat. For the first time in his life, he knelt down and kissed the ground as soon as he stepped off the boat. The land in Japan is not the most solid in the world, but it was a better place to be than at sea in the middle of a typhoon, that much he was sure of.

The boat wouldn't be going anywhere for a while. There was no question of a quick fix before sailing off again. And more to the point, it would be expensive, certainly more than Jim could afford. Looks like he'd be spending a bit of time in Japan. Wonder what job opportunities there are for someone like me? One week later he walked into Mega.

"Hello my name's Jim Parker I'm from South Africa and I'm looking for a job as an English teacher."

And he was hired.

"You see, they really do take on anyone, including the marine trash dumped on the beach. How am I supposed to feel any pride as a teacher when they'll take the likes of you!"

I was of course jealous because Jim had an incredible story to tell of how he got the job.

And as we learned more of Jim's ordeal lots of things started to make a bit more sense. I assume Jim had been a Christian all of his life, but his near miraculous survival could only serve to deepen his faith; it also explained the zest with which Jim threw himself into everything. He'd survived! He'd stared down the barrel and had come out the other side. It seemed like he hadn't been in a bar for years because, in fact, he hadn't. Well, for months anyway. And those hours in the eye of the storm must have been spent wondering if he'd ever lay eyes on another beer. Another human. Another pair of tits. Eccentricities like walking naked around the apartment and muttering to himself were also neatly explained, along with observations of foul smelling land toilets: Habits ingrained by life on the seas. And his constant sorties on his sorry little scooter, poor substitute for sailing though it may have been, at least allowed him the sight of shifting spaces. Where his hatred of Kiwis comes into all this is slightly unclear. Just a simple rugby rivalry thing, I guess. But Jim had survived, thanks to a boat that was just sturdy enough, just possibly with some divine assistance, and certainly a lot of luck.

He didn't know it at the time, but that was to be the end of his life as a sailor. His boat remained in the marina for almost a year until finally Jim, unable to pay for the repairs or the harbour costs, found a buyer.

Swapping sailing for teaching must have been a big anti-climax, but Jim always maintained an admirably healthy perspective on life, and I think he probably enjoyed his new job as much as anyone in the office. But equally, it wasn't likely to be a long term solution. Jim's eyes were always looking for a new opportunity, so it was no surprise when he moved into a partnership with a young Japanese entrepreneur, trying to set up a car import company. Soon he was off on business trips to China with increasing frequency, until they set up a permanent office there, which Jim worked in full-time.

After that, it all becomes a little hazy. I heard he was back in South Africa for a while, but got screwed by his business partner (not marriage partner, this time). And then next thing I heard he was living in Bulgaria of all places, setting up some business venture there, although I have no idea what it was.

Then in 2015 we got a message from his daughter on Facebook, telling us that her father, now in his mid-sixties, had suffered a massive stroke, but was recovering in hospital.

Terrible news, but I could picture Jim in his hospital bed, blue eyes still twinkling, even though he'd lost use of the right side of his body. Down but not out. I could imagine him convinced that it was The Almighty that had saved him again.

"Are you OK, Jim?"

And from his hospital bed, I can clearly see him struggling up onto his elbows - his whole flabby, ageing body straining at the seams - looking me in the eye and saying:

"Does the Pope have hairy armpits?"

4) Douglas: End of the Road

Kumamoto Mega was getting crowded.

Jim's arrival proved to be the start of a rush of new teachers. It was almost as if word had got around: Hey, if that guy can get a job, surely anyone can. And they could, of course. Murray was next - the bald guy. He'd trained in a catering college in Edinburgh, but instead of seeking honest employment in a British hotel, had been led on a complicated route around the world - Go East, young man! - in pursuit of various ladies, ending up in Kumamoto after meeting a Japanese girl in Singapore.

Then there was Elizabeth, a sweet, mild-mannered New Zealander who'd come over with her New Zealand boyfriend. He'd found a job teaching in an elementary school - another popular entry route for first-timers in Japan. "Let's go together," he'd told her. "You can get a job there too, for sure." So she did. And a few months later he decided to ditch her, having found a new Japanese babe. "Can't help falling in love," he said. "Bloody Kiwis," said Jim. For once you had to agree with him.

Helen was next in through the doors. A Canadian girl, who'd trained as a social worker, but before starting her job, had gone to Brazil on a whim - her first foreign adventure - and decided she wanted more, leaving her Canadian boyfriend back home. "Monogamy is overrated," she liked saying, sending a loud signal that she was available. Nobody took her up. She delighted in tormenting the male staff, especially Yasu. The newly married Yasu seemed to take it well, but there was the odd occasion when Murray or I had to come to his rescue. Don't be cruel, we said. Don't take advantage just 'cos the poor

107

guy's too polite to tell you where to go. Pretty girl, Helen, but I think most Japanese guys were frankly scared of her. Just a little too wild. Murray, Elizabeth and Helen clearly differed from Jim in age and mode of arrival. The thing all four had in common, other than a total lack of teacherly credentials, was an eagerness to join in our socializing. They were party people. Welcome to my world, we said.

The sheer variety of the new arrivals added an exciting dimension to our daily lives, but it was still quite a shock when the newest teacher walked through the doors: Elvis Presley. An English Elvis, his jet black hair greased and combed back in a way rarely seen in the wider world since John Travolta's memorable performance in Grease. Elvis was a throwback in so many ways. I couldn't remember seeing anyone looking like him throughout my teenage years in Yorkshire. He was kind of out of place and definitely out of time, that was my first impression. But while your eyes were initially drawn to his hair, his most impressive features were his high-arched eyebrows, frequently raised in a kind of surprised "what-the-hell-am-I-doing-here" expression, which not only inadvertently revealed his innermost thoughts, but also neatly mirrored the reaction he would often provoke: What the hell was Elvis doing here in Kumamoto?

"I'm an architect," he was almost too quick to say to anyone he met. "Trained in architecture, was working in an architect's office in Guildford before I came here."

"So you're planning on becoming an architect here, then?"

Maybe he was, probably it was his Grand Plan all along. Or perhaps - looking at those eyebrows - he didn't really have a clue what he was doing here. What was true was that he'd somehow agreed to trade in his real trade for a possibly slightly less attractive career in teaching. It didn't seem to make too much sense neither to us, nor apparently to him if that expression was anything to go by. But there was another important thing about Elvis, the main reason in fact for having chosen to turn his back - temporarily at least - on his budding career back home. Elvis was married and he had two young sons. He was: A Family Man!

This was another first in the Kumamoto office. Our university bubble was slowly but surely being popped. First Jim, the unfeasibly old guy, and now a man who had come with family attached. At first glance, Elvis was much more one of us than Jim - he was in the same age bracket, just about to hit thirty. In spite of his family situation, he seemed ready to throw himself into the swing of things. Not as much as Jim, maybe, but then who was? But he had a balancing act to perform. His wife and kids were after all waiting for him at home every day. He needed little persuasion to come out though, and when he was given permission to do so, he certainly seemed ready and willing to party. Those eyebrows seemed to relax just a little as he threw the beers down. And upon reaching a certain hour, we were understanding when he announced, somewhat sadly, that probably he should head home. Of course, you don't have to make excuses: Off you toddle, we said. It's midnight. See you next time. And so he returned, torn between the desire to get well and truly shit-faced and his responsibilities as A Family Man. You could almost hear the jukebox turning from *Blue Suede Shoes* to *Are you Lonesome Tonight* as he walked out the door to get on the last tram home.

Elvis's name was Douglas. And Douglas fell into a brand new classification of Gaijin. I'd already sub-consciously started dividing Gaijin I met into loose categories like: Teachers/Not teachers,

American/Not American, Dicks/Not dicks, Lifers/Going home tomorrow, Young/Jim Perkins. But now, finally, here was a really useful distinction - the only one which really mattered, as I was to find more and more over the next few years. It was almost Darwinian, it was so blindingly obvious. Those like me, who had come of their own free will: Alone, single, adventure seekers. And the others: Attached, nervous, suspicious. Fished out of their natural habitats. By predators. Dangerous predators. Dangerous predators posing as harmless sweet-faced Japanese ladies, who'd fanned out around the world and come back with their prize, a non-Japanese specimen they could keep in their cages for others to come and marvel at. "Ooh, he's taller than mine!" or: "Wow, he's even shorter than most Japanese!" "Ah, he's so cute!" or: "His eyes are so big!" "He's so hairy!" or: "Why is he bald already?"

Douglas's gaijinological classification would probably be: "Elvis Architectus Brittanicus: Speaks English. Non-venomous. Mostly docile. Expanding belly. High eyebrows."

"I know you have trained as an architect, I know you have no interest in Japan, but if we go there you can get a job easily. All you have to do is talk - you like talking - and we can make a nice life for ourselves." This was the line he fell for. Spoken by his wife one evening after a tough day in the office, snuggling together on the sofa with a bottle of Italian sparkling wine. The line appears towards the end of the handy 40 page *How to catch a Gaijin* manual, a must read among Japanese ladies, married and unmarried alike, who are trying first to catch a Gaijin partner and then lure him over to their home country. It starts with a list of attractions Gaijin can offer those single ladies who've given up on a baseball player or a *salaryman* for a husband, including non-aversion to domestic chores and a typically "Ladies First" mindset. The opening few pages list the different Gaijin species: European, African, South-East Asian, Indian, etc, with particularly detailed descriptions coming under the most highly sought after category: "Native English Speakers." Chapter 3 is devoted to some of the less attractive traits which are sometimes encountered: Illogical aversion to unfamiliar foods, complaints about any non-English language comedy being by definition unfunny, refusal to get out of bed before noon at the weekend, along with a useful list of home-made cures. And towards the end comes a list of the hard-sell lines only to be used once the subject has been buttered up and is unlikely to offer any resistance; once formerly suspicious minds have been rendered suppliant. The line quoted above is the standard formula, the most tried and tested; indeed it is virtually guaranteed to succeed. Tempt him over with the promise of riches which require a minimum of effort beyond his Gaijinity, which he has in abundance.

What chance did Douglas have? He should have said no, should have told her it was a ridiculous idea; that they were perfectly happy in England, that after a few years he'd be earning a nice salary. He should have added that even if he was apt to moan about it a little too often, he actually really did enjoy such English things as nights in the pub, meeting his slightly odd relatives and watching TV which, even if it was sometimes a bit crap, at least it was in English. Then there was the not unimportant fact that he'd never spent more than two weeks outside England before, so wasn't it a huge leap of faith to expect him to be able to settle down in a brand new country with its own customs, traditions and quirks which were entirely alien to him? He'd never been to Spain, but he'd been on holidays to Greece and Italy, which he would happily admit to enjoying very much - lovely weather over there - but he'd tended to stick to English food wherever possible, and he'd never bothered himself about learning more than a handful of words in those languages - what was the point when everyone spoke English? So yes, he was happy to leave his home country for a few weeks at a time, provided some conditions were met; but to say *sayonara* to England, to make a clean break, with the prospect of only ever returning for a couple of weeks every summer - wasn't that one of the way down dumbest ideas he'd ever heard in his life?

These are the words he should have said. But he didn't. He didn't even wriggle too much on the hook. Next thing he knew, he'd said goodbye to his friends and his relatives and he was sitting with his wife and kids in his new house, in a country he barely knew anything about, surrounded by people speaking a language entirely unfamiliar to him, in which he couldn't even ask where the toilet was. How the hell did that happen? It was too much. The surprised look which usually flashed across his face once or twice a week back in Surrey had already started to etch itself into his face, his new permanent expression.

"So, why did you come to Japan again, Douglas?"

"Well, basically it's my wife's idea. Her parents are getting older, so she wants to be near them. She says that once we get settled here we can make some serious money."

"And how old are the kids?"

"Well there's Matthew, he's four and he's a bit wet, then there's little William. He's only two, but he's strong. Loves breaking things."

"And do you think you'll be teaching here for a long time?"

"Oh, good gracious, no. Did I tell you I'm an architect? No training as a teacher. So just find my feet, and then look around, see what other options come up. In the meantime, Wifey can make good money as an English speaking engineer, doing specialist translations and the like. And I'll have time to try to get to grips with the language."

"I see. Sounds like you have plans, Douglas. That's wonderful."

And why wouldn't he have plans? This for him was serious. He had a family to support; this was not just some jolly post-university jaunt, like it was for us single types.

"Wifey", as I was later to find out, was one smart cookie. A doll-faced, hard-headed woman. I'd never met anyone Japanese with such mastery of English. A perfect TOIEC score, one of the best measures of English ability. Not to mention a mastery of how to control her husband, for which there's no test I'm aware of, but in which she would also doubtless get a maximum score.

Now all of this is not to say that Douglas was totally against the idea. There was little doubt that Wifey had been the driving force behind the move, but Douglas may well have been not too difficult to persuade. He had a chirpy up-for-it, try-anything-once character. He was genuinely sociable, always trying to find someone in the office to go out and have lunch with.

"Come on, where are we going today?" he would ask, never taking no for an answer. On my own, I'd be more than happy to munch on some homemade sandwiches or grab something at the convenience store and read a book in the park, but with Douglas around, there was no chance of that. We'd be practically frog-marched to one of the Chinese, Italian or Indian joints across the road. Wow, this guy needs company, I thought.

There was no mistaking his Britishness. Or rather his Englishness. He was quick to crack the kind of jokes about the Scots, Welsh and Irish that you're not really supposed to say in this day and age. There was nobody more British in Kumamoto than Douglas, we used to say. Quite a character. A Bona Fide Englishman, the type of jovial geezer you expect to see in every pub up and down the country, good-naturedly justifying the reasons why he'd traded in his happy single life for matrimonial prison. "Bliss! Cor blimey. Wouldn't have it any other way. Bliss, I tell you!"

Yep, there is A Family Man, I thought. What a responsibility, to take your young family and re-locate to a country which you know next to nothing about. And still retain your sense of humour! Can't be easy at all. Just as well he has such an easy-going nature.

"Ooh, you single guys are lucky here. All these beautiful single ladies. Not complaining of course, love Wifey to death, wouldn't change anything for a second. But I tell you, if I could have my time again, cor blimey."

But at the same time, there was something I couldn't quite put my finger on. Behind the jocularity, there was a sense that it was all an act, a feeling that something wasn't quite right. Well, surely that's perfectly normal, I told myself. After all, it must be quite a wrench to turn your back on everything you've known and join this unlikely bunch of people pretending to be teachers in a small city in Japan.

In Douglas's favour in those early days was this: He may not have been in England any more, but he almost could have been. With a group composed largely of foreigners, there was no real need to dip too deep into the culture of Japan. Thousands of Gaijin stay for years, decades even, barely getting their toes wet. You can float on the surface, sometimes pretending you're not in a foreign country at all. Doubtless this softened the blow considerably for Douglas. He had a ready-made set of non-Japanese to hang out with. Maybe he did sometimes forget he was in Japan. It wasn't so hard to do.

Lunchtime was the undoubted highlight of his office day. Things went downhill once the afternoon classes started. "Back into the firing line"; "Over the top we go"; "The final push", he always used to say as the bell rang announcing time for the next lesson. Sometimes there was a feeling that he would actually have chosen to face German snipers and be done with it rather than spend fifty minutes talking about banal everyday things with Mr. Uemura or Mrs. Takahashi. A quick glance in his direction and he would be sitting there, a barely concealed boredom written all over his face, eyebrows pushed up as far as they could possibly go. He seemed to be holding his breath and counting the seconds, willing the end to come that bit sooner. A little less English conversation, please. And he must have frequently asked himself in between the jokes, "What am I doing here?" and the passing of time didn't provide any easy answers. In truth there was also a touch of self-superiority. That this teaching lark was beneath a man of his talents, and a hope that it would all be over - the sooner the better - and he could get back to his real job. Yes, inside the school, it wasn't hard to see he was struggling to come to terms with things. Away from the school at least - on those occasions when he was allowed out - he was more successful at keeping on his mask of conviviality. But just on occasion you sneaked a glimpse at what lay behind.

"Not coming out tonight, then Douglas? Rushing back to Wifey?"

"No, actually it's a private lesson tonight."

"Again? Careful, now, you don't want to end up like Charlie."

"No, no chance of that. It's just the one guy I teach. Friend of Wifey's cousin. Company president, actually."

"Oh, really?" Here was news indeed. "Suppose he pays more than your average student?"

"Oh yeah, wouldn't do it otherwise. $100 an hour."

"Wow, and that's a once a week gig?" My tongue started to hang out, this was way over the going rate.

"No, it's whenever he's free. Maybe 3 or 4 times a week. Like a bloody prostitute."

Nothing jovial about the way he said that. The guy was genuinely complaining about being "used", rather than rubbing his hands at landing such a dream private. I couldn't think of anyone who'd turn down that kind of money, let alone sound so spiteful about it.

"Well, gotta pay for the kiddies I guess," I said. "Hope everything works out for you," I added, trying not to smile too broadly as I walked out of Mega for the last time. It was July 1997.

During my sabbatical in New Zealand, my mind frequently wandered back to all those weird and wonderful folk back in Kumamoto. Charlie and *The Hokey-Pokey*; Rie unbuckling her bra; Daisuke's *Pachinko Man* routine in karaoke; Douglas willing the clock to speed up. Thousands of memories, both hilarious and banal, which continuously flashed before my eyes, triggering a sudden chuckle here, a snigger there. "What are you laughing about?" my girlfriend asked as I stood there, tea towel in hand, engaged in the enormously unfunny task of drying the breakfast dishes.

Then, in summer 1999, a letter materialized in our mailbox which was to rekindle my relationship with Douglas. I was just at the point where I was contemplating the next move in my life. Two years in Christchurch had been a kind of outdoor paradise, but I was pushing 30 and I didn't have any skills to peddle: I was no architect. It looked like teaching English would be my lot in life. New Zealand didn't seem to offer much for my career. The pull of Japan was still strong. I genuinely liked the country and I knew I could earn far more there, but I absolutely intended to avoid Mega, so I needed a foot in the door. And it arrived.

"Hi Peter. Hope things are going well for you. We have exciting news. I just opened my school and we need someone to help out. This is no run-of-the-mill place; we've already signed contracts with some big companies. I heard you're thinking of coming back to Kumamoto. Would you like to work here? Return to sender."

Talk about fortuitous timing.

Three short months later, I was back in my old city.

Napoleon English School was the name of the place he and Wifey had opened together.

Arriving at the school for the first time, I was impressed by the show of Union Jacks flying outside the front door. These, coupled with the rather grand name, promised more than the modest suburban one-room school which it turned out to be. At first glance, it didn't quite live up to the image I'd formed from reading Douglas's letter. I tried to hide my disappointment, but Douglas had it covered.

"Oh, this is just for the locals. The main business isn't here · it's in the firms where we teach. We've got these big contracts, so we'll be mostly going off to teach at the companies, but at the same time we have this office, mostly for show, but we have a room for teaching kids and adults. We want to give something back to the community," he explained, maybe a touch too self-importantly, I felt.

"And what are you teaching at the companies?"

"Well, talking in business situations."

"So, like English conversation."

"Yes, but much better, obviously. Not like Mega. God, don't know how I survived that place. And our big point is using British English. You know all the other schools here teach American English? It used to drive me mad. The textbooks we use are all British English. That's why we want you. Only British teachers working here."

"I see."

"Can't offer you too much right now, maybe five or six hours a week, but it's gonna expand quickly. The sky's the limit. You in?"

What was I going to do? "Where do I sign?"

I wasn't entirely convinced that it was the Americanisms that were driving him mad, more the fact of sitting down and exchanging vapid conversation with people he really didn't give a shit about, but I decided it was maybe not my place to make this point.

But a lot of what Douglas said made good sense. In spite of the overwhelming preference for American English, a number of Japanese people seemed to have an innate snobbery for which the idea of "Queen's English" was ready made. You could always get a few heads nodding when you mentioned that British English was superior to American English, that it was somehow purer and classier (a cheap trick, I admit).

The differences in vocabulary, spelling or accent never unduly bothered me. If it had done upon arriving · I remembered spelling "aeroplane" that one time with Sam · I was way too lazy to waste time worrying about it anymore.

Spell "color" with no "u"? Whatever. Elevator? Sneakers? Diapers? Sure. Be my guest. No skin off my nose. You really had to make an effort to stick to your linguistic roots if you didn't want to drown in the Americanisms that abounded in the textbooks, an effort I was unwilling to make. It did admittedly land me in trouble with my London nephews on my summer trips back to the UK, casually asking about the latest soccer scores.

"It's not soccer, it's *football*," they hissed back, and I was taken aback by the venom, aware that they'd be talking disgustedly about their uncle "talking like a bloody Yank" for months after I left.

Douglas was cut from a different cloth. Douglas was a true patriot. He was still the most British man in Kumamoto, of that I was sure. Just look at the flags!

"No, that's just marketing," he insisted. "Love Japan, me. Love the place, but you have to make the school stand out."

There was just the name which I was curious about: Napoleon. It was hardly the most English of names. There was a brief pause before he said, "Well, I know he wasn't from England, but it's just a name and it's easy to remember. That's the important thing. What was ever logical about names anyway? Why are Belgian chocolates called

Godiva? You know, you're the first person who's actually asked me that. Everyone else just tells me what a good name it is."

So there. Choosing to name the place after a major military figure was slightly odd, but calling it "Wellington" or "Nelson" would probably have raised more eyebrows. Napoleon, even if England was one of the few European countries he'd never set foot in, needed no introduction, and just maybe Douglas was contributing to the re-writing of history whereby at least a fraction of the population of one small Japanese city might start associating Napoleon with England instead of France. In any case, I personally liked it, often having thought of myself as being born on the wrong side of the Channel.

Douglas himself had naturally changed a bit. His surprised expression was still there, but he was doing his best to adapt to his new role as successful manager. It was a role more in line with his self-image. His spiel contained a hint of pride, but not too much. A vague promise of a share of the spoils, but nothing specific.

It appeared that his dream of doing something architectural had fallen through - but hey, he was his own boss now. Or at least, his wife was the boss: Keeping it in the family. And if he'd turned his nose up at $100 an hour before, presumably he was - they were - doing better than that. Which only meant that they were doing very nicely indeed, thank you.

"Are you still teaching that president, by the way?" I asked, innocently enough.

"Oh yeah. Bend over backwards and do me," he spat out, shaking his head.

Still not enjoying that so much then, it would appear.

So, I was ready for my first assignment in my new school, under my new big boss, man it was all rather exciting.

"Tomorrow we'll be team teaching. This is the course outline," he said, handing me a file and explaining a few of the details, while I asked a few questions about the format of the lesson. "You'll be fine; it's the same as...it's the kind of format you'll be familiar with. We'll drive up there, it's out near the airport. I'll pick you up tomorrow at 9:30. Don't forget to wear a suit and tie. Can't be scruffy. Got to look the part. This is the real thing."

"OK. What colour is your car? Don't know much about makes and things," I added unnecessarily.

"It's red."

Back home, I gushed to my girlfriend, "It looks like they've got things set up nicely. It's not full time yet, but I can work a few hours. Seems like we did well coming back now. This is a real stroke of luck for me. I think the empire is expanding."

I probably had some dream that night about being appointed junior commander at the Toulon blockade. Would my early start guarantee my position at his side during the Imperial coronation?

The next day, I waited at the assigned meeting place, absent-mindedly practicing poses for future statues in my honour when a Ferrari pulled up. A red Ferrari. It was Douglas's. I opened the door and got in.

"Holy crap, Douglas. You didn't mention your car was a Ferrari."

"Well, it's not as if I have anything else to spend money on. It's one of my conditions."

He didn't elaborate, but I guessed he meant conditions of staying in Japan. Had he tried to convince the family to move back to England? Had he been bought off by his wife? Blimey, I don't think that appears in the original fishing manual. I guess they were beyond that by now.

In the car, Douglas filled me in on a few details of Napoleon English School. The pair of them had been around to a number of companies and managed to secure some rather lucrative contracts teaching half-year courses in English. "Huge contracts, huge," he said, eyebrows oscillating, as if he genuinely couldn't believe the kind of money he was raking in now. His enthusiasm was genuine, but he should probably have made an effort to tone it down a little. It's good to know that your erstwhile friend and colleague is doing well, but slightly less impressive when your own hourly wage is of distinctly Mega (the company, that is) proportions. I figured that Douglas was actually starved of people with whom to share his joy.

And it was hardly surprising, for as soon as I started to get into the new routine, some lessons taught at companies, but mostly conversation style classes at his school, I was starting to feel a slight nostalgia for Mega, and specifically its location slap bang in the centre of the city. All the shops and bars were right outside the door. Napoleon's suburban location felt in a way like being back in Saitama: Nothing doing. Each day I arrived there were Douglas and Wifey, all welcoming smiles. When I left, there they were, still grinning away. Sometimes there was little William throwing blocks around or shooting things with a variety of toy guns, Douglas proudly looking on. And other than a few students who came through the door, that was it. I felt slightly stifled. And little by little, distant dreams of empire building notwithstanding, I felt that overall I was happy to be only working part-time here and started sniffing around for lessons in other schools located more centrally. There was the niggling sensation that this was possibly not a healthy move for Douglas. In escaping Mega - for which his contempt, now he'd opened his own business, knew no bounds - he'd inadvertently given up the only kind of social life he'd had in Japan. It may have been a poor substitute for the one he was used to back in Surrey, but it was a chance to have a laugh with a few other Gaijin and blow off some steam. In his new school, a 200 metre walk from his house, he was alone. Was this really the blessed relief he insisted it was? Was it good for his health?

Actually, health was a real issue for Douglas. He'd mentioned it a few times at Mega, something about a bone disease. Incurable, apparently, just something he had to live with. Naturally, he blamed it on Mega. It had got worse owing to the stress of working at that bloody school, he said. I didn't contradict him, as images of him twitching during some of those lessons came flashing back. It probably really had aggravated his condition. But just maybe Mega was not entirely to blame. If it was magnified by stress, maybe it was the more general dislocation of his life, and his underlying Englishness, unable find a focus in this foreign country, that was doing the damage.

"So, is your bone problem any better these days, now the stress has gone?"

"Not really, no. It's a chronic condition, you know. I take medicine for the pain, but it's never going to go away. Bloody Mega."

But even his pride in the school, his school, was also at least partly about putting on a brave face. A few months later, on our way to some (for him) high-paying business class, he suddenly confided in me. "You know the real reason why I call it Napoleon?"

No, I had no idea. I decided not to share with him my theories connected with pomposity, imperial yearnings or a simple love of brandy. Most schools went for something more snappy, like "Apple", "ABC", "Magic", or chose a geographic location, "London Bridge", "Sydney" or "Golden Gate."

"Well," he said with a slight sigh, "I feel like Napoleon. Condemned to living on an island where I don't want to be. But at least I'm the master of the island, make no mistake about that!" He jabbed his finger on the dashboard for added effect.

Cripes, I wasn't sure how to reply to that. Here was effectively a frank admission that he had in fact been captured, forced to live here against his will. Sad too that it was such a private joke that I was probably the first person he'd shared it with.

Had he chuckled to himself when he thought of the name? If so, there was nothing funny about it now; it was just a sad confirmation of my suspicions. Why not just call the school The Slammer? Alcatraz? The Jailhouse? Rock of Gibraltar if you wanted to keep to something more imperial. That would carry with it the added bonus of it being in the British Empire too. But no, Napoleon it was, and I was wondering which island he had in mind, the larger one he escaped from or the tiny one where he ended his life?

As I hopped on my bike at the end of the day, having shared a beer with Douglas in his kitchen, the uncomfortable feeling returned that finding financial success may not be the best thing for Douglas's sanity. He was becoming a marginalized figure.

The uneasy joint role of Napoleon's solitary (part-time) employee and (full-time) Doug's Last Link to the World of the Gaijin continued. I was expected to join in his self-congratulatory remarks, as if their success and my success were connected. It would have been nice if it was, but I'd worked out by now that was not going to be the case. Lucky I wasn't really a car person. Nor even a money person for that matter. I was happy making what was still undeniably a decent wage packet, even if I was unlikely to be going out and buying a fancy sports car any time soon. Still with no family to provide for, it's fair to say I was very content in my own little way. A few Dougisms started to grate though.

"We've given you a little sweetener," he announced when I was given a new class. "It's a little way out, so we've paid you slightly above the normal rate." Examination of the next monthly wage packet confirmed that Douglas was not exaggerating at all with his use of "slightly" while also explaining why he had chosen not to tell me aloud the exact value of the "sweetener" for risk of me bursting out laughing.

No, I was unlikely to become a rich man just working for Douglas and Wifey, I decided. They were kind of holding me at arm's length, but ultimately that suited me. It didn't feel like a smart move to give them too many of my precious hours and I was happy to continue building up other lessons elsewhere.

Napoleon continued to expand though, and soon it became apparent that new blood was necessary. A quick ad in Douglas's hometown back in Surrey, an interview by his brother, and our new teacher was flown over.

"Alright? I'm Lucy," came the surprisingly strong Manchester accent, spoken by the blond, short-haired young lady standing in front of me in a rather low-cut white shirt revealing the tops of her freckled breasts. Definitely not from Surrey. Definitely not what I was expecting. Lucy was the first full-time member of staff and she would become the face of Napoleon English School.

"How can I get her to cover her tits up?" asked a visibly worried Douglas a few days later. I was unable to offer any advice, but the next day there was (sadly) no hint of cleavage, presumably thanks to a quick word from Wifey. Douglas was still chewing his fingernails though, nervously observing his new employee. "I can't believe my brother sent over someone with such a strong northern accent. Do you think she's gonna be OK?" he asked almost every day, obviously not believing she would be.

"She'll be fine. She's new to this. Remember your first few days in Mega?" A sharp look from Douglas. He preferred me to not even mention the place by name any more. He would have been happy to pretend it had never existed.

One week later, eyebrows raised comically high at the frustration of watching his protégé's slow progress, he asked, all shook up, "Why can't she say "Hello" or "How are you"?" This was indeed a notable feature of Lucy at this stage. Her greeting to all and sundry was invariably, "Alright?" A laudable refusal to surrender your linguistic roots it might have been, but for Douglas it was just impossibly frustrating.

It was hilarious, both Lucy's stubborn insistence on it - "We never say "How are you" in Manchester," she explained - and the way it riled Douglas. You could see his bone condition deteriorating by the second as he watched Lucy make her way through the lessons. I laughed about it at the Izakaya later that week with Charlie and Murray. It would have been hysterical to Douglas a couple of years back, but there was only a trace of the Jovial Geezer remaining. The Humourless Business Manager had taken over.

Douglas had maintained a thread of contact with the Gaijin community. There were by now few colleagues remaining from his Mega days and he increasingly lost touch with even these, through a combination of hard work (in the office) and inertia (outside it), topped off with a healthy dash of paranoia.

"Murray asked me if I could give him any hours," humphed Douglas one morning. "They all think you owe them something once you become successful." It was a shame to see Douglas choosing to cut contact with everyone, assuming that they were all out to lay their hands on his cash. He was not one of them anymore, even if he had pretended to be at the start.

"You should see how much profit we made last month," he said, not showing me how much profit he'd made last month. Lucy hadn't turned out badly after all it seemed. I thought about retorting: "You should see how similar my pay check is this month compared to last month." But what's the point, really?

Things seemed to be slipping away. I had to face the sad reality that my statue would never be erected in recognition of services rendered to Napoleon or Elvis or anyone else. In any case, I had other things on my mind. I was getting married, busy sorting out all the arrangements. I proudly announced the wedding plans to Douglas.

"You're coming of course. Most important person, really. Boss. And friend," I added, handing him the invitation.

"Of course, wouldn't miss it for the world," he said. Not hard to detect the lie there. The truth was probably the exact opposite. Nothing less than a tiresome nuisance, forcing him to emerge, however briefly, from his little island in the corner of the city. Probably have to come face to face with some of the plebeians as well, no doubt.

"You know, Pete, don't think we're going to be able to come," he said casually one evening as I was getting ready to go home, about three weeks before my Big Day. "So much work to do, Wifey's in the office almost 18 hours a day sometimes."

It took me a while to realize what he was talking about: The wedding, my wedding! He was trying to get out of it! Now, having been around Douglas for almost two years now, I could read him pretty well. I understood it was not high on his list of priorities, and that he would have gladly skipped it if at all possible. However it would have been absurd for me not to invite him and it was even more ridiculous for him to decline the invitation. I was stunned. Despite my years in Japan, I hadn't come close to mastering that native art of hiding one's emotions. I could hardly demand him to attend, but I could certainly sulk. Which I did, basically refusing to speak to him for two weeks. Not come to my wedding? "Lots of stuff to do"?! How can he not come? There's no way you can *not* attend your employee's wedding. Especially in Japan. Especially when you only have two employees. Especially when he is a friend; or at least when you're pretending to still be friends.

It worked. He got it. The next week, he took me to one side. "Sorry mate," he started, somewhat sheepishly. "We made a mistake. Do you think it'd be OK if we came? That's if we're still invited." It was a nice, humble apology, and I was thrilled that he did in fact seem to realize he'd been in the wrong.

"Of course you're still invited. Took your time though, didn't you?" And that was enough for me. The man had been out of line, but he'd seen the error of his ways - and I was the last person to hold it against him. All forgotten, all in the past, see you next Saturday.

So it was a very strange mix of emotions indeed when, on the day of the wedding, the only two invited guests who didn't show up, among people who'd flown over, not only from England, but also from Tokyo, Osaka and Okinawa, were my boss and his wife, who lived twenty minutes up the road. Disbelief and anger, bafflement and hurt.

"Sorry about yesterday. An important translation came in," said Douglas rather casually on the phone the next day - after lunchtime I think it was. I can't remember if I said anything or just hung up straight away. I do remember that a week later, with the relatives safely back in England and all the festivities over, I returned to the school to place my letter of resignation on the desk. I was no longer an employee of Napoleon. I'd escaped Elba.

Not surprisingly, Napoleon went from strength to strength after that; they were never going to miss me! Lucy turned out to be a wonderful teacher for them, and they had soon hired another lady. Lucy brought her out one evening.

"This is Claire, she's from Adelaide."

"G'day," said Claire, her smoky Latin looks at odds with her accent. Wow, Douglas had decided to end his Brits-only policy on his third member of staff. I wondered whether Claire was forced to censure her Ozzie greetings while in the school. I allowed myself a smile as I pictured Douglas twitching nervously. "G'day, mate! Streuth. Fair dinkum." Another lady followed only months later; Tracey from Glasgow, with curly, shoulder length red hair, twinkling eyes and a delectable accent guaranteed to cause further squirming. The ad appeared in the local paper once a month, looking for all the world like Charlie's Angels. Douglas had that trademark surprised expression. The ladies were all suitably buttoned up. I became friends with all the girls, the Angels; they were only too happy to escape the suburbs, come to the city centre and hang out at the bars at the weekend. Napoleon's latest news was a frequent topic.

"How is business doing over there?" I asked Lucy.

"Oh, it's great. We've got a new contract with Tokyo Alliance starting next month. Douglas says it's huge."

"And how is Doug himself?"

"Well, he's OK, but his hands are playing up. You know he has this chronic bone condition?"

"Yes, he often used to mention it. Poor guy. Does he get out at all? I haven't seen him even once since I quit."

"No, he's a real homebody, no change there. Oh, but there is one thing. He's building his own house."

Now this was interesting. A local architect had joined the school as a student while I was still working there and I knew it was maybe the only hour of the week that Douglas truly cherished. How could it not be, talking about something he cared about? One hour a week to talk to his heart's content about, I assume, topics exclusively related to architecture, so Douglas could feel, however briefly, like the architect he was trained to be. And he'd hired him to build a house. I would love to think that Douglas's input was significant and the house was built largely around his own ideas. I passed by sometimes, on my way elsewhere, and it was certainly not a modest abode by any standards. When it was finished, it stood out proudly - both in style and in size - from all the surrounding houses.

Like a sore thumb.

It was hard not to get lost in metaphors here. Was it a palace or a prison? Was its red brick exterior a proud expression of the nationality of its owner, or was it two fingers in the general direction of all the other Japanese style houses? "I am not like you, I do not want to be like you and I will never be like you." Was it a pleasure building it, or was Douglas crying inside that his dream house was being put up in the last place where he wanted it? Did it offer him genuine escape within its four walls, or did it just reinforce the feeling of being held captive every time he stepped out? Did it just give him one extra reason to never leave? This really was his St. Helena: Entirely self-built, entirely self-inflicted.

"So I guess the house is all done? Doug must be proud as hell," I said to Lucy at the bar. Somehow or other and in spite of my best efforts, the conversation always came back to Douglas at some stage.

"Yes, it's finished. It's amazing. You should see it!"

"Yeah, I drive past sometimes. Quite impressive. So I guess he's probably getting out even less often than he used to, now he's built his castle?" It was hard to understand why I continued to crave Douglas's latest news. He was always on my mind. It would have been preferable to forget him completely. Was I genuinely interested or was it just a conversation filler? Was I hoping for his success or secretly praying for some disaster to befall the company?

"No, he never goes out, just stays home and plays video games with the kids when he's not working." He had the car. He had the house. He had a profitable business. But it didn't appear that Douglas was exactly basking in his success.

A couple of years later, Lucy told me that little William - already ten years old - had spent some time in hospital. He wasn't able to go to school. It seemed like he'd inherited his Dad's bone condition, but it was a more severe form of the disease.

This was a little too much for me to take. *Oh no, not Billy*, I thought. His Dad's pride and joy. My Boy. The little tank. Douglas was never prouder than when he was talking about his son terrorizing the other kids. I sometimes felt he was Douglas's little avatar. *Go on, Billy, give them one from me. For making me come to this damn country. And another one, serves them right for trapping me in this hell.*

Funny how time slips away. Now there was to be another wedding, the third of the Napoleon Angels, Tracey. It had been six years since my own wedding and as soon as I got the invitation, my first thought was, naturally: Would Douglas come?

"Of course. He and his wife are both coming. Actually he's going to make a speech," assured Tracey.

I didn't share Tracey's confidence. But surely history couldn't repeat itself?

As the day got closer, I wondered what it would be like seeing him again. Would we ignore one another? If he came in the first place, that is. We occasionally bumped into each other in the streets around the city. Or more accurately, a few times as I was walking or cycling somewhere, there'd be a toot and a quick wave as a red Ferrari zoomed past. There was virtually zero chance that we'd ever find ourselves in a face to face situation by accident: Douglas's world was the 200 yards that separated his house from his school. I had no reason to go there. And I'd be as likely to bump into him in a shop or bar as I would to run into Elvis himself. Wow, how long ago that seemed, meeting him and his hairstyle for the first time, listening to him constantly cracking jokes and pestering everybody to go to lunch with him, demanding that someone keep him company. Mr. Joviality. Was it really the same person?

The day of Tracey's wedding came. Upon arriving, I scanned the room. Surely, surely they couldn't pass another wedding in favour of a sudden important translation. That would be verging on Guinness Records territory. But no, there was no mistake. There he was, with Wifey, sitting down at a table on the far side of the room. We gave each other a distant, nodded acknowledgement and settled in our respective corners. It must have been a slight worry for Tracey, having a warring boss and ex-colleague. My daughter had been given a starring role as a bridesmaid. Surely there wouldn't be any unpleasant scenes between us which might spoil Tracey's special day? She needn't have worried. I'd long since forgiven Douglas for his strange absence. Things had turned out well for me, I was enjoying my life, juggling a number of different jobs, not for one second feeling anything approaching nostalgia for the years I'd spent working at Napoleon. The overwhelming emotion I felt for him was pity. How had he managed to cut himself off so spectacularly? Everybody needs to let off steam, have a change of scene once in a while, and Douglas · the most British guy in Kumamoto, the unfailingly sociable geezer · more than most, especially once you took his disease into account. He simply wasn't the kind of guy who could tolerate such isolation.

For the first half of the wedding, we stayed in our different corners. I watched as Douglas got up and made his speech. He was clearly not enjoying himself, but he got through it, did what he had to do. He managed to smile, cracked a few jokes, went back to his seat next to Wifey and helped himself to a deserved cold beer. *Dear me, how much longer before I can escape from this, be back in the safety of my house*, he was doubtless thinking. There was clearly no way he was ever going to come over to my table, so I picked up my beer and headed over to say hi.

"Mind if I sit down here?" I asked, pointing to the empty seat.

"Of course not."

There were a few seconds when his guard was up. *What's his motive in coming here and talking to me?* he seemed to be thinking. He was maybe bracing himself to get an earful about not showing up all those years ago, but that was never my aim.

"Hey there stranger, how's everything? Hear lots of things about you from Lucy and Tracey. Looks like you're doing really well."

And we started chatting. Douglas visibly loosened up by the second as he saw I was not going to go on the attack, not going to accuse him, not be sarcastic, not going to ask him for any work. I'd just come over for a simple chat like we should have been doing every week for the last six years. And after a few minutes, there was the guy I'd known back at Mega, laughing as we talked about a few of our colleagues, some of whom were still living in the city, none of whom he had any contact with at all.

"Remember Helen chasing Yasu around the office? Or Murray and his stalker? Jim and his odd expressions?"

"Christ, Peter, how long has it been?" he sighed, his guard now 100% down, and just enjoying a chat with a friend.

Indeed, I thought. How long *has* it been? Since you had a laugh about the old times. Since you relaxed enough to forget you were trapped in a place you didn't want to be.

After that, I still saw him once in a while, zooming around. Red Ferraris are not hard to spot in provincial Japanese cities. And I still got all his news from his ever loyal Angels. Having met him again I felt much more interested in offering some advice.

"You should bring him out. It'd be great to have a few beers together like we used to in the Mega days." But of course he never came.

"He's getting worse. Sometimes he says the pain's so bad he can't think," a concerned Tracey told me a year later.

"Tell him to take a break. He's never enjoyed teaching anyway. I have a friend, Sally, who's looking for some work. She's a trained teacher, she'd be perfect. As long as Douglas doesn't mind Americans?"

Next thing I heard, Sally had indeed got the job. Douglas's dream of a British only staff seemed to be getting further and further away. I wondered if he still cared.

"Douglas is taking a break for a while," Tracey announced a month later.

It could only be a good move for him. Why not take a back seat role, leave all the teaching to people who enjoyed it more than him? Spend some time away from the office. Maybe even try and leave the island once in a while. It would surely do him a world of good.

"Any improvement?" I asked, the next time we were out.

"No, it's really awful. He can't even hold a pen, the pain is so bad. They found him a doctor in Kobe and he's spending a few weeks up there getting treatment."

Oh dear. It seemed like things had got worse quickly. At the wedding, he had brushed it off in a quick sentence. He hadn't seemed affected by it any more than when I worked for him. But now he was getting specialist treatment.

Poor Douglas. One by one everything seemed to be being taken away from him. He couldn't even retreat from the world and pretend it didn't exist.

I continued asking after him. He was back home, the treatment seemed to have been successful. Then he was back at work for a few days, just teaching a few lessons, not on a full schedule. Doing things sensibly. Not rushing anything. Getting better slowly.

And then one morning, I woke up and turned on the computer to check the emails and I noticed a message from Sally. Hmm, that was a touch unusual, I thought, and clicked it open.

"Terrible news about Douglas. He passed away last night," it simply read.

I was dumb-founded. He had just turned forty.

I was straight on the phone to Tracey. "What on earth happened?" I asked.

"I don't know," said Tracey. There was a long pause. "I don't know," she repeated. I could imagine her opening and closing her mouth like a goldfish, barely able to form any sentences.

I drove round. When I got there, Tracey was sitting motionless on the garden bench. She was clearly in a state of shock. She'd been working at Napoleon the whole of her time in Japan; the school was her world. She knew Douglas better than anybody else.

So what had happened?

It seemed that the night before, Wifey noticed that Douglas was late in coming back from the school. He would usually walk down there to lock up after the last lesson, maybe check a few things on the computer, enjoy a few moments of solitude before returning to the safety of his castle. An hour later, slightly puzzled, she went to investigate and found the school empty, unlocked, all the lights still on. With a sinking feeling, she opened the door, went inside and found her husband lying on the floor behind the sofa.

He was dead. He'd simply collapsed.

Poor Douglas. Lonely Man. I saw Elvis again, the fun-loving party man. I saw the patriotic Brit. The proud father. The manager of the school, both in those exciting early days after it opened, then as the boss, Charlie and his Angels. It was difficult to see which, if any, of these roles had come to him naturally. There was always an element of an act, of pretending. But ultimately, there was only one person who needed to believe: Himself. And he failed in that task. So when the toughest role of all came along - that of patient - he was ill-equipped to fight it. Had he done a better job convincing himself he was where he wanted to be, had he been able to congratulate himself on building such a successful school, and enjoy the fruits of all those sacrifices, he might have believed in his ability to put up a fight against his condition.

But he didn't. He couldn't. There was no pleasure to be had. There was no fulfillment. There was no point to anything. He just seemed to crumble. One thing on top of another. Imprisoned in a country he never felt any affection for. Quick to blame everything and everyone: The country. The company. His students. Life. He tried to joke about it, but that was just a veneer, and only beneath the surface was the real Douglas, the one with the eyebrows permanently raised, initially in an expression of surprise, then increasingly set as a form of endurance, then just loathing.

And even then, he might have just about been able to manage. The real, fun Douglas was still in there, ready to relax and share a joke, given the opportunity. I wondered how many times he'd managed to do that since our conversation at the wedding.

But the pain had started to take over. Who knows how closely related it was to stress? Perhaps it would have hit him even if he'd never come to Japan and was happily working as an architect in Guildford.

But living in Japan certainly didn't help.

The strain of enduring his life turned into the real physical pain of his chronic disease. The pain of seeing his son suffering from the same condition must have been the final straw. Pain everywhere he looked. No solace anywhere. The weight of everything had simply crushed him. His body just shut down and refused to go on any longer.

The funeral was, obviously, awful in just about every way. None of his family had come over from England. Half a dozen of Wifey's relatives. A handful of students, some of whom I recognized, others whom I'd never set eyes on before. And aside from his three employees, that was it. I felt Sally's hand on my shoulder as I started sobbing. Jesus, I thought. This was proof, if any was needed, of how small his world was. And there was William, now maybe 12 or 13, hobbling down the aisle in leg braces and crutches to peer into his father's face one last time. Don't Cry Daddy. You're safe now.

I went to take a last look at my friend. Shit, Douglas, if you ever have your time again, whatever you do, don't come to Japan.

5) Thomas Meets his Match

And the world keeps turning.

The seasons come and go. The misty March morning frosts change to pink as cherry blossom fever sweeps the land, then the late June rains fall, seemingly heavier each year. Summer burns harder than you ever knew it could, but then the first cool winds of autumn blow and you're safe again.

While the Japanese seasons turn in largely familiar patterns, there is plenty of the exotic to savour in the native annual festivals and traditions. New Year is barely over before the *Coming of Age Day*, when newly turned adults parade around in their kimonos. Colourful festivals are the rule, liberally sprinkled throughout the year.

The *Hina Dolls* Girls' Festival in March is a sight to behold. The Boys' Festival in May is even better, brightly-coloured carp streamers everywhere, some towns stretching thousands of them across the rivers. Countless *matsuri* - fiestas - are held in every town at the height of the summer heat and then the *Shichi-go-san* festival for young kids in November is charming, thousands of mostly pre-school kids visiting shrines, all adorably dressed up in traditional attire.

It takes surprisingly little time for these native Japanese customs, initially excitingly exotic, to feel strangely familiar.

You'd think they'd be busy enough with their own homegrown traditions, but it seems there's always room for more. Several events and customs have been imported from the West which at first seem reassuringly similar to the ones back home but which upon repeated annual inspection start to feel distinctly odd.

Imitation is the most sincere form of flattery, runs the phrase · and Japan would seem to be living proof of this. There are so many aspects of America which have been absorbed into Japan's culture that the Gaijin sometimes forgets that Christmas and Valentine's Day are recent commercial additions, having absolutely no meaning within Japan's Buddhist society. They simply look cool. Who doesn't love a Christmas tree all proudly lit up (and looking far better, incidentally, than most of the sorry specimens on show in most towns around the UK)? And by the way, why bother actually celebrating Christmas Day itself? "Christmas" in Japan ends abruptly · and to the Gaijin, rather confusingly · on December 24th with a box of KFC chicken wings the typical climax. On December 25th it's business as usual, the focus already having firmly shifted to the more serious New Year holiday one week later, most emphatically not connected in any way to Christmas. How many times have I lazily mentioned the "Christmas holiday" only to be corrected: "Not Christmas. New Year!"

And on Valentine's Day, you won't find roses or declarations of love. Everything is simply about chocolate. The shops fill up with heaps of expensive chocolates in lavishly imagined packaging, which the Japanese give to express their "respect" to the people in their lives, rarely with any romantic connotations and also, rather improbably, always a gift from female to male.

All of this does inevitably cause moaning among some of the more pedantic Gaijin. "They're doing it wrong!" they'll complain. For me it's simply odd that they're doing it to start with. I can hear Boy George and Bono singing, "Do They Know It's Christmas Time At All?" Well thanks to the decorations then yes, they do; but when you mention the Three Wise Men, the shepherd watching his flock, or Mary riding on a donkey, you'll draw blank stares. These play no part in the Japanese take on Christmas, and then again, why the hell should they?

You won't find me doing any grumbling. I love being allowed to enjoy the pleasingly Christmassy atmosphere conjured up by the ubiquitous illuminations and festive songs of both Western and Japanese artists, without being swept up by the throng of weary panic shoppers. And I'm not averse to being given several boxes of extremely tasty chocolates every February.

And the seasons keep turning.

You suddenly find that you're not young anymore. The next stage of life beckons. The wedding invitations start pouring in. And it's time for you to observe that weird hybrid mix of native and foreign influences at work again, in the form of the marriage ceremony.

This was the point I was at. The wedding rush was in full flow and showed no signs of letting up. At first sight, weddings in Japan seem to be very similar to those in England. Look a bit closer and you'll notice some differences - but not so many. The bride wears a white or cream dress; the groom, a suit. Champagne and beer flow freely. In fact, it all seems just like back home. But weddings never pretend to be authentically Christian ceremonies; they merely focus on the more idealized, visually captivating aspects of the Western version.

In fact the Japanese wedding, like so many other things in this country, is nothing less than a work of art. The various stages of the wedding are choreographed to a certain kind of perfection, the bride and groom often seemingly mere actors following well-rehearsed moves.

The traditional shrine has no place in a typical modern Japanese wedding. Hotels compete with purpose-built "Wedding Halls" for hosting rights. Both always feature a Western style "chapel", whose sole use is to offer an "authentic" backdrop in which the couples can exchange their sacred vows in a twenty minute ceremony, before moving to the main hall for the banquet. And to complete the illusion, extra "authenticity" will be added by the presence of a foreign "priest".

The first time I came across one of these, at my wife's friend's wedding in Osaka, I was impressed by the sudden appearance of the young, handsome American who managed to look at the same time very priestly and yet very unpriestly. He smiled his way through the ceremony, his fluent Japanese and smooth professionalism had me completely fooled: I had no idea this was not a real priest! This was an English teacher who was earning a few extra bucks at the weekend doing a turn as a holy man.

The bride and groom are as blissfully unaware of the total lack of any priestly credentials held by the man guiding them through the sacred vows as I was on that first occasion, but it really doesn't matter. It's not a scandal waiting to break. Nobody is under any illusion that the "chapel" has any religious meaning to start with. So when you mention the fact during a lesson that your colleague and hell-raiser Terry dons a frock at the wedding chapel every Sunday, you will never get anything as satisfying as a shocked reaction.

The same Gaijin who criticize Christmas's lack of authenticity will be over-quick to point out the ways in which the Japanese wedding is artificial - and therefore stupid.

Well, that may be very true, but what's also true is that every one I'd been to was rollickingly good fun.

But today's was very different. We were not in a Wedding Hall; there was no chapel, no fake preacher. We were in a bar. I wasn't feeling excited - quite depressed to tell the truth. It was the first time in my long experience of weddings to have the overpowering sense of not wanting to be there. I couldn't really put this down to the location. It was more to do with the couple themselves.

How many weddings was I up to now? Too many. There were no signs that the rush was slowing down quite yet, which could have been annoying if I'd analyzed it too much, but actually just felt like the new normal. It was that time in our lives. Everybody was doing it and why shouldn't they? It's a universal thing, even if it's not a universally beautiful thing.

I couldn't think of any I'd been to which I hadn't enjoyed. I had some precious memories: Hiro and Tamami in Yokohama, Hiro having learned to play the piano especially for the occasion and not playing a false note! Shizue marrying her New Zealand boyfriend in Hiroshima, her parents' stunned reaction - only learning of the ceremony a month before - priceless. Even Takako throwing up into a bucket as I congratulated her on her marriage with Kieran had been strangely touching. It was simply nerves after all. The personalities of the couples had always ensured that each occasion had a very different feel.

This one, however, was a complete departure. Why exactly were we gathered here at *The Red Zed*, waiting for the couple to step up and exchange the vows of their eternal love to one another in front of the serving counter?

The simple answer was that Thomas and Cindy were getting married.

But that was kind of missing the point. The more pertinent questions were:

Why had we been invited?

Why had we accepted?

Why was anybody else here?

Did anybody actually like Thomas?

"It's your fault," I said to my wife. "You know too many people." That familiar look of light hurt shadowed briefly across her features. She returned the accusation, slightly more sharply.

"Hey, he's your friend!"

My friend? Thomas? The idiot whose wedding we found ourselves at now, the one we'd agreed to come to through some frustrating lack of efficiency at sorting between invitations, simply saying "Sure" whenever one of these missives showed up in our mailbox?

"No, my darling, my eternal salvation, he is most certainly *not* my friend."

But Asami wasn't listening. She'd zoned out of our brief conversation. She, at least, was enjoying things. One of her more exasperating gifts was an ability to not only endure, but to positively take pleasure from what for many count as tortuous situations. Not realizing that for most people this is not a natural skill, she therefore

146

expects me to be able to do the same. But I can't. It's something I always mean to work on, but I fear it's a lost cause. The whole notion of "self-improvement" leaves me cold and so I'm in a Catch 22 situation: How can you self-improve if you're allergic to the very concept?

But back to the problem at hand: How we'd ended up here. I tend to look for the good in people, that's one of my better points. I'd love to write some good things about Thomas, I really would, but sadly there isn't anything. He was Canadian, but I couldn't tell you from which province. He'd been in the city for some years, but I didn't know how long. Where did he work? Absolutely no idea. Just not at any of my schools, thank God.

On the surface, he seemed mature, confident. He had the kind of face which in a photo might even suggest the perfect son-in-law. One glance at the picture on the mantelpiece and you could imagine him being funny, smart, popular. But upon meeting him, all of your assumptions would quickly go up in smoke. More than being neither smart nor funny, he had that rare ability of irritating absolutely everyone. One of those people who, while not bad in an evil, kill-all-your-children kind of way, simply had no redeeming qualities. I hadn't found one yet, and judging from the stories about him, maybe nobody else had either.

One of his "friends" (*"He's not my friend!!"*) had invited him round to his place a few years earlier. Walter was the proud father of two: a five year old daughter plus a baby son. He was still coming to terms with balancing his newly domestic life with his desire to stay in touch with his old, still single buddies and had misguidedly asked him round to the house. I'm sure Thomas was over the moon to be actually invited, but was less happy to have these stupid children get in the way of just shooting the shit with his pal. Why did people go and have kids? Where was the fun in that?

A couple of hours later, aware that this was not going to turn into the bingeing session he'd been hoping for, Thomas stood up to leave. Kind of a relief for Walter too; maybe Thomas wasn't really the kind of person he wanted hanging around his kids too much. As they went to show him out, Walter patted his daughter on the back, encouraging her to practice some English.

"Go on, ask him what he's going to do now!" Which she obediently did.

"So Thomas," she said, glancing up at her Dad for approval. "What are you gonna do now?"

Thomas turned around, bent down slightly (not worth stooping all the way down to her height), looked her in the eye and said, "I'm gonna go home and masturbate."

Walter's horror only last a few seconds, long enough to realize that at least it was nothing a five year old would ever understand. And Thomas, doubtless congratulating himself on his wit, walked away and · we have no reason to presume otherwise · went home and masturbated. This was after all before Cindy was around to lend a hand.

And talking of Cindy, what was her story? It takes two to tango, right? Well I can't say I ever spoke more than a few words to her. There was no particular reason for this; I wasn't really trying to avoid her. Not at first, anyway.

She'd suddenly beamed up from somewhere. There they were, the group of party girls I knew well; Mayu, Risako and my own Asami, all dancing at *The Red Zed*. And then one day, hey presto, there was Cindy! It seemed that this was, in spite of Asami's protestations otherwise, the tenuous link which had drawn me in a little closer to Thomas's sphere. While always enjoying chatting with Mayu and Risako, I had never got any good vibes from Cindy. One scan of her heart-adorned bag, coloured hair ribbons and Hello Kitty t-shirt told me that this was a lady whose company didn't seem to offer any prospect of enhancing my own happiness in any way.

One aspect of Japanese life which leaves me cold, and I'm confident I'm not alone, is *kawaii* - "cutie" - culture. This insistence on plastering stickers of adorable animal characters over everything may be acceptable up to junior high school. One might argue that, in small doses, it's a healthy thing for high school girls. But I would contend vigorously that beyond that (and honestly speaking years earlier) it should be banned. The number of otherwise sensible Japanese ladies in their twenties, thirties or even forties whose ears, key-holders and mobile phones are adorned with Minnie Mouse or Moomin accessories is more than confusing, it's actually rather alarming - and Cindy clearly embraced this fashion more than most. Combine this with a voice deliberately pitched slightly too high ("kawaii!"), sparkly face glitter (*"kawaii!!!"*) and the self-consciously cutesie gestures and expressions (*"Chooo kawaiii!!!!!"* - soooo cute!!!!!) and it was not hard to see that any bonding between the two of us was never really going to happen.

Then there was the name: Cindy. That's not a Japanese name, yet Cindy was clearly as Japanese as they come. A nickname, it would seem...but why? Had she hit upon "Cindy" to make her seem slightly more exotic? More enchanting? ("Cindy? Wow that's so *kawaiii!"*) I'd have to assume so, but I was always petrified that if I asked her, she might open her eyes wide, tilt her head slightly, put on an angelic smile and with a quick flutter of glittery eyelashes say it was short for Cinderella and expect me to say, "Ah, I see. How *kawaii!!*" I just couldn't take that risk.

"Having an annoying name" should never, of course - however tempting - be a valid excuse to ignore someone. Ultimately, people's names are only annoying if they themselves are annoying (which she *absolutely* was). But - and leaving aside her choice of partner for now - there was the infuriating way she pronounced it.

The difference between 'shi' and 'si' is one of the classic Japanese pronunciation pitfalls. For those Gaijin not satisfied by the endless opportunities for punning provided by the more famous inability to differentiate between 'l' and 'r' (SAMPLE #1: "The singer came on stage and everybody started crapping." SAMPLE #2: "This is a big erection night for Clinton." SAMPLE #3: British customer (complaining): "This chicken tastes rubbery!" Japanese waiter (smiling and bowing): "Thank you very much!"), just try riffing on some of the even more low-brow opportunities offered by *sit/shit*, or *city/shitty*. Cindy seemed to rejoice in pronouncing her name "Shindy," under the apparent belief that it was even more adorable like that.

"Nice to meet you. My name is Shindy," she would say, stretching out her bracelet-adorned arm. *Shilly girl*, I thought. I cringed as I imagined her patting the seat next to her: "Come and shit down next to Shindy."

So, to surmise: In what amounted to a perfect storm of slightly irritating bits, Cindy was, shall we say, not my cup of tea - and this was resolutely nothing to do with what seemed to be a pretty well established fact, namely that Cindy was not the most difficult girl to pick up. It's worth noting that she was indeed pretty and, underneath all those cartoon character garments, possessed a very attractive, shapely body which she was maybe a little too generous with when it came to letting Gaijin explore it. I usually did my best to ignore all the gossip, but even I could have named at least three other guys who had been "with" her in the brief time since she'd appeared on the scene. Not that it mattered. The moment I discovered she was going out with Thomas, I felt a release. Any guilt I had felt about allowing myself to get irritated by her name, appearance and voice evaporated. I had been right all along! What more proof was needed? The world made sense. I now had legitimate grounds for ceasing to be interested in anything connected with her.

And then we accepted the invitation.

I assumed at least that Asami and Cindy were friends, but Asami was quick to deny any connection. "No, never had anything to do with her outside the bar."

"So remind me why we're actually going to the wedding?"

"Because we got an invitation and he's your pal and it's rude to say no."

"Look, I keep telling you he's not my "pal". I really don't think he has any pals."

It was hard to tell if Asami was being willfully deaf or just taking pity on the guy. Was I exaggerating about the lack of friends? I think not. You could feel it in the smirking faces of the gathered guests. It was kind of like someone had come into the bar, told the random customers to get changed into a suit and tie and then get on with the wedding. In fact it was exactly like that: That's pretty much how it must have happened. All the guys here were bar-flies, mostly ones that I didn't know very well and had little desire to get to know any better. Were they really his friends? Was it possible? It did seem rather far-fetched. But at the very least, surely *some* of them liked him more than I did?

"Why are you getting married in a bar?" I had asked a few months earlier one night out, taking a break from dancing and suddenly finding myself with Thomas sitting in the chair opposite me. You have to say something, right? It was an innocent enough question.

"You know, Pee-tah," he said. He started every conversation with me in this way. It irritated the hell out of me. "It's very important for me to be real. You wouldn't understand." He paused to take a swig. It could have been an impressive opening, but I knew otherwise. I inwardly sighed, and braced myself for the inevitable monologue.

"Weddings in this country are just fake. They're worthless. They don't mean shit."

Here Thomas was, true to style, insulting me to my face. OK, so I obviously hadn't invited the guy to my wedding - the thought had never remotely crossed my mind - but he did remember that I had just got married, right? All be it in a fake, worthless kind of way. He ploughed on. "I've never been a churchgoer, so why should I get married in a chapel? I'm a drinker: That's my religion! And I want to keep things real." The more Thomas warmed to his argument, the more strongly I could sense my desire to escape.

I heard him drone on. "Our relationship so far has played out in the bar, the highs and lows have been experienced here." A pause now to allow me to observe the sincerity he was exuding, before a final flourish.

"This place is the symbol of our love. What could be more fitting, more real, than to get married here?"

Replaying this conversation in my mind as I stood among the other guests, trying (and failing) not to look too bored, I was reminded of one of those Oasis wannabe bands from the early nineties going on about how their music was "real" because they didn't play too many notes, had a snarly vocal style, appeared angry in photo-shoots and took lots of drugs. No, wait - that was Oasis themselves, wasn't it?

I sniggered a little to myself as I looked up and winced as I saw Thomas's horribly insincere wedding smile, rather at odds with the leather griminess of "real" in a British nineties rock band sense. This was just as he too glanced over and misinterpreted my smirk as a smile of support and approval at the proceedings so far.

Going back now in my mind to my own wedding and the journey there was as good a way as any of checking out of this painful display of nuptials unfurling before my eyes. It had been a year since we'd tied the knot, so possibly some of the details were already starting to get a little fuzzy, but it had certainly seemed "real" at the time.

Oh, the mysteries of marriage! Few people would argue that this marks the point when you are forced to realize that wherever you happen to be - and no matter how hard you've been trying to pretend otherwise - the time has finally come to start taking things more seriously than you used to. From here on in, "Bit of a larf" is no longer an acceptable life perspective.

The dating phase of life in Japan never seemed much different from the same phase back in England. Young people are out, meeting other young people. The existence of "love hotels" (where you pay for your stay by the hour), among other establishments, only seems to encourage the free and easy aspects of any budding relationship. The first hint a Gaijin usually gets that something different is at play here is when the parents get involved. This will usually be towards the end of the dating phase, frequently only making an appearance once the couple gets engaged. *Surprise!*

This stage, the "meet the parents" bit, actually occurred rather early on in our relationship and didn't go particularly well. News that I'd started dating a Japanese girl didn't cause the slightest stir with my own family back in Yorkshire. We flew over together, only six months after we'd started going out, and my Mum and Dad chatted with her in her broken English. No fuss was made of her being Japanese - and why should it have been? I was 26, for Christ's sake.

But parents in Japan are parents for life. There's no "letting go" / "let them make their own mistakes" philosophy. Until she's married, whether she be 18, 28 or even 38, she's the property of the parents who will frequently block their daughter's preferred choice of partner if, for whatever reason, he isn't deemed suitable.

In my wife's case, her choice was particularly badly received - and it wasn't even that I was a Gaijin. She'd been in a three-year relationship and had made the mistake of introducing him to her parents, which is tantamount to an announcement of imminent marriage. Her Dad had taken to the young chap and was ready to welcome him into the family. Asami too was resigned to heading down this route, but then - poor thing - met me, suddenly saw other possible futures open up - and called the whole thing off.

It actually got even worse. When I invited her to Yorkshire, I was unaware that even a mature young lady was expected to clear everything with her family first, even less that she'd announced, rather improbably, that she was heading off for a week's holiday in December to visit her female teacher in England. When her parents got wind of the reality of the situation, the storm really started. An elaborate web of deception, they fumed. Stringing along her poor unsuspecting perfectly decent boyfriend, suddenly dumping him for a British man - a *Gaijin*! - lying to her father's face about the reason for her trip abroad. Ouch. When you put the hard facts down, I couldn't help agreeing it was pretty damning. Should I in fact trust somebody as manipulating as that?

The words of fury from her father, once he'd got tired of calling up and yelling at me to go back to whichever Buddha-forsaken country I'd come from, were rather decisive.

"If you leave, you never come back to my home!" he spat out at his daughter. She returned with a cheery, "OK, see you then!" and next thing we knew we were sitting on a plane heading for the Southern Hemisphere. Holding hands and rather excited about what the next chapter in our lives had in store.

But three years later, still together and back in Japan, he had come around. Asami had in fact read the situation correctly, another of her many talents. Her Dad had got tired of keeping up a rage for three years, and it had burned itself out. In any case, I'd got to know her mother and she didn't seem to consider me the dangerous monster, the scheming, corrupting ne'er-do-well of her husband's imaginings. Maybe she slyly fed him a few positive comments and in the end he even gave me a smile along with his consent.

That had all felt rather real, I felt like telling Thomas, but couldn't be bothered. What did I know about real? What was a five year "fake" dating period compared to a dozen "real" dates down the pub?

Our wedding, if truth be told, did actually feel a little fake. One curiosity of Japanese-Gaijin weddings is that they tend to have a far more "Japanese" flavour than an all-Japanese affair. Even before I discovered that the priests were phoneys, I had an aversion to the idea of a Western style ceremony. I could imagine my family coming over and being kind of disappointed: "Oh... It's just like in England." No, if I was going to get married in Japan to a Japanese lady, I wanted it to be as Japanese as possible. Naturally, many Gaijin reach the same conclusion. I would guess that out of the very few traditional shrine weddings which take place in the country these days, an astonishingly high number would include one foreigner. The accusation that we are every bit as guilty of play acting, of not having any appreciation of the core values of the Shinto faith, is entirely valid. I will not argue.

We went to the shrine - Asami dressed up in a kimono, myself in a *hakama* - had a real Shinto priest (as far as I could tell), had to learn all the different points of the ceremony; the correct way to drink the proffered sake, including numbers of twists and sips, not to mention the lines I had to memorize, all the time trying to ignore the sweat trickling down my back, a combination of the residual October humidity and the bodily reaction to the importance of the occasion.

So, fake or not fake · I was as resoundingly un-Shinto as I was un-Christian · it had at least been an unforgettable experience. If nothing else, it had been quite a show for my family and friends over from England. Asami's Dad was impeccably behaved throughout, never looking anything other than incredibly proud of his beautiful daughter as he had every right to do, all previous threats having been definitively consigned to the past.

Then after the ceremony, the failure of Douglas to show up to the reception had actually been slightly deflected by the absence of a couple of other friends I'd invited from England, both of whom would have been making their first ever visits to the country, but who were · unlike my boss · given a pretty reasonable form of excuse in the shape of the 9/11 terrorist attacks.

It's fair to say that there were a few things swirling around on our Big Day. But we got through it, enjoyed it. My family's decision to brave the threat of the terrorists was amply rewarded. The family in Japan had given their blessing to their wicked (but delectable) daughter. It felt good. It felt solid. It was all solemn enough to make me understand the significance of the moment, even if all that stuff about the correct number of turns of the sake cup was a load of codswallop.

So...a wedding in a bar? I liked bars, and I liked this one more than most. *The Red Zed*, the best Gaijin bar in the city, the default place to go to for a beer after work. The scene of many a memorable night out. But as a suitable setting for a wedding? A little bit light, no? One glance up at the rows of whiskey, tequila and gin bottles right behind Cindy's head seemed to confirm this. Other weddings were fake? Well sorry, Thomas, I guess we'll just have to agree to disagree.

This was the first one I'd ever attended to which that word would seem to apply. More than that, it was what the whole occasion seemed to scream out.

But while undoubtedly Asami and I had far more pre-marriage history than Thomas and Cindy, there was another recent wedding which I couldn't help harking back to. Akiko was one of Asami's work-mates in the Honda School of English. Single and outgoing, she quickly became a firm friend. Aside from being exceptionally pretty, she was endearingly innocent and months later, when we commented on it being strange that she didn't have a boyfriend, she told us that actually she did.

"Oh. You do? So who is he?"

"He lives in Spain."

That was a good reason for us never having met him, then. In fact, even Akiko hadn't seen him for over four years. It turned out that the two of them had started dating while exchange students studying English at Liverpool University and had stayed in touch upon returning to their respective countries.

"Poor girl," I said to Asami. "What a waste. She's deluding herself." Even if she thought they were still a couple, it was hard to imagine him having the same notion. "There's no way he's sitting there back in Valencia munching on his tapas and pining for her."

Then, one New Year, she went over to see him and we got the tissues ready for when she returned, sobbing and wailing. How badly we had misjudged! When she came back, she was in fact even more ecstatically in love than ever. One year later, it was his turn to come over - a first trip to Japan - and the year after that he came over again, this time with his family and friends - because they were getting married.

Quite a wedding that one, just a few months ago. The image of a radiant Akiko dancing flamenco with Diego's father was one of a number of moments that had seared themselves into my brain on that happy occasion. It was the nearest thing to true love I'd ever seen. Imagine only meeting twice in six years and then deciding to tie the knot?

The contrast with today's ceremony could hardly have been any greater. Every word, every movement on that day spoke plainly and unambiguously of the strength of the bond between them, and it was a very powerful thing to observe.

I could feel a tear coming to my eye just thinking about it and moved to brush it away just as Thomas looked over once more in our direction. *Oh God, bet he thinks I'm moved by today's frankly pathetic gathering.*

"*Please* let this be over soon," I thought. I could feel my enthusiasm for marriage ceremonies shrinking by the second. Until this morning, the word "wedding" had always conjured up exclusively happy thoughts. I love a chance to get tanked up while enjoying some seriously good food - who doesn't? - and on occasion I get quite emotional. But today, there was no food other than a few plates of cold stuff, and it did seem a touch cruel that even though we were at the bar, the staff were not serving during the "ceremony", which in spite of the different surroundings had somehow ended up including the worst aspects of a more conventional event - notably the long, boring speeches. Here was yet another of Cindy's friends stepping up with

one more long-winded episode of her life pre-Thomas. ("I remember
the first time I met her and I thought, Ooooh!! She's sooo *kawaiii*!")

Once more I cursed our decision not to simply offer an apology and
stay home. I had thought many times about not coming, in fact it was
pretty much the only thing I'd thought about since first noticing our
clerical error. I had seriously pondered telling him that I got the
acceptance slip mixed up with another wedding, one I actually wanted
to go to. Then when it became too late for that, the spectre of
Douglas's no-show returned. There shouldn't have been any
comparison: I was not Thomas's boss. I wasn't his colleague. I
absolutely wasn't his friend. I couldn't care less if I never saw him,
them, again. (It was my dearest wish, no less.) But there is something
sacred about a wedding invitation. I'd missed my chance to refuse
when I'd first received it. Plus, my wife might slap me.

Even that final, unspeakably awful night out - and how much
more of an excuse does anyone really need? - had not, incredibly,
sufficed. How long ago had that been now? Three weeks? Four? Christ,
two tortuous evenings in the space of a month: Two more reasons to
dislike Thomas even more.

The Japanese have an expression, actually quite a recent one:
Kuki o yomenai hito. This translates quite charmingly as a person
who can't read the wind and refers to a person who says inappropriate
things in a given situation. I take pleasure imagining it was made
with Thomas specifically in mind. He is truly special in the way you
can put him in any situation and it's almost guaranteed that he will
say something or do something unsuitable, causing offence or
irritation. I'd usually been spared this, working hard as I did to spend
as little time as possible anywhere near him. But last month my lucky

run ended. The tragic sequence of events that had led me here was easy enough to trace: Cindy materializing from nowhere, "befriending" Asami, inviting us to their wedding, us accepting...and now · what the hell? · it seemed that we were suddenly expected to "hang out"! With Thomas!! And bloody Shindy!!

They announced their plan to have a karaoke night. "Hope they have fun," I said sweetly. Asami listened as I matter-of-factly restated my obvious intention of not going.

"Of course," I continued. "I don't like them. I don't like karaoke. What possible reason would I have to go?" But Asami had other ideas.

"We're invited to their *wedding*!" she said in that exasperated tone people use when forced to explain elementary matters of basic politeness to a child.

At this early stage in our married life, it's fair to say that she possessed the moral high ground. This was no mean trick, and I was occasionally tempted to remind her of her despicable actions in dumping her previous boyfriend so coldly when choosing to start dating me, but never quite managed to find the courage to start this argument.

So, I failed to get out of it.

We arrived at the karaoke box. My sulking meant that I'd neglected to check who else was coming and I was slightly horrified to discover that all the other people there, sitting around the table looking up at us as we walked in the door, made up a kind of role-call of the people I least cared for in the city.

I had assumed, somewhat illogically, that there might be a couple of people I vaguely got along with, but that didn't seem to be the case.

161

As soon as I entered the room and took one look at the assembled members, I was strongly tempted to back straight out. There was nobody here who I would usually choose to start a conversation with. It was hard enough to say "Hi, how are you doing" to Thomas.

"You know Pee-tah, we're really busy," he said, clearly delighting in his "hilarious" spoof British accent. How could anyone be so effortlessly infuriating? The guy possessed a truly remarkable skill. "So many things to do, you wouldn't understand, but can't turn down a night at karaoke with all my friends now, can I?"

Asami sat down and started talking to Cindy, the most natural thing in the world for her. "*Kawaii!!!*" I heard her say. Unsure of - and uninterested in - what particular adornment she was referring to, I plonked myself down next to her, the sinking feeling already somewhere near my knees. I sensed I needed her to stay close to me that night. Someone had already started singing the first song. The thing which struck me as I glanced around was that all the other faces looked as awkward as I felt. It was not a typical karaoke vibe; more like being among a group of patients in a dentist's waiting room. Other than Asami, Cindy and another girl - all busy comparing accessories - the assorted guests were barely talking to one another. I guessed that none of them had exactly jumped at the invitation. Thomas was rather smug in that over-important way he had. He viewed everybody there as his friend - weren't we coming to their wedding after all? Weren't we all here on this special occasion tonight to support him and Cindy in this beautiful moment, to experience the wonderful blossoming of "real" love?

It ranks not only as the worst karaoke experience in my life (by a country mile), but one of the worst experiences of any kind I've ever suffered. Nobody even forced me to sing anything. I probably did my usual bland rendition of Blondie's *Call Me*, rather happy when it was over and I was allowed to put the mic down, having done my duty to contribute in some small way to the event. At the forefront of my mind was the absolute necessity of making sure that this agony was limited to two hours. There will always be someone who'll insist on extending by one more hour, but I knew I was incapable of putting up with such sustained torture and resolved to leave Under Any Circumstances.

We passed the half-way mark and I was already fully focused on my escape. Thomas had been a surprisingly passive participant so far. He hadn't even been allowed any canoodling on the sofa next to his fiancée. She was one of those girls who seemed - rather ironically, you might think - embarrassed by any public show of affection. But nonetheless he was enjoying playing the host, grinning a little too much, saying "Man, this is fun!" way too often, while I was trying to work out if he really was enjoying himself, and if so, why? He'd sung a couple of American classics - maybe *Born to Be Wild* or *Eye of The Tiger* - and then, with the ladies threatening to steal the limelight with their near perfect renditions of recent J-pop fare, and with a suitable amount of beer having passed his lips, felt the time had come for his big moment. He reached for the control, typed in a few numbers and *Bolivian Parody* appeared on the screen. Before I was able to compute the potential for disaster these two words implied, I even let out an exclamation of pleasant surprise: Huh, fancy him picking this song!

Before continuing, I should clarify that I had never, obviously, been to karaoke with Thomas before and, equally obviously, would

never go with him again - my point being that I don't know if he
sometimes sang it in front of others. What soon became clear though,
was that he often sang it in his car, in his room, in his head, imagining
the day when there would be a crowd of people watching him,
cheering him on. And this was that day.

"A Canadian singing *Bolivian Parody*! Should be fun!" This was
my feeble effort at bonhomie. It must have sounded hollow. I can't
imagine ever thinking Thomas doing anything which "should be fun."
In any case he ignored me, fully focused as he was on the song whose
opening refrain had just started.

I have had moments in my karaoke career which I'm not proud of.
Ill-advisedly choosing Eminem or Sting and getting lyrics and/or
melodies hopelessly wrong or trying comedy takes on Michael Jackson
or Prince that fell well and truly flat. I still cringe now occasionally
remembering my pathetic attempts to sing a particular song years
ago, and pray that the people who witnessed it have erased it from
their memories. Maybe I'm being spoken of right now by someone in
Dublin or Perth. "When I was in Japan we went to karaoke one night
and there was this middle-aged balding English guy who tried to sing
Take On Me. God, what a dick." This is entirely possible. Who can
ever be sure? The only thing I am absolutely certain of when it comes
to karaoke is that I have never come close to embarrassing myself to
even a fraction of the level that Thomas took it to now.

The first lines, *Look at my new wife, oh she's so fun to see,* gave no
real hint at the suffering to come; but once the second part cut in, a
horribly over-emotional *Papaaaaaaaa!!* followed by an even more
hideous *My llama's deeaaaaaaad!!!* already started to get most people

scratching various bodily parts, aware that we may be in for an uncomfortable few minutes. Oblivious to this - oblivious to anything at all in fact - Thomas continued. The song is of course, apart from being long - never more so than that night - multi-layered; and even though Thomas started with the dial jacked up to Level 11 on the embarrassment scale right from the off, each subsequent bit he just somehow managed to ramp it up one further notch. The Spanish operatics were astonishingly awful. His falsetto *Atahualpa* was actually painful. I couldn't even enjoy the aptness of some of the lyrics:

Todos me odian! - "everybody hates me!"

Dejame salir de aqui! - "permission to get out!" - *No, no, no, no, no!*

I think I actually stopped breathing during *famiLEEEEEEEEEE!!*

You realize that if anyone here did in fact have any empathy toward the guy - and that was still an outside possibility - they could have thrown in a hoot of laughter, or maybe an ironic "Go Thomas, go!" to ease the tension. Even better, some quick thinking near-buddy might have spared him any further shame by pressing the "cancel" button on the remote. It was there for a reason after all.

But there was just an appalled silence which took hold remarkably quickly and which held throughout the following six minutes. Amazingly, things didn't improve during the inevitable air guitar part which Thomas could theoretically have used to take a bit of a break, maybe a sip of beer and a suggestive wink at his fiancée. Instead he decided to take things down to barely imaginable depths, unbuttoning his shirt - oh God no - all the way. Next, he was on his knees, dangerously close to Cindy who, trapped, seemed no less horrified than the rest of us by this astonishing display of poor taste.

As he squealed on his imaginary guitar, thrusting his head back at every high note, his tongue wiggling around suggestively, you could imagine her calculating already if it was still strictly necessary to go ahead with the wedding. Oh Jesus, and look now he's writhing around on the floor, shirt off the shoulders and down to the elbows.

Just gotta leave, gotta leave before I heave.

And when that heavy bit was finally over - was it really usually this long? - what was he going to do? Surely not unbutton his leather pants? No, fortunately the pits had been reached already; I think it would have been literally impossible to go any lower, congratulations on that at least. Now he was just standing there, shirt completely off, revealing a hairless, oddly androgynous chest, breathing in and out, hair dishevelled, glasses somehow still on, the total silence belying the fact that there were about fifteen drunk thirty-something's in the room. As I looked through the gap in my fingers which had been shielding my eyes since *Pizarro, Pizarro,* there was a feeling of release being mere seconds away.

Whichever direction Andean gusts puff, sang Thomas. Silence. And it was over.

I think Asami was the only person who even attempted to clap and there was suddenly a general fidgeting around for bags and coats. Even though nearly fifteen minutes remained until we got thrown out, nobody could wait to escape this torture chamber.

Leaving karaoke, people will normally start discussing which bar to go to next. This didn't seem to be the case on this occasion, but it wasn't as if I was checking. It was all I could do not to break into a sprint as I left the room. I was aware that Thomas was standing there, very alone, quietly buttoning up his shirt and Cindy was sitting, semi-frozen in her chair, waiting for somebody to go over and break the spell.

That had been a mere month ago. And now we were at their wedding. Lord give me strength. At least it was apparently nearly over. And looking on the bright side, it had actually been entirely painless compared to that night in karaoke. I remembered my father's favourite saying: "Be thankful for small mercies." Never truer than on this occasion.

The highlight of the whole wedding came towards the end during the ring exchange, when a few of the guests, bored with pretending to give a shit about it, started chatting.

"You shagged Cindy too, didn't you?" I heard someone behind me say to the guy standing next to him.

"Sure," replied his friend. There was a pause. "Who hasn't?" he added, with a barely suppressed guffaw which, rippling through the other guests, Thomas picked up on, nodding appreciatively in our direction at our efforts to keep the mood "real".

It was not long afterwards that I heard some gossip about Thomas and Cindy. I saw him one Friday sitting at the counter and found myself uncharacteristically marching over to greet him. It was a chance to confirm things.

"I heard you're planning on leaving?" I asked. It came out a little more cheerfully than I intended.

"You know Pee-tah, I wanna open my own bar. I feel it's what I should be doing with my life."

"But not another Gaijin bar in the city, right?" I asked, nervously.

"No. I've thought things through. I know I could run a great place here, but my heart says I should go back to Canada. My country's calling me. I've had fun here, but I'm a nature boy at heart. The wilds of Canada are in my blood. You wouldn't understand. It's always been my dream to open my own place. You know Pee-tah, there's more to me than just a teacher: I'm a businessman too. I feel there's a huge market for someone with my skills to open a bar in Canada, combine it with some Japanese elements - you know, a karaoke room, Japanese style snacks. Cindy can help, she'd make an amazing waitress. I think we'd be a great team. I have this vision of exactly how it should be. I feel it's like a calling."

I agreed heartily that it was an absolutely perfect plan, that there was no reason at all for them to stay here, that Canada was indeed calling them hope they find a perfect location pray the bar keeps them busy forever good luck bye!

One wonderful Thomas-free year later, a disturbing rumour reached me that he was back in Kumamoto. My heart sank. Back in Kumamoto? Thomas? "*Thomas and Shindy*" Thomas? Assuming it wasn't a wind-up then surely this was just a quick trip to visit the in-laws?

Well actually no, apparently it wasn't. He'd returned to live. *Nooooo!!!* I looked up and shook my fist towards the heavens. *Why?!!* Had his Canadian karaoke bar dream come to nothing?

In fact, even though I successfully managed not to bump into him for another full year, snippets of his news filtered through and I put together a picture of what seemed to have happened. Cindy had - entirely predictably in fact - met someone else a few months after arriving in Canada with her new husband and they'd split up. Simple as that. I remembered once more the look of mortification on her face after Thomas's karaoke performance. It was the first time I'd ever felt any sympathy for either of them. I couldn't work out if dumping him for another Canadian counted as another plus in her favour? On balance you'd have to say yes, it probably did.

Maybe as a reaction to his failed marriage or probably out of horror of being back in a country where people were not shy to tell him what they thought of him to his face, he'd packed it all in and decided to head back to Kumamoto. Fuck. I could understand what the attraction of Japan was, but why did he want to come back to this city? Weren't there bound to be painful reminders everywhere of his ill-judged, short-lived marriage? Couldn't someone go and suggest him to try starting anew in a different city? Couldn't he combine Japanese and Canadian elements and open a bar in Tokyo? Or Northern Hokkaido?

It was bound to happen sooner or later. I walked into *Jake's Bar* one Friday night and there was Thomas sitting alone at the counter.

"Hi, Thomas," I said, heart sinking. *OK. Don't ask anything about Cindy or his brief stay in Canada. Don't get him started. Just keep it simple.* "How's it going?"

He took a deep sigh and, adopting a suitably "being philosophical through the dark memories" expression - got started.

"You know Pete, I'm doing OK. Things were pretty hard for a while back there but I feel that coming back here I have lots of friends who have helped me to get through it." He finished, nodding his head slightly, giving a wry smile in bittersweet reflection of the fluctuations

169

of life and the whimsical reality of his being back in a bar in Kumamoto by himself. I scratched my head metaphorically, wondering who these "friends" could possibly be, while I waited nervously, wondering which overused cliché he'd select for his next comment. Maybe "strength through adversity" or "coming out stronger at the end of it." Just please, please avoid anything like "And you know what the irony is, Pete?" I just don't think I'd be able to take that.

Whatever it was, I've forgotten. I am not exaggerating when I say I don't care at all.

I'm simply grateful that I miraculously managed to avoid meeting him again. Now it's something I don't even need to worry about as he (Hallelujah!) actually left a few years back. Perhaps the memories were too harrowing after all. Maybe the call of Canada was too strong to ignore. Whatever the reason, I'm sure I wouldn't understand.

So where did he go? Was it in fact Canada? Did he open up his bar elsewhere in Japan? Might he have "done a Charlie" and relocated to China? I'm unable to enlighten you and make no apologies for the fact. All I know for sure is that he is no longer here. I'm safe. The last I heard about him was that just before he left, a British friend (Oli-vah: My hero!) punched him during a barbecue in the park because he was "annoying". It's one of the rare times in my life when I almost feel there may actually be a God. On the whole I sense that this is unlikely, but you never know. So just on the off-chance, let me offer up a prayer.

Please Lord, forgive me all my sins. May Your greatness shine ever more radiantly with each passing moment; and may You keep

Thomas out of my path for the rest of the days that You choose in Your wisdom to grant me.

    Amen.

PART TWO: LEAVING

6) Ben: The Man with a Plan

The longer you stay in Japan, the more dangerous it becomes.

Have you ever seen · or preferably read · *The Beach*? You know the story, about the "perfect" beach hidden away from the masses on a small island in Thailand and when the American protagonist finds it, there is that initial moment when he beholds it, maybe a couple of extra days when he and his friend are allowed to enjoy it. Not only that, there's free marijuana! But then it doesn't take long for the whole thing to unravel and we discover that of course the drugs are not there by accident; in fact this paradise is nothing more than a fortuitous byproduct of the drugs that are grown there. The drug lords of course care nothing about the scenery, and everything about the importance of maintaining the secrecy of the island. There's no such thing as a perfect place; beauty comes at a price; and a dozen other clichés, yawn yawn.

In a somewhat different way, it sometimes occurs to me that Japan could be viewed in a similar light. *Where communism works* was the provocative title of a book about Japan I occasionally flicked through without ever buying in my first few years of living here. Fair play to the author too. If you're looking for the model of the perfect economy, whether it be communism without the dearth of productivity, or democracy untarnished by those tiresome social ills like crime, poverty or gang warfare, Japan may well be for you.

In the case of the movie version of *The Beach*, Leonardo's joy was sadly ruined almost as soon as he got there. Poor bastard, after spending all that time securing the maps, swimming all that way and everything. Probably better if he never bothered in the first place, although I'm sure he enjoyed his few moments in the water with that naked French chick. But even if he'd been able to stay, he'd surely have tired of it after a few months. "Yeah, I found paradise. It was OK for a bit, but all that fruit for breakfast was a bit much. I miss my fried bacon and sausages."

One interesting point here might have been to see how he would have re-adapted to the less perfect world from which he came. The movie never touched on this. It didn't need to. His idyll was over almost before it started. And besides, it would have made a boring movie even more so.

But just say for argument's sake that Japan is that perfect beach. You arrive, you fall in love with the place and with nobody chasing you away you decide to stay. Before long you've developed an all-consuming irrational passion for origami or bonsai. Then one day many years later, you cock your head up, finally paying attention to that little voice inside your head which you've been doing your best to ignore. "That's right," you nod, "I'm not from here. I was only ever planning on staying a year or so. But can I make a living back home folding paper or growing tiny trees? No?" Oops. What to do?

I'm not saying for a minute that Japan is a perfect place. There are plenty of Gaijin who positively delight in ripping the place to shreds. In fact you could ask anyone here to make a list of most annoying things, and there will be hardly anybody who doesn't fill a sheet of A4. But interestingly, you'll find some things which most people would class as virtues twisted into negatives. "People work too hard." "People are too polite, too fussy." Other complaints might be about the crowds: "Two hour queues for a ride in the amusement park!" or "There's never a seat on the trains!" Then there are the downright trivial ones: "Strawberries in sandwiches? Corn on pizza?" "The milk has a funny taste." Or "The desserts are tiny!" Hardly a damning profile of an awful place. I think it's fair to say that most people here could probably grudgingly agree that at least certain aspects of the country get much closer to perfection than most places.

I could tell you the names of three of us for a start.

Things continued changing in Kumamoto, but we could hardly blame it on the new faces. It was just us and that unavoidable fact of life: Getting older. Spending every available evening drinking at the bars downtown had somehow stopped being the most appealing way to pass time. It wasn't even that we were specifically trying to avoid Thomas, at least not as far as I can recall; more a simple matter of changing circumstances.

In my case, other things were competing for attention, most notably fatherhood. Playing with my two young daughters, watching them growing daily and reading bedtime stories was of course my new Number One Absolutely Favourite Thing to Do in the World. Who would have thought there'd be anything more rewarding than drinking yourself into a stupour at a bar? But even as recollections of those evenings at the Izakaya with Charlie, Murray and Douglas's angels were becoming an increasingly distant memory, a night out drinking beer had never lost its appeal. Au contraire. Once little girls were safely tucked up in bed, the call of the amber nectar and the need for some Gaijin companionship were stronger than ever. And what did you know? As luck would have it, a group was waiting, tailor-made for my requirements: A bunch of guys who had for their different reasons decided that drinking at home was the way to go. God had pulled another one of his tricks. The age of the shindigs had started.

First up was Bill, hailing from Alabama. With his easy manner and boyish grin, he'd been one of the most visible Gaijin in the bars in my early years in the city. He had a hectic social life, always on his way to another bar, another party, so we rarely chatted for more than a few minutes, but they were always a fun few minutes. A talented guitarist, he'd hooked up with some other musicians and had quickly become a familiar face on the local music circuit. No evening out was complete without one of Bill's live shows, where he'd be resplendent in a pink, silver or rainbow wig. He'd made the most of his local rock star celebrity while it lasted, leaving a string of girlfriends in his wake.

But one fateful Saturday night at *The Red Zed* all that changed. He got involved in a scuffle - for reasons which remained the source of much speculation for years after - leaving him with two black eyes, a few hours in a prison cell and an acute sense of injustice. He decided to shun the Kumamoto social scene completely, instead choosing the more sheltered environment of a home party. What could I say? I was more than happy to hang out with Bill and if he refused to hit the bars, well that suited me just fine.

Bill introduced me to Gary. It was quite a shock to discover his existence. Gary lived a couple of blocks away from my flat, had been in the city for over ten years, but his face was one that I'd never seen.

"He's a bit of a hermit," laughed Bill unnecessarily on our first meeting. "Not many people get to meet him."

Gary didn't fit the profile of your average recluse. For a start, he was chatty and well-informed. He was never short of an opinion on any subject and as a bonus had a seemingly endless supply of hilarious anecdotes. Secondly, he had a partner he had been with for many years. Kumi, with her friendly smile and great line in vulgar t-shirts, became the only constant female presence at the shindigs. Gary's downtime was built around the twin pillars of music ("Eddie Van Halen is God!") and old US comedy reruns ("Saturday isn't Saturday without Saturday Night Live!"), but the overriding motor driving his life was stinginess. He never went out. He and Kumi spent every single evening at home, drinking the cheapest (and foulest) whiskey imaginable, with either the CD or the video on. Their home arrangements were sparse, to put it mildly. Living in Japan gave him the chance to pass it off as "Zen", but this wasn't fooling anybody. It didn't take much to realize that both the lack of furniture and the refusal to ever go out - even if he claimed this was because of a simple lack of interest in events beyond his four cheap walls - were just twin manifestations of his scrooge-like miserliness.

We got into a routine of taking turns hosting shindigs. It was undeniably nice to belong to what soon came to feel like a secret society, although the only real danger here was limited to your musical preferences being exposed. Bill and Gary were as one on this. Acceptable tastes were not up for discussion, they were set in stone.

"Queen? Daft Punk?" A stony silence would frequently follow when I unthinkingly let slip what I'd listened to the previous week

Thinking before opening my gob rarely helped. "Man, that's an awful song," they fired back when I declared my love for *Jump.* "A synthesizer on a Van Halen song? How dumb is that?" Yikes, these guys were hardcore. Over the years, alongside the chatting, the teasing, the 80s American music, SNL videos and round-up of local gossip, the subject of the future would inevitably pop up.

"Never gonna head back to Alabama then, Bill?" I asked.

"Why would I?" said Bill. "Nothing over there for me." Subject closed.

"How about you, Gary? When are you taking Kumi back to Hawaii, start living in the style you both deserve?"

Gary looked back and blinked a few times, not understanding the point of the question.

I loved hanging out with these guys, but I often asked myself what they - and many other people I knew - actually got out of living here. It was far from obvious. They worked at different schools in the city, which paid the bills, but they had no interest in anything specifically related to Japanese culture, including - as far as I knew - origami or bonsai. We had all chosen to side-step the question of what we were really still doing here in Japan, and even more conveniently avoided confronting the logical follow-up of just how long we planned to be here. Were we actually doing anything useful? Did teaching English satisfy our life goals? Hmm, "fulfillment": Here was a concept which rarely strayed into our chats. Had any other ambitions we might have once possessed completely evaporated?

What would we say in our defense if we were led, shackled, in front of the jury at the Court of Gaijin Laziness (and Other Crimes) and faced those exact questions?

"So how do you plead?" the judge would bellow accusingly.

"Guilty as charged, your honour," we'd be forced to reply, hanging our heads in shame. Guilty of accepting an easy life over a more meaningful one.

My old friend Murray had a term which he used disparagingly for those who'd fallen victim to Japan's simple charms and had stayed here too long: Wash-ups. I remembered laughing in agreement. It was the exact word I would have used for Thomas a few years earlier, but suddenly he wasn't here yet we still were. What did that say about us? Nothing very positive, it could safely be assumed, had we chosen to analyze things more deeply.

But we didn't.

For better or worse, and for our own different reasons, Gary, Bill and I saw no need to justify our continued existence here.

But there was a fourth shindigger who didn't quite share this rather limited vision of the future.

Ben was a no-nonsense Australian. Short and stocky, with kind features oddly reminiscent of Gene Wilder, he wasn't afraid to call a spade a spade. He dissed *The Beach*. "No surf there. What's perfect about that?" he sneered. "Stupid movie. That girl had nice tits though." Here, typical of Ben, he managed a near perfect eight word critique of the movie without even trying. How could anyone not agree with that? Ben enjoyed living in Japan, but he was also far more critical of the country than me. Everywhere has its faults, but maybe in my eyes Japan's were considerably outnumbered by those in England.

I have always struggled with my patriotism, which only ever emerges during football or cricket matches, and even then it's a rather painful, wish-I-was-from-somewhere-else-so-I-would-be-spared-the-pain-of-having-to-watch-this version. Away from sports, I'm happy to be as far from England as possible. I have to stop myself sometimes when I extoll the virtues of the French countryside, Swiss friendliness, Japanese cleanliness or German humour (this, obviously, just to wind everyone up) to an unsympathetic British audience. Sports aside, the only thing I really love about the UK is the weather. Even that gets me in trouble.

"You like the weather? The summers with no sun? Are you crazy?" Shit, if that's controversial, I'd probably best keep my thoughts on the crap food, boring towns, gloomy gits and overrated TV to myself. And just be grateful that I have no yearning whatsoever to return to my homeland. Its call falls on deaf ears where I'm concerned, and thank Jesus or the Buddha for that. I'm not sure if I've exactly found paradise here, but I'm content in my adopted home. And therefore I don't need to pay too much attention to the previously mentioned dangers of living too long in this country. While Ben seemed far readier than me to condemn his entire cricket team to the fire - "Bunch of fucking idiots" was his scathing commentary even when they won a game (which they always seemed to do against my England heroes) - he was undoubtedly more a man of his country than I have ever been. He actually wanted to go back. He happily confessed to missing Australia and was formulating strategies for how best he might return there. What's more - and unlike Thomas - these were firmly rooted in the realms of the possible. The guy clearly had his feet on the ground. No flights of fancy for Mr. B. He knew what he was doing; he had a plan B, C, D and most probably E.

When I first met Ben, working at my first post-Napoleon language school, he, like me, had already been though the Three Holy Stages of Gaijin: 1) Come to Japan. 2) Meet a Japanese girl. 3) Get married. He never progressed to the Fourth Stage: He didn't have any kids. His wife Harumi had some medical condition apparently, unable to have children. I'm sure that was a big blow for both of them. It didn't take a big stretch of the imagination to see them as doting parents. But if it wasn't to be, hey, there was no point in moping around. And Harumi wasn't doing any moping. She was in insurance, working her way up within the firm and doing very nicely indeed, thank you. It was only shortly after meeting them that they bought a very handsome, brand new apartment with a lovely wide balcony, just downstream of one of the local beauty spots.

While Bill's bachelor pad may have been modest in size, it seemed rather luxurious compared to the place Gary and Kumi called home. But Ben's new flat was in a league of its own. It was a veritable Versailles. It was a reason for staying.

"This is seriously cool," I cooed at their house-warming party, leaning over the balcony and staring down into the constantly changing ripples on the crystal clear stream gurgling a couple of metres below. It was the best of all the shindig locations, by miles. I'd take this over Di Caprio's "perfect" beach any day.

"Looks like you're here for the long term, then?" I asked.

"Oh no, not at all," Ben shot back. "Piece of cake to find a tenant for this kind of place. No, I'll be heading back to Oz at some point and when that happens, we can rent this out, keep the money coming in."

"You're scaring me. You make it sound like you're leaving next month."

"Well, if something comes up, then yeah, I just might. I've been here for eight years now. That's long enough. Not staying here forever."

You see? The guy was always making plans. Buying a place just when he was getting ready to leave? Smart couple, Ben and Harumi.

"I bought a bungalow in Australia a few years back. I rent it out to tourists by the week, but when I go back, I've already got a place to stay," he told me.

"Shit, Ben. You own a house in Australia?"

More than anything, this unremarkable statement showed up how embarrassingly badly organized I was in running my life. We were not teenagers anymore; he'd just turned forty and I was only five years younger. But I was probably the more typical type of Gaijin. One of the reasons many of us found ourselves here after all was a general horror of the world of mortgages and insurance that seemed to go hand in hand with regular employment back home. It was nice to pretend we were out of it here, even though of course we were doing little else than storing ourselves up for a major shock at some unspecified point in the future. Some of us had kidded ourselves into believing that being here in Japan was a valid reason for not thinking about scary things like pension plans, which may have been true if we were talking about two months, less so when it was two decades. But not Ben, it would seem. Compared to everyone else I knew, Ben seriously had his head screwed on. He seemed to have all his options covered.

"Well, you have to make plans, right? Never know what's round the corner."

Wise words indeed. Spoken like a true insurance salesman.

"Oh no, that's the wife. She's the one who plans everything. She's got God only knows how many insurance plans taken out on me. She'll be one rich lady if I kick the bucket."

Either he already had a healthy sense of financial prudence before he met Harumi, or else a lot of it had rubbed off. I thought about Charlie's stalker and Sam's surprise. Douglas's shocker hadn't happened yet, but so many people I knew here seemed to have lives made up almost exclusively of a chain of unexpected events. God knows how I'd managed to avoid all these pitfalls so far. Yes, it was a wise thing to be thinking about your future.

It wasn't as if Ben hadn't had a good time here. He'd first come over as an exchange student, had liked it so much that he'd decided to stay on a bit which turned into a bit longer. Then, during a third "bit longer" stage he'd met his future wife which was just another reason to stay on a bit longer still. It wasn't as if he'd been idle during his time here, either. He'd been around the country working in various jobs, always earning money, saving money. He'd even done some work at the Nagano Winter Olympics. In his own quiet way, he'd adapted to life in Japan very well. He was more immersed in the country's culture than most Gaijin. But he knew that while he'd enjoyed his time, he didn't want to spend the rest of his days here. Plus - like all of us - he was not getting any younger.

Given our years spent here, we were only too aware of the little known phenomenon of Reverse Culture Shock. You move to Japan, you kind of brace yourself for a shock. Sometimes it hits you in a big way, sometimes it's more of a slow burner. Of course! It's rare to find a Gaijin who doesn't start complaining about something within an hour. The noise, the humidity, the traffic. The crap TV, the cheesy music, the odd customs, the food. I still haven't met any Gaijin who's happy swallowing a live wriggling piece of squid. It took me years to appreciate raw horse meat, the local delicacy. You spend years studying the language, think you're almost up to native fluency and then make a dumb mistake that would embarrass a five year old. Things are different here, of course they're different.

But Gaijin returning to their home countries are not braced. Even if they are not expecting any fanfare, they kind of assume they'll slot back into their old lives, forgetting nothing stays the same. Their countries have moved on without them. Nobody pressed a pause button while we were away. Their friends have embarked on new careers and made new friends, on top of which those imperfections in society which they barely noticed before they set foot in Japan suddenly seem glaringly obvious. The dirty stations, the dog shit in the parks. The ridiculously early closing times. The lack of manners, the general rudeness of folk, the aggressive youths.

"I can't remember it being this bad," they'll say.

Wrong! It really was this bad, probably even worse, you just didn't notice it. You just got softened by those years in Japan where you weren't forced to stare these things in the face every day.

And it gets worse. You go for your first post-Japan job interview.

"And so, erm, Mr. Turner, what have you been doing for the last decade? English teacher? Hmm, I see. Well we have a couple of road sweeping vacancies."

Ben was fully aware of this and like someone waiting to cross a busy road, he knew it could be suicidal to dash across. It required careful thinking, timing, planning. No point in rushing across if there was nothing waiting. Something would appear. And in the meantime, things weren't so bad here, once you headed out onto the balcony with an ice cold stubby.

I for one found his insistence on wanting to leave Japan hard to fathom.

"What is there in Oz that's so great you want to move back there anyway? Shit cricket team, rank beer, spiders hiding in your slippers, crocodiles leaping out of the rivers, kangaroos falling out of the skies. Jeez, stay here, mate!" I'd never been to Australia and had no plans to either.

"Surfing's not so bad," said Ben with a smile. 'Cos our Bennie may have been of a more modest disposition than Bill, but he too was the possessor of a rare talent. A talent nurtured on the shores of his native Newcastle. The guy was a surfing star.

"Legend," corrected Ben. "Legend is the age category for surfers over forty." Ben had a purpose built van, with space for his surfboard and room to sleep, and as often as work would allow, he'd be off to one of his favourite surfing locations on the eastern side of Kyushu. He'd fallen in with the local surfing crowd and started entering competitions held all over Japan. Coming back from one event in Kochi, on the neighbouring island of Shikoku, I casually asked him how he'd got on.

"I won," he said. I waited for a few seconds, assuming this was some kind of joke. He calmly continued leafing through the surfing magazine in his hands, no further comment seemed forthcoming.

"You're shitting me, right?" Ben looked up at me and gave a slight shrug.

"You're not? You won? This was an all-Japan event, right? Holy crap, Ben, you're a God!"

"No, only a legend," corrected Ben once more, patiently and kind of modestly. "The waves were a bit of a joke, mind. Still, I got a couple of good rides and I guess that was enough."

Yep, no champagne return for Ben. Just winning a national surfing event and then quietly getting on with things. He was happy enough just to be able to get out in the waves, but it seemed that surfing in Japan was a poor substitute for The Real Thing in Australia.

"No sharks here, though," I offered. "And at least they speak some English in Japan."

"Shut up, you bloody Pom."

And so Ben's clock was ticking down on two main fronts. Every season without hitting the Ozzie surf was a season lost. And there was that age thing, knowing that every extra year makes it that bit harder to find a job and to re-establish yourself in The Country You Once Called Home.

It was a path laced with danger. The road to hell is paved with good intentions, and the journey back home is littered with the ossified corpses of former English teachers who've attempted unsuccessfully to reverse the effects of Japanification. There were scores of examples any one of us could quote. Friends who had really struggled to fit back in. Three years seemed to be a watermark of sorts. There was Charlie Peach. He'd surprised nobody with his inability to readjust. Kenny had done all right in America, but he'd only been in Japan a couple of years. Murray meanwhile had washed up on the southern shores of England, where he was now running a hotel in Folkestone · seemed very successful too · but he would frequently warn me off following suit.

"Oh God, you don't want to come back to England. Nothing here. Much better off staying in Japan." This was unnecessary advice, as I was one of the rare few who had precisely zero plans to leave Japan. But if Ben had anyone similar warning him against going back Down Under, he was not to be deterred. Ben had made up his mind.

There was one cautionary tale which resonated above all. Another mild-mannered Australian, a genial sort called Kyle, had made the decision to take his young family back, shortly after the birth of his third child.

"I've had ten happy years in Japan, but it's no place to raise children. They aren't taught to think for themselves," he would say. He loved the idea of his three kids running around in the wide open spaces of the Sydney suburbs. He'd found a plot of land and construction of their new house had already started.

"Do you have a job to go back to?"

"No, no point in looking here. I'll look around once we move back. Bound to be shitloads of stuff. Sydney is a huge city."

Japan had treated Kyle very well. He'd enjoyed his time here, was comfortably set up, and would probably have stayed if it hadn't been for his family, but kids come first, right? He was still only in his mid-thirties, young enough to start over again. He had no great ambitions, just wanted a job that would pay the bills. They'd sent lots of money home.

"Yeah, had a great time here, but can't wait to get back to the snakes, spiders and crocs." These were probably not the exact words he spoke (I wasn't there) but he certainly said something, and with whatever it was he said as a final farewell, he vanished, never to be seen again.

"Hope they're OK," we said at a shindig a few months later.

"He'll be fine. He has a couple of years' worth of savings. Smart guy, Kyle. He just needs to get some part-time work to start the ball rolling. He'll find his feet soon enough."

One year later, someone asked, "Did you hear anything from Kyle?"

"Not good, I'm afraid. Sounds like most of his savings have gone. They couldn't finish the house and he still has no job."

Another year later, we heard he'd found a job, but it was two hours away from Sydney. He only got back to see the family at the weekends. After that messages dried up completely.

This, more than any other, was the model that kept Ben from darting across the road at the first sign of a gap. We were under no illusions as to how hard it could be. That was the main reason why the likes of Bill or myself were still here. We'd probably both at various times vaguely considered leaving Japan, but when we paused for a moment to reflect on the effort that would be involved - and with no burning desire to return - we'd chosen the easier option of staying. But Ben was smart. The man had a plan. Multiple plans. If anyone amongst us was likely to succeed, it was Ben. He probably spent hours every evening refining an infallible strategy.

"It may take a few months, years even, but I'll get there eventually."

I was kind of surprised that Harumi was also hoping to spend the rest of her days in Australia. Would she be able to find work? Just what did she plan to do there? She spoke very little English - Ben's Japanese was fluent - and seemed to live for her job, doing crazy hours which Ben didn't mind complaining about. Was she really willing to pack it all in and head Down Under?

"Yeah, she loves it over there. And she's ready for something new. She's worked her tits off all her life, it'll be paradise for her to be able to take things a bit easier, put her feet up, enjoy a pina colada, let me take care of her."

These were noble sentiments, but I found it a little difficult to picture Harumi relaxing on a beach, cocktail in hand, for the last 30 or 40 years of her life. Aside from rarely drinking alcohol, she was a certified workaholic. At least that would be the diagnosis back in Australia. Here, working 14 hour days was just considered normal. I'm not sure if my gleeful comments about the dangers lurking in every corner did much to firm her resolve to take early retirement and follow her husband to the Land of Eternal Sunshine.

Then, one day, it happened.

"I found a job on the internet," said Ben. "Working in a factory, down the road from my place. The location is just perfect. Couldn't be better. I sent off the application, just got to wait to hear back from them. I really think this is the one, though. So could be our last shindig this weekend. At my place?"

This was sad news indeed. "Well I guess that means congratulations. So, you're going too, Harumi?" I asked.

"God, no. Not that stupid," she laughed. "No point in throwing everything away, putting all our eggs in one basket. He'll probably hate it, quit after a few weeks. No, I'll stay here, then if things work out for him, once he's got everything sorted, I'll start to think about tying things up at this end and moving over."

There spoke a wise woman. She didn't seem to have complete faith in her husband's ability to hold down a job. The voice of prudence resonated throughout. Again, I was impressed. These two really were covering all their angles, not taking any undue risks at all. I remembered my own escape from Japan with Asami almost ten years earlier, with absolutely nothing waiting for us and an underwhelming total of $3000 in savings, half of which I spent on a car a week after arriving in New Zealand. The amazing thing is that I can't remember feeling even slightly worried. And everything had worked out fine, hadn't it? What it is to be young!

Actually on this occasion, we had jumped the gun. It turned out that Harumi wasn't the only one not leaving. Ben wouldn't in fact be going either. It was a false alarm.

"Didn't get it," he said, not looking too sorrowful if truth be told. "Lucky I didn't book my ticket. Shindig at your place next week?"

It seemed that we'd been a touch over-hasty to see him off.

His second leaving party was similar. He'd found another job, this time in the town next to Newcastle. He was even more optimistic about this one as it required someone with Japanese speaking ability. "Not too many Japanese speakers in Newcastle. Think it's in the bag," he said confidently.

It fell through.

"Just as well I didn't hand in my notice. Looks like I'll be here a bit longer."

I think it was Ben's sixth leaving party · almost a year after the first · which became the official one. This time he'd quit his job, booked the flight, he was leaving the following week. There was little doubt this would be the last time for us to sit out on his balcony, watching the shimmering translucent waters below. For a while, anyway.

"So, all the best, Ben."

"Yeah well, gotta try these things, eh? Don't have my hopes up too high for the job, to be honest, but it doesn't matter. It's a first step. There's sure to be all kinds of stuff once I get back there. And if things don't work out, I've got a house and wife waiting for me back here."

"Hear those poisonous cane toads are reaching the size of small sheep these days. Wouldn't want to be heading somewhere like that!"

"I'll keep a stick in my car."

"So suppose this is it, then."

"Guess so."

"OK, well it's no secret I'm going to miss the house like hell, but I might miss you a bit too: Who can I talk to about cricket now?"

And with that Ben was off to start his new life. Days later he found himself in Newcastle Airport proudly decked out in a crisp new uniform, working as a representative of All Oz Airlines.

That lasted precisely three weeks.

It wasn't the most promising start to his post-Japan career.

"They just put you in the firing line," he complained. "You have to stand there and basically get abused by the passengers when their flights are suddenly changed. No, couldn't have stood that any longer."

But he was back in Australia at least. The first stage of the plan had come to pass. Now he just had to wait for something else to come along. And in the meantime it was relatively easy to get a few part-time jobs. He started in a café, working lunch-times. It was kind of fun too, certainly compared to the airport job. But you could hardly see Harumi giving up her carefully cultivated career and flying over to start a new life on the other side of the world with her husband waiting tables. Definitely upside down, in more ways than one. No, this was obviously just to kill time, earn a few bucks while keeping an eye out for the right opportunity.

Then it came. There was a guy in the area who'd built up his own gardening business and now wanted to sell it. Gardening; now that was something Ben knew a little about. He'd always been an outdoors guy. That was one reason why he'd never found teaching English truly satisfying. It had its good points of course, but at the end of the day there was always that staring out of the window, the yearning to be under the blue skies instead of in a stuffy classroom. As a young man back in Australia, he was constantly looking for any excuse to be out of doors, whether it be surfing, fishing or bushwalking. Now he was back again, didn't it make sense to be looking for something along the same lines? OK, so he didn't have any gardening experience in a professional sense, but how hard could it be? And then there was the fact that he'd be his own boss: A self-employed businessman. That appealed to Ben's sense of pride. Yes, here was a real opportunity.

The more Ben thought about it, the more he liked the idea. He'd already done his time sitting in conversation schools in Japan teaching grammar. The thought of never again having to put on a suit and do time in an office sounded grand. As a self-employed gardener, he'd be outside all day. Zigzagging up and down on a mower. There was no shortage of large gardens in the neighbourhood. And buying the enterprise would give him that head start, rather than the slow, painful process of building up a business from scratch. He could effectively save years of his life by taking over this existing concern, with its all-important client list. He'd probably have too much on his hands, maybe even have to turn folk down. With a bit of hard work, he'd surely get the money back on his outlay in no time and then everything else would be pure profit.

"I've found a great gig. This guy has a small gardening firm which he wants to sell. I think I'm gonna buy it. I'll have my own business! Give me a few months, and let's think about you coming over and joining me," wrote Ben in an uncharacteristically upbeat message back to Harumi.

"Are you sure this is a wise move?" asked Harumi, clearly meaning: "There's no way this is going to work, sunshine. You really expect me to throw away my life to come and watch you mowing some lawns? Don't make me laugh. I'd be surprised if you can make a quarter of what I earn."

Here was extra motivation for Ben. *She doesn't think I can hack it. She doubts me. She doesn't believe in my vision. I'll show her. I'll make her proud.*

And so he paid $10 000 and became Ben the Gardener.

"Worst decision I ever made in my life," moaned Ben.

Now this didn't necessarily mean much from a person who rarely made bad decisions.

"No, but I mean, just a huge cock-up. Disaster." He shook his head with shame. Maybe someone with a longer record of cock-ups could have shrugged it off more easily. But this was a new situation for Ben.

It didn't take long for the proud brand new self-employed business owner to realize that he'd paid way over the odds for a concern which on close inspection looked far from healthy. For a start, most of the tools were shockingly out of date. He needed to replace virtually everything. "No matter," he thought. "Everything worthwhile needs an investment. In for a penny in for a pound!"

But it only took a few more weeks to see that doing up people's gardens wasn't as easy, fun, or profitable as he'd imagined.

"I was earning better money serving beer."

The mails to Harumi quickly lost their initial optimism. That sinking feeling had started. Would this really provide a living for him? The image of Kyle appeared over the tulip bed. *Ha! Told you so! Not just me, you see!* Ben picked up the bag of fertilizer and there was Harumi looking back at him, a slight sneer on her face. *Take care of me? You really think you can take care of me?*

There was of course the final option: The Retreat.

Of course, if it doesn't work out, I always have a house and wife to come back to in Japan.

Weren't those his exact words the day he'd left Japan? Something like that anyway. It was one of those throwaway comments, one you assume you'll never hear again. But now, something he'd mentioned almost in jest was starting to loom as the most likely outcome. The last thing he'd wanted was for that to happen. It wasn't a Plan C, D or E at all. It was an F, an admission of Failure. He'd gone away, full of optimism, low on self-doubt - and had Fallen Flat on his Face. Triple F.

There was one last throw of the dice. He had his holiday bungalow. Could he use his Japanese contacts to make money there? Australians were into the self-catering thing, that's how he'd kept a steady few bucks coming in over the years; but with the Japanese love of being pampered, wasn't there a chance to increase profits? He could offer a week or a two week plan. He could be the tour guide, drive them around to places of interest, offer swimming, surfing or English lessons if they wanted. Hell, he could dress up in a kangaroo suit, polish their shoes and brush their teeth if they were willing to pay for it.

We tried to help him at this end. We pointed a few people in his direction. I tried my best to stop my natural tendency to revel in the less appealing aspects of Australia.

"Great country," I told anyone who seemed interested. "Always wanted to go there. You know Ben's got a flat, great view of the beach; Wow, it'd be a wonderful place to visit. Koalas in every tree in Newcastle. No snakes or spiders there. Always sunny too, no winter where he lives."

And a number of people did go. Had a great time too, I heard. But maybe Ben wasn't able or willing to go to the next stage, market it to the general Japanese public. The line between students and friends is a very grey area. Lots of students become friends - that was one big reason why many were interested in going over. But to charge "friends"

- wasn't that mean? The guilty feeling was hard to shake off. And in any case, word-of-mouth would at best only reach a dozen or so customers. No, all things considered, that avenue would never amount to anything more than a bit of pocket money. Welcome enough, but no solid income there.

He was running out of options and rapidly losing motivation. Everything he tried seemed to lead to a dead end. There was no magic solution. I bumped into Harumi around town occasionally. "Anything to report from Down Under?"

"Well," she said, not wanting to appear too harsh. "No." Sounded kind of harsh.

"Good thing you didn't pack in your job too."

She gave a wry smile. "That was never going to be very likely now, was it?" she said.

"All kinds of horrible bugs and viruses over there anyway."

"Yes," she said, turning her nose up. "Much better here in Japan."

"And it's just non-stop sun over there too."

"Yes, just ten minutes outside and you turn black."

"Small city too, Newcastle."

"Yeah, nothing to do there. No good shops. No karaoke."

"No sushi."

"No, only steak. I'd probably put on ten kilos in the first few months."

This seemed rather unlikely; Harumi was always very careful with her weight. But it certainly seemed that she had lost any interest in Project: Move Together to Newcastle that she might once have had.

And suddenly Ben was back in the Land of the Rising Sun. I was delighted. Bill and Gary were happy too. One of the toughest things about Gaijin life is the near constant procession of friends away once they've got bored with the place, or run out of reasons for being here anymore. To get a friend back was an unexpected bonus. I hoped Harumi was glad to get her husband back. If she was disappointed that her Australian dream was over, at least for a few more years, she did an excellent job of hiding it.

After a few weeks of feeling a little down, Ben too brightened up considerably. OK, so this turn of events had never featured in his plans, but he certainly wasn't badly off. His apartment was there and he had a genuine bunch of friends. His self-deprecating humour helped a lot too.

"You know what the worst thing was?" he said.

It turned out that it wasn't anything to do with being rejected from job after job in spite of his long list of qualifications. The worst thing, he said, was the lack of curiosity about what he'd been up to in Japan. Friends, even family, had barely shown any interest at all in what he'd been doing for the last decade.

Here is the reverse culture shock in action. Everyone had been busy getting on with their own lives. Whether this was inside or outside the country made little if any difference to anybody other than Ben.

On his first evening back in Kumamoto, what a different sensation to have everyone crowded around, eagerly listening to every twist and turn in his fortunes since we'd last seen him. I can only assume this helped a lot in restoring a portion of his lost confidence. We weren't going to judge him on his lack of success in carrying out any of his plans A-E. How could we? The very thought of me trying to launch a new life for myself in England was simply ludicrous. Of course, it was a rare opportunity to indulge in a bit of gentle mocking which I for one was hardly likely to pass on, blowing raspberries at the nearest available Ozzie being the fastest way to regain some modicum of pride following England's latest cricket humiliation. But more than anything we were overjoyed to welcome a friend back.

And so the weeks continued. He got his old job back. It was as if he hadn't been away at all. The main thing missing from our conversations now were Ben's future plans in Australia. He wasn't going to be staying here forever, but the focus had shifted to early retirement. Get enough money together to look forward to a comfortable retirement in the sun, cocktails optional. But that was a long time away. And the thought of Harumi retiring...hmm, that was hard to imagine. She'd probably get bored after two days. Definitely not a beach girl, Harumi.

"It must at least have been nice to be surfing in some proper waves again," I asked, a few weeks after he'd come back.

He paused and smiled. "The funny thing is, I maybe got to go surfing three or four times tops the whole time I was there. When I was working I didn't have time, and when I had time I just didn't feel like it. Weird. Never happened to me before. Usually just get on the board, head into the waves and forget about the world. Those cane toads really are fucking scary, too."

Effectively then, the fall-back option had worked. If you were a politician, looking to put a spin on things, you'd easily be able to present the whole experience as a resounding success. That a plan was in place all along just in case he wasn't able to settle back in. He'd been, he'd tried - it hadn't worked out. Now he was back; he was safe. Sure, maybe he'd lost a few thousand dollars, but in the grand scheme of things, what was that? He'd come back wiser. He wasn't built for risk. Maybe he hadn't heeded his natural instincts. Live and learn, that was the lesson. From now, it would be a more cautious Ben. No more running after impossible dreams.

We were quickly back into the reassuringly familiar rhythm of the monthly shindigs, watching the usual comedies, listening to the usual tunes. It was obviously paying off. Ben was perkier by the week. Not only that but he was getting back to the beach more and more often too, until one day at his place, something seemed amiss.

"What's up, Ben?" I asked. "Not getting homesick for bloody Australia all over again are you?"

"Well no, not really. Actually it's Harumi."

Harumi? What could this be? Was there trouble at work? Were her insurance sales lower than usual? A missed promotion? A smaller than usual bonus? Any of these would be sure to put her in a foul mood. Or - surely not - nothing between the two of them now was it? Harumi could be, if not exactly cruel, then certainly somewhat cool on occasion. Surely there was no talk of separation? All of these possibilities hung in the air, unvoiced.

"She went to the hospital. Routine medical check. Goes every year. Well, this time they spotted something. Cancer."

Uh-oh. Wasn't expecting that one. That c-word came right out of nowhere. We waited. How bad was this going to be?

"Well the good news is that it's in the first stage, so the chances of dealing with it are much better."

"Well yes, that's why you do routine checks, right? So they should be able to get it before it spreads. But...the bad news?"

"The bad news is that it's pancreatic cancer. One of the deadliest kinds."

Shocked silence. It had been only a year since Steve Jobs had passed away, and his untimely death had done a lot to make people aware of this horribly aggressive form of cancer. Even if I didn't know much about the grim statistics, I had at least heard of it.

"But you said about the good news - it's been detected early. So the chance of recovery is high?"

"Not high. But higher than if it had been left unchecked. She's already booked in at a clinic in Okayama. Top clinic in the country apparently. We checked it out. She's off up there this weekend. I managed to convince her to take some time off work. She'll stay a month; they've got this aggressive chemotherapy treatment. But even then..."

"Even then?"

"They say there's only a 10 to 20% success rate."

We all went out together a couple of months later. Harumi had come back from the clinic. She'd responded well. She was looking good. That night she was the leader, very powerful. A lady on a mission - a mission to forget? I was half-expecting a frail lady who'd need help walking from one place to the next. Not a bit of it. There she was charging across the road, signalling to the rest of us to follow her. Then she was heartily tucking into her fried rice at her favourite restaurant. This was not a sick woman. It was not something she wanted to talk about, either. Any subject OK, but not the c-word, please. It was very rare for us to be going out together. For Harumi work was always first. She was a very occasional member of the shindigs, usually returning from the office about the time we were heading home. In any case, Harumi didn't hold much by crowding into each other's flats. She liked to do things in style. It was easy to forget how outgoing she was. With her limited English, she usually came across as rather quiet, patiently tolerating the drunken Gaijin husbands' rather rowdy silliness. But on this occasion, here she was, leading us through the menu, cracking jokes. This was much more her world. The woman had style. And money. If you're going to go enjoy an evening out, for Christ's sake go somewhere decent! What's the fun of staying in and drinking cheap beer like a bunch of adolescents? You could virtually see the words passing through her brain. A bit harsh, but at the same time, spot on. We all got a glimpse of the real Harumi that night. A classy lady. A fighter.

And it was to be the last time I ever saw her.

A few weeks later, a test revealed the cancer was back. She took more time off work, went back to the clinic for more treatment. Didn't respond so well this time. The cancer took hold and spread.

We got updates from an increasingly forlorn looking Ben and it wasn't looking positive at all. When she wasn't getting treatment, she was throwing herself even more into her work.

"She just refuses to slow down," he said, in that weary tone of a person who's given up trying to persuade someone, realized the sheer futility of it.

"Why doesn't she quit, try and make the most of whatever time there is left to her?" This was the question that all of us asked each other.

What would you do if you only had a few months to live? How many times had we used that conditional sentence for grammar practice in lessons? How odd, how awful to be asking the question when it was deadly serious.

Was Harumi choosing work? Or was she just choosing to carry on as normal, pretending it wasn't real?

How much longer would she be able to continue to pretend?

Not long. Her condition was rapidly worsening. The treatment had obviously failed. Now it was just down to pain management. Next, she'd finally quit her job. She was just too weak to continue. Days later she was in hospital. Then she was moved into a hospice. I was still unaware of the nuances in meaning of the different medical facilities. Ben spelled it out to me. "It means you're going to die soon," he said. And then, one weekend when I was out hiking, I got a phone call. "She's gone," said Ben. "Passed away this morning."

Shit. What can you say?

The funeral, as it happened, was only a couple of years after Douglas's. At this one, at least, hundreds of people had gathered to pay their last respects. Her section chief lost it completely during his speech extolling her virtues as an exemplary employee. On the coffin behind him stood a picture of a youthful Harumi smiling pleasantly, a young lady in control. Ben's brothers and sisters, all three of them plus spouses, had all flown over from Australia, just arriving hours before she breathed her final breath. Harumi's ageing parents bravely contemplated their daughter, lying in her final resting position. Surrounded by friends, family and workmates, the grief was palpable, but it was a fitting send off.

God only knows what was passing through Ben's mind all this time. It had been barely three years since he'd left on his ill-fated return to Australia. Two years since he'd come back, tail between his legs. Only ten months since the initial diagnosis. The speed with which the disease had taken hold was entirely in line with the doctors' predictions. Nothing can truly soften the shock, but he'd been able to brace himself, mentally prepare for this day. And with the arrival of his siblings, there was that somewhat surreal holiday feeling surrounding the whole proceedings. It was their first time in Japan. It was almost quaint to hear of their experiences: The astonishing abundance of vending machines. The wonder of the Japanese toilets with their washlets. The first time confronted with raw fish. And not least the incredible politeness and patience of Japanese confronted with a foreign rabble, unable to speak a word of their language between them.

"And no snakes, spiders, crocodiles or cane toads either," I wanted to say.

And no Harumi either.

The time for grieving came once they'd returned.

We tried to increase the number of shindigs. Ben bore up bravely all things considered. Probably the hardest thing was at work. How can you continue teaching English conversation when your wife has just died? But he managed it. Sometimes in the office, I'd catch him, lost in thought. Doubtless pondering on this thing called life, and how, despite his best efforts, his own had ended up doing such a spectacular 180 degree turn. He should be in Australia now, coming home from a hard day's work mowing lawns, looking forward to cracking open a can of VB and watching the latest episode of *Home and Away*. Maybe Harumi might have thrown together a plate of his favourite noodles.

How - why? - was he still in Japan?

Gradually, as the magnitude of everything slowly sank in, he started to turn his attention more and more to the ".why." And there was no "because." Not anymore. He had shared the numerous mourning ceremonies with Harumi's family, but he wasn't one of them. They were no reason for him to stay. Now at least he was able to go back to Newcastle on his own terms, without the pressure of providing for a wife who was used to a certain level of lifestyle. Ben certainly didn't mind roughing it, if that was what was called for.

Mum was the final reason. "She's getting on. Stupid for me to stay here. I can spend time with her, look after her." On his first return to Australia, he'd left most of his stuff behind, but this time he was going for good. It's crazy how many things you acquire after a dozen years in Japan. Unless you're Gary, that is. Everything had to be sent back or thrown away. Lots of work. Even so, barely one year after the funeral, Ben had left.

We only had three false leaving parties this time. Ben sold the apartment. I don't even think he was particularly sorry to see it go. "I thought you were planning to rent it out?" I said, trying not to blubber like I really wanted to.

"Yeah, well plans change," he said simply. Indeed they do, nobody knew that better than Ben. The time had come for a complete break. There was to be absolutely no return to Japan this time.

And Ben is still in Australia now. He comes back to Japan occasionally, catches up with his many friends here. Always great to see him. And back in Oz he still lives with his Mum, works as a lifeguard in a pool and keeps two pet cane toads, Shane and Mervyn. No suit and tie for Ben. He catches the surf when he can. Must be in the "Demigod" category by now, I'd imagine.

And I hope that Harumi is looking down on him from her deserved place in heaven, proud that her husband kept to his original plan after all.

I wonder what cocktails they serve up there?

7) Odie: The Happiest Man in Japan

In Japan, land of earthquakes, eruptions and countless other natural disasters, the biggest danger may actually be one of its biggest attractions: Flattery. You will be praised on the size of your eyes, the colour of your hair. Your style will be admired and your height will draw gasps. And that's just your appearance! Once you open your mouth and talk, your (pathetic) attempts in the language will cause amazement, your professed love of green tea and tofu will generate bravos and your (amateur) appreciation of the finer points of Sumo will probably set a few people swooning. Better not mention your post-graduate thesis on the Meiji Restoration and your ability to use shuriken like a Ninja for now. Leave those for later, just in case you cause a scene.

Japanese are masters of giving compliments. It's undeniably nice how the smallest "achievement" can be met with a fanfare of applause, but at times it can be quite baffling. Egos brought up in the west have evolved a protective mechanism, so when any modest feats are met with sarcasm, silence or downright insults, we are prepared. Far less impressive acts in Japan will get the opposite treatment. Fragile egos which may be crushed in less forgiving cultures can find fertile ground in which to flourish.

"You can use chopsticks? Wow, that's amazing. You've heard of Ichiro? How knowledgeable you are! "Arigato, Konnichiwa, Oishii" - your Japanese is fluent!"

Even for someone who has never set foot in the country, this seems rather excessive, but for those of us who actually live here? It's just a difference in culture, the flattery is entirely well-meant, but here's the thing: It suddenly becomes necessary to develop a strategy to cope with this unfamiliar barrage of praise. Smiling "Thank you," while thinking, "C'mon, please, did you take me for a total idiot?" is my policy on this. I like to think it's protected me against becoming a self-important twat, but you can never be sure. You'd have to ask people who know me.

The sad thing is that not everybody realizes the importance of this mechanism. Certainly, it is tempting - like a mother whose baby forms its first words a few months earlier than others of similar age and is briefly convinced that she may be nurturing a future Einstein - to let such words of praise go to your head and persuade you that you really are a little special. It may be forgivable for a mother, whose hopes will anyway soon be dashed as she slowly realizes her little darling is just as useless as all the other brats, but it's unpardonable — aside from being entirely ridiculous - for the unexceptional Gaijin who, having spent a few months in Japan and is unsurprisingly able to perform some of the most basic cultural and linguistic functions, convinces himself that he has achieved something extraordinary. The accolades only seem to confirm what he so desperately wants to believe. That's when the baby ego gains the potential to turn into a monster.

With that, I'd like you to meet Odie. A very ordinary specimen of the human race, most people would concur. A nice guy, to be sure. Handsome in a conventional young white American way. Tall by Japanese standards. I venture he would go entirely unnoticed back in his hometown. But in Japan, nobody told him to reset his ego defense switch. And he succumbed.

The first time you meet Odie, you'll probably get a good impression. He's not shy, he's chatty, kind of interesting. He has a nice happy face. Actually he was a dead ringer for one of my old friends from Hull University, Dave, leader of The Lesbian and Gay Society. Dave too had a very happy, unmistakably gay smile, and Odie's was almost identical. Therefore I kind of assumed that Odie too was homosexual. Stands to reason, right? Same facial expression, same sexual orientation. I was always waiting for him to come out, but he never did. Totally wrong on that account.

But in spite of that first impression, there was something about him which suggested you wouldn't be too upset if he didn't come to the next party. Weirdly, this feeling never left me the whole time I knew him, spanning over fifteen years. For a long time I couldn't quite put my finger on it, until it finally hit me: The guy never asks questions.

"I'm Odie, from Tennessee, USA."

"Right, I've never been there. Down near Florida, isn't it?"

"Well, sort of...."

"I'm Pete, from Yorkshire, England."

"Oh, OK, I know Yorkshire."

"Have you been there?"

"No, never been there, but I have a friend here in Kumamoto from London."

Or, many years later, a typical conversation would run,

"Hey, Odie, did you have a good weekend? DJing again?"

"Yeah, it was good. Quite a big crowd out on Saturday."

"Sorry I couldn't go. Big night out on Friday, I was exhausted all day Saturday."

"No worries."

You see? It's very subtle. It's actually so normal that you don't notice it for months and months but then once you identify it, it becomes mildly irritating. The balance of conversation gets slightly skewed, which is the whole point in the first place, because in Odie's brain nobody is more interesting than himself.

He's also one of those people who talk slightly louder than they need to. Is it because he's sub-consciously angling for a bigger audience? Does he feel that his words would be wasted if there was only one listener? Just a tiny bit annoying. That and the slight pause he gives before pronouncing his views on a particular matter, which - assuming he's not just slow - I guess he employs to give his words more gravity.

Oh yes, Odie is a happy man all right, and that in itself is a wonderful thing to see. I met him at a small school downtown just after I started working for Douglas. And it was clear right away that Odie had found himself the perfect job. For Odie, the class is his audience, the students are his fans. The curtain goes up and Odie is on the stage every hour. He doesn't have to work hard to search for subjects for the lesson; words come naturally to him. He's no wordsmith, but he can single-handedly keep a conversation going almost indefinitely. Usually the teachers are constantly checking the clock, working out how much more material they have time for (or how the hell they can drag things out until the bell). In Odie's lessons, it's the students who are busy glancing at their watches, wondering who's going to draw Odie-Sensei's attention to the fact that the lesson has already overrun by ten minutes.

It's curious really that Odie doesn't ask questions. It's a staple of almost every teacher. "Have you ever... How often do you... When was the last time you...?" I shudder to think how many times I use those three alone in the course of a single week.

In the school where we taught, a young lady always came in on Friday night before the end of the last lesson and waited for Odie.

"Is that your girlfriend?" I asked one time, genuinely curious that he might actually be straight and just managing to catch myself before I started asking any embarrassing "how often" questions.

"Oh, that's my wife, Erika. We got married last year."

"Your wife? Really?" Wow, that threw me. Here I am complaining about Odie never asking any questions, and I'd never got far enough to find out his marital status. I guess I'd never even asked him about girlfriends before. Must have been that sub-conscious gay assumption.

So young Odie had been snapped up already, barely a year after setting foot in Japan, still only 24.

"You know, we met, we're into the same music, we started going to karaoke, and then just kind of tied the knot," he explained, pausing way too long after each comma. I guessed that this probably wasn't much of an over simplification. She didn't seem like a regular Wife-of-Gaijin, if such a thing exists; definitely on the quiet side.

"I think she gets a bit jealous. She kind of wants to stay home most of the time. We hardly make it to karaoke any more since we got married."

Oh dear. Sudden post-marital personality U-turns don't bode well for a long happy life together. Once I'd discovered her identity, I tried some small talk but it was painfully obvious that she had no interest in me at all. Her husband was her whole world. I could picture her, hands clasped, hanging onto his every word in conversation, straining to catch every note he sung in karaoke. I guessed she probably couldn't believe her luck · and the whole thing was mildly confusing to me too: A proposal is usually a question, right? Was Odie capable of that?

I have two theories about Odie which I'd like to present now. First, his name. It sometimes crossed my mind that Odie's over-healthy interest in himself might have been somehow connected to his slightly unusual name. Nobody gets too excited when meeting a Chris, Mike, John or Peter. It's not a conversation starter, more of an eye-roller, whereas Odie was unusual. It seemed to be missing a letter. Cody, Jody, Brody: OK. But "Odie"? Just downright O.D: Odd. It was almost impossible not to ask a couple of follow-up questions.

On top of that, one of the most popular songs in Japan at the time, on heavy rotation, was *Oh Dear My Sweetheart* · which instantly became *Odie My Sweetheart*. Boy did he love that. "You're sooo vain," I wanted to say, "I bet you think that song is about *you*. Don't you? *Don't* you?"

Second is my theory of relative skills. Odie wasn't too proud to admit he had zero hand-eye coordination skills. One time he was invited by some Japanese friends to play badminton. It was one of those situations where they simply wouldn't take no for an answer.

"I can't play," protested Odie.

"That's OK, we're not very good."

"No, but I don't mean I'm not good, I mean I really can't play."

It was futile. Odie went along and gamely tried not to make too much of a fool of himself. He picked up the shuttlecock and tried to hit it. The shuttle dropped to the floor and his friends burst out laughing.

He picked it up again and tried once more. Another swoosh of air, and more laughter, just a ripple this time. Third time, same result · and silence. It's a good story and instructive that Odie didn't mind telling it. He wasn't bothered by being a duffer at racket sports. Why should he be when he shone in so many other areas? So my theory is that Odie measured his other meagre talents alongside his sporting prowess and reached the erroneous conclusion that he was a gifted musician, this essentially by virtue of not being tone deaf.

Music: The love of Odie's life. He didn't actually play anything. No guitar, violin or trombone for him, but he wasn't going to let that get in the way of him carving out a name for himself in the local music scene. He decided to launch a two-pronged attack. DJ ODIE was there spinning the discs every Saturday night to a packed dance floor in *The Red Zed*.

Now I have to rein in my natural skepticism here as I don't know much about the skill requirements of a local weekend DJ. Playing Chemical Brothers, R.E.M, and Blur records one after another doesn't strike me as a massively difficult task, but credit where it's due, these were fun nights. If there is a skill among DJs which separates those who can get people onto the dance floor from those who can't, then he had it.

Unluckily for everyone though, it was the second prong that really appealed and it was into this that he poured most of his energy. His dream was to be a singer: ODIE the Rock Star. A Saturday night local DJ is usually a marginal figure, the majority of those shaking their thang under the strobe lights probably even unaware of his or her existence. But the singer is the centre of attention, the focal point, drawing all eyes onto him. This is where Odie believed he belonged.

And watching him on stage for the first time was when I really understood that Odie would be in Japan forever. There was no safer bet. He was loving every moment, punching the air à la Freddie, doing slightly provocative hip moves à la Mick Jagger, and singing 100% à la Odie. Which means not terribly well. You could see the audience gamely clapping along; you could see the other band members trying to avoid looking at their singer. And there was Odie taking the applause, as if it was a genuine appreciation of his talent rather than just something polite people do when a song stops. This scene could only possibly be in Japan. No way would he last one night back in the US, but here he and his band, *Butter Fingers*, had got a monthly slot at one of the local live houses. I knew the other band members and tried to go and see them when I could.

After the performance we'd go over, have a chat. "Good show, guys. Interesting gyrating movement you were trying out there, Odie. Where did that come from?"

"Well you know," he said earnestly, "I want to try to reach out to some of the younger fans. (pause) Give them a little excitement. (pause) Set their pulses racing."

Or after another resoundingly ordinary show:

"I think we nailed that last song." (pause) "But on our second album we should aim for more of a dance sound." (pause) "I think our fan base would like that."

Fan base?! What the hell are you talking about, Odie? You're taking the piss, right? There were barely forty people at the show and most of them were friends or family. But no, Odie didn't do irony. There was no modesty. He really believed they were heading for stardom. Florence Foster Jenkins had been re-incarnated.

"Don't think much of the singer," said Ben's brother on a final night out before flying back to Australia a couple of days after Harumi's funeral, his Australian twang carrying a little too easily to the ears of the musicians on stage. No, I don't think anyone thought too much of him - but what can you do? He was enjoying himself, he was happy, who were we to pop his bubble?

And then, to complete his happiness, there was Risako. For readers wondering what became of Erika, I am unable to enlighten you. I have no idea. She was not connected to anyone of my acquaintance besides Odie. It appears they got divorced as easily as they had got married. There was no lasting legacy, other than the honing of Odie's unique singing talent in the pre-marriage karaoke dates. If she has any place in this story then that is it. There were no children. I guess she either entered a convent, convinced that Odie was the only one for her and if he didn't want her, she didn't need anyone. Or more likely, a few years later she married a salaryman and led a very normal life raising two kids, never mentioning her strange former life quirk to anyone.

But Risako's role couldn't be more different. Once Risako steps on the scene, Odie's life will never be the same again. Odie even has to make room for her. Risako may not have been a natural show-off but her role was not merely the adoring wife, smiling benignly at her hero from the side of the stage. Risako, you will see, has quite a personality of her own. We should probably rename Part II of this chapter, *Risako: The Siren of Kumamoto*. Terribly sorry Odie, it's time for you to step aside; Risako becomes the main protagonist in your story from now.

Risako was one of the regulars at *The Red Zed*. She loved dancing and was genuinely pretty and sexy. Which is more than you could say for her husband. You see, Risako was already married. She'd spent a year studying English in Texas. No fishing manual necessary for Risako: She'd met Howard in a bar, attraction had been instant and mutual, they'd had a torrid love affair and Risako had brought the goofus back with her to Japan.

Howard would win the unofficial *Least Attractive Gaijin in the City* award by some distance. Aggressive, edgy, unable to hold a job down - even in Japan! - Howard was the kind of Gaijin who gives us a bad name.

Love is blind, you may say, but on this occasion it was just Risako whose eyes were not functioning properly. But the good news was that they were rapidly recovering. It appeared that way too late, she was starting to reach the same conclusion as everyone else. There are only so many times you can hear, "What's a gorgeous girl like Risako doing with a moron like Howard?" without asking yourself the same question. And it didn't go unnoticed that she seemed to rather enjoy sidling up to the DJ and spending rather longer than strictly necessary to request the new Mylo record. Maybe she liked the way he talked to her. Perhaps Risako had had her fill of the Macho Gaijin and she was attracted to the softer version which Odie incarnated. She started staying longer and longer at the DJ's booth every night out. No surprises there for Odie; for him she was just another of his adoring fans. What could be more normal than for some Japanese chick to be interested in the cool guy spinning the discs? Wouldn't it in fact be odd if he didn't have his circle of groupies? And Risako was indeed interested in many things about this showy, confident young

American not the least of which being that he had already been through a divorce.

"*Divorce...*"

Was this the first time she played the sound of that word around her lips?

Odie started playing a very dangerous game, spending more and more time with Risako. Howard may not have been the Dumbest Gaijin in Kumamoto - the man wasn't greedy in his trophy hunting - but he wasn't smart. And yet the signs were clear enough to anyone watching. You could see the collision course, and you had to fear it would not end well for Odie. Odie had quite a meaty build, but I imagine his boxing/kung-fu skills would be more on a par with his badminton than his DJing skills ("I'm a lover, not a fighter"). Howard had a track record. He'd been involved in a few scuffles in the bars and always ended up on the winning side. He was one of those I was wary of. Always be polite when Howard's around. Keep away as far as possible. Keep any conversations with his wife brief. Keep any negative thoughts to yourself.

"Fascinating, Howard," I smiled sweetly as he stood there at *The Red Zed* one Friday evening, trying to impress us with his ludicrous flat-Earth theories. "You're so smart!"

The end came inevitably, Howard confronting Risako one night about the exact nature of the relationship between her and Odie - and Risako admitting that basically the marriage was over. And to Howard's credit, in his storm of fury, the violence was limited to objects. He ripped the cash register out and hurled it across the counter, he smashed a few of the whiskey bottles, kicked over some tables and chairs, generally made lots of noise and disappeared out of the bar and into the night. Not a scratch on Risako, and even if it crossed his mind, he didn't head to Odie's house with a hammer, knife or chainsaw, which he could so easily have done. Instead, the next day he simply moved away from Kumamoto, never to be seen again. Boy did Odie get off lightly there. And that *Least Attractive Gaijin* trophy was once more up for grabs. (Thomas, anyone?)

And so it was safe for the two of them to come out openly as an item without risking a fork in the neck. They were suddenly The Celebrity Couple of the Kumamoto Gaijin community. ("Brad warned me about those paparazzi.") And only months later, after presumably Odie's second and last use of an interrogative during his time in Japan, they tied the knot. For Risako, if she'd been listening carefully it may have been a sense of déjà entendu - some non-believers cruelly whispering that Odie didn't seem a huge improvement on husband number one. Certainly you tended to think Odie, like his ex-wife Erika, probably couldn't believe his luck - or then again maybe not. Self-confidence was one thing he didn't have a problem with. Thinking about it, he probably wouldn't have raised an eyebrow if Beyoncé had declared her love for him ("She wants to do a duet with me"). But there he was with a drop dead gorgeous wife, to be followed one year later by a cute-as-anything little baby son.

And so, Odie was set. A perfect job, a perfect wife, not quite such a perfect singer ("Two out of three ain't bad"). But now for his greatest role yet: Dad. I think it's fair to say that Gaijin Fathers tend to be more involved in raising kids than their Japanese rivals. This is even one reason why they are sought after (by some). Away from the exhausting demands of rock superstardom and in the more humble domain of the daily grind, Odie had gravitated to teaching kids. The guy had endless reserves of energy. He loved playing, adored dressing up, spent all his time bouncing, jumping, singing, running - no ball sports obviously - and he became the ultimate kids' teacher, opening his own school, ODIE'S KINGDOM. It might have been perfect training for parenthood, but it wasn't necessary. In the realm of fatherhood, Odie really came into his own: He was a natural. Nobody I knew could hold a light up to him in this regard. It was a seamless transition, the vote is unanimous. (Drum roll) *The Best Father in Kumamoto* award goes to...ODIE!"

It's so good to see a genuinely happy family. It warms the heart. Risako had also, somewhat surprisingly, transformed from hard-core party girl to soft, patient mother. She was positively oozing maternal goodness, which only flowed even more abundantly upon the arrival of another truly adorable baby, a daughter this time, two years after the first. You'd have to have a heart of stone not to be happy watching them, even if the feeling of not, in fact, minding too much if Odie wasn't around at the next party had never left. Like a family of owls, you didn't want to get too close, but neither did you want any harm to come to them.

Yes, even if I still wasn't about to join Odie's inner circle of chums, the new Odie was certainly an improvement on the old version. But wouldn't you know it - Odie going up in my estimation due to his heroic turn as a Dad coincided almost exactly with him going down in my estimation owing to his excessive use of Facebook.

God only knows why I ever agreed to join Facebook. It seemed like a dumb idea at the time, and it was. "It's great," enthused a friend. "You can keep in touch with all your family and friends in England."

"I already keep in touch with them. We talk on email about three or four times a year and that's plenty."

"But you can send photos, do live chats!" she gushed.

It didn't even sound remotely tempting, but unable to come up with a strong enough argument against it, I allowed her to set up my account.

Once there, I quickly discovered that none of my friends or family in England even seemed to be on it, and the posts were almost exclusively put up by acquaintances living within five miles of my house, the majority of whom seemed to like nothing better than uploading the most inane crap. And the Worst Offender was of course Odie.

Jeez, I really did well to never get too close to this guy, I thought every time I read his memes or some "hilarious" package he'd spotted at the local supermarket. I had seriously underestimated just how annoying he really was.

Facebook was made for Odie. Yet another platform from which to perform, to spread The Word of Odie. And now, thanks to Facebook, there was ODIE grinning at me in a Sponge Bob outfit, ODIE expounding his thoughts on the latest episode of some US TV show I'd never see, or ODIE declaring his love for some new soda product, virtually every bloody day. I started to occasionally wish a tiny bit of harm might come to him.

Odie's roots in Japan just kept getting deeper and deeper. He gave up the DJing, but would still perform regularly at the live houses, now with *The Shape Shifters*. Time sadly had not turned him into a more watchable performer. The years went by, the kids grew quickly, his son reached 6th grade in elementary school and he was already a dead ringer for his Dad. Rather miraculously, both kids showed a remarkable aptitude for sports. Tomoki was the school baseball team captain no less, while Michiko had joined the basketball club. Risako was suddenly busy ferrying them around every weekend to matches all over the city · Odie didn't have a driver's license · and somehow found the time to open her own small shop selling "American" cookies. She never seemed to have a moment's rest. There seemed to be multiple Risako's. On top of the mother, the driver and the cookie maker, she had to help Odie with the running of his school. Odie spent all his energy on useful things like dressing up in superhero costumes and jumping around with kids. Risako spent all her energy on useful things like cooking, driving and managing both businesses.

Life went on. I didn't care much to see Odie every time I turned on the computer, but there's always a certain comfort which comes with life maintaining a regular rhythm. I'd managed not to let myself get too irritated. It's just a part of life. Owls go "towit-towoo", and that's cool. And if Odie feels a compulsion to post stupid stuff on FB, so be it. Let it be. As long as you don't sing the damn song. It's a sign that things are normal, nothing more.

If someone had told me that inside two years, the whole family would have left Japan and Risako would be filing for divorce, I would have told them to go away and stop wasting my time with such blatant nonsense. That dude was a lifer. He'd die if he left Japan. He'd suffocate. He was a model of Evolution of Gaijin. He needed to breathe Japanese air, needed his karaoke and his sushi, his stomach would refuse non-Japanese food. He had adapted completely to his environment and would never be plucked out. Divorce? Well, we never know what goes on behind closed doors, but these two were so dearly devoted to their kids that whatever problems might develop between them, there was nobody less likely to separate. Ladies and Gentlemen, let me present the winners of *Couple Least Likely to Leave Japan* and *Couple Least Likely to Divorce*. It's a hands-down decision. Two more trophies right there to add to the collection. Odie's scooping them up left, right and centre.

So it would not be much of an exaggeration to say that it I was dumbstruck when they not only moved to USA but also broke up.

Their problems can be dated back with remarkable precision to one fateful night, 2016 April 16 at exactly 1:24 am.

We all had quite a shock that night in Kumamoto. I went to sleep with my seven year old daughter, Eri, who was still young enough to want to share my bed on occasion. My wife had passed out on the sofa. Eri was prone to kicking and punching in the middle of the night, so I could never get a truly peaceful night's sleep whenever she was there. What I was not prepared for however, was to wake up with the bed shaking violently from side to side and the sounds of heavy things crashing down and human screams, these sounds coming both from within the apartment and from outside. My daughter, bless her, was not to blame for any of this. Various sirens and bells were going off, but this was all only vaguely perceived, my attention more concerned with wondering why the hell my bed had suddenly become a bucking bronco and trying not to get thrown off. It continued for what felt like several minutes before blessed stillness returned. A quick check: Eri - OK. Wife - OK. Risa - in her bedroom, also safe. Relief. But we had to get outside. We somehow crunched our way in pitch blackness through the piles of fallen furniture to the front door and joined our neighbours walking down the outside steps of our apartment building to the road below, then got into our car and drove to the nearest open space. We spent the rest of the night inside the car, doing our best to ignore the shrieks that went up every time one of the occasionally powerful aftershocks hit.

The Kumamoto earthquake was one of the strongest post-war earthquakes in Japan and it changed life in the city for weeks. It caused miraculously few deaths, largely due to the time it struck, when most people were safely in bed, but the destruction was everywhere. In a country with the strictest earthquake regulations on house-building in the world, you'd see at least one collapsed building every block. Yes, on the whole, we could count ourselves very lucky indeed. Eri even claimed to have slept through the whole thing. Many friends' houses had suffered structural damage, but only a month later, aside from a few of the more severely affected villages to the east of the city, life had mostly regained its pre-earthquake rhythm.

But there were exceptions. Mentally, people had responded in different ways. The relentless aftershocks were nerve-racking. There was no guarantee that another mighty tremor would not hit.

One family was affected more than all others of my acquaintance: Odie's. The entire contents of his house had been unceremoniously dumped all over the floor like everyone else, but they hadn't suffered any damage. His daughter, on the other hand, was suffering extreme panic attacks. Every aftershock that hit would send her into fits of terror. She shut her eyes, blocked her ears and started moaning and stayed like that long after the shaking had subsided. More than that, in between quakes she became mute, refusing to engage in conversation with anyone, simply awaiting the next tremor with dread. Odie and Risako panicked. The reports were very confusing. Nobody could predict the future, but dipping into Kumamoto's history, the last substantial earthquake seemed to have occurred some 400 years previously, sparking a period of seismic activity which apparently lasted "years". Two days was bad enough, but months or *years*? That was way beyond imagining. So, supported by friendly calls from his family in the States to "get the hell out of there", that's exactly what they did. It wasn't easy either, but after a series of frantic phone calls, they managed to get their hands on some of the last precious tickets, and next thing, they were on the plane.

I'm sure it was with a huge sigh of relief that the wheels of the aeroplane left the liqueous concrete Japanese runway and an even bigger one when they landed on the reassuringly solid concrete of JFK. A wise decision, no doubt about it. It was the start of a long recovery process for Michiko. She slowly and surely started to re-emerge from her cocoon, but it would take many months for her to recover completely, let those terrifying memories subside.

Anyway, now they were nice and safe in Tennessee. The kids always loved visiting their grandparents' house. They were spoiled rotten naturally, but more than that · the house was BIG. A true castle compared to their exceedingly modest Kumamoto apartment. The grandparents loved spending time with the children. A couple of weeks once a year was woefully short, always over much too quickly. "You kids going back already?" they would say sadly, and it was a genuine sadness. Why did Odie have to live so goddamn far away? All the other grandkids were in the same city.

So who was it who made the suggestion first? Probably Grandpa or possibly Grandma. Must have been one of them. "Why go back to Japan? Why not stay here? Lots of space, everyone gets along just great. Haven't you been in Japan long enough already?"

I can hear the kids shouting, "Yeah!" I can see Risako looking on and nodding approvingly in her motherly way. And I can see Odie glancing around nervously at everybody, suddenly aware that he was in a minority of one and in need of some masterstroke if he was going to turn it around and get back to his beloved Japan, his adoring students, his devoted fans.

"Well, it makes sense to stay here for a while, I guess, and once things settle down in Kumamoto, we'll be able to go back." It was a very sensible thing to say, so why did nobody seem to agree with him?

"Tomoki wants to meet his friends again," he continued, smartly identifying his son as the one least likely to contradict him. A base to build on.

"I have friends here too," said Tomoki, a little too defiantly for Odie's liking. Oh dear. This would be an uphill battle. His biggest potential ally might have already gone over to The Other Side.

And Risako wasn't hanging around. Without even telling him, she was already getting all the documents together she needed to apply for residency.

When Odie arrived back on Japanese soil a couple of months later, he'd lost. He was all by himself, his family had stayed in Tennessee and he had a simple briefing: To sell up and move back.

"Unbelievable," I said, glad that I hadn't bet any money on this turn of events. "Odie? Moving back to USA? What can he do there?"

There were definite tinges of Charlie here, where just one unforeseen event sets in motion an unstoppable force, and what seems a solid, immoveable existence is revealed for its true transitory nature. I pictured in my mind Odie singing *How fragile we are*, but managed to get rid of the image before he got to the chorus.

So what would the future hold for them? Well, now that the unthinkable had happened and Odie and his family had gone back to live in America, then all bets as to what was to happen in the next few years were well and truly off. My confidence in my core beliefs had been shattered. Who was I - who was anyone - to bet against his face suddenly appearing on MTV? He might be ushered in by popular demand to replace Adam as lead singer of Maroon 5. I had no right to assume that Odie wouldn't be representing the USA in badminton at the next Olympics. Evolution might be proved to be false. Nothing was impossible.

But for now, Odie had work to do. He had to sell his school, cut all his other ties. His students were probably no less shocked than he was. How could they find another teacher like Odie? He tearfully informed his band members, voice cracking, that they'd have to go on without him. (They did, found a replacement one month later and everyone agreed it was a big improvement on the previous singer.) He held a few garage sales; we tried to help him get rid of all the stuff that he couldn't take back with him. In truth he didn't have a huge amount of stuff. The apartment where the four of them had lived really was small, almost owl-size in fact. Easy to see why the kids were so happy to be living in Grandpa's. There were a few goodbye parties. He tried to put a brave face on things, but it was clear that if he'd had any say, this wouldn't be happening. At his final farewell bash there was a pretty good turn-out. We wished him, them, the best of luck and went home. I may even have felt a touch of sadness finally that I would be unlikely to see him ever again, which was quickly replaced by the depressing realization that I'd be seeing him on an almost daily basis on Facebook, even if this time it'd (hopefully) be with news that I actually wanted to hear. But the overriding sensation was simply being dumbstruck that the LAST guy who would EVER leave Japan had actually left Japan. Maybe I had just inherited his trophy…

Sure enough, over the next few months Odie was never far from our thoughts, thanks to the constant stream of photos showing the family setting out on their Great New American Adventure: The kids beaming, Odie wearing a Spiderman costume, Risako standing to one side, trademark half smile on her lips. I realized I had never been more interested in him and was itching to know what the next few months held in store for the family. By any reasonable measure, he was at least ten years beyond the point of no return. He'd never held down a full-time job in the States. He had big responsibilities, providing for two kids just short of their teenage years. The odds were stacked against him. "Rather you than me," I thought, thanking my lucky stars once again that my daughters had regarded the whole earthquake and its aftermath simply as a bit of a jolly with less school and more board games than usual. But there was always the thought at the back of my mind that Odie tended to defy logic. Might he actually come through the whole thing unscathed?

It was fun going through the various different scenarios that might play out. Perhaps the kids gradually start to miss their old life in Kumamoto, Michiko finally puts her trauma behind her and the family announce their triumphant return.

Or: Odie lands a plum position either in a university or a nightclub and loses interest in Japan, realizing that you can actually wear Incredible Hulk costumes in America too. (Duh!)

Or: Odie accepts that his family are set, they're never even going to contemplate The Return, but he's unwilling to give up his love of Japan and they settle on a compromise whereby he spends most of the year working (and singing) in Kumamoto, returning to spend time with the family as often as he can. They don't need him so much now that they're older anyway.

Oh what fools we were! Hadn't we by now had enough experience of life to know that the only thing that would happen would be the one thing we never even considered? Apparently not. All that "Will they come back? Will they stay in USA?" turned out to be totally irrelevant. The post-script hit everyone blindside, none more so than Odie.

The second wave of Facebook posts seemed to confirm a happy transition. The smiles and the superhero costumes were a constant, but now these were accompanied by some positive news. Odie had found a position in the local college. Risako too had found a part time job. The kids had settled remarkably quickly into their respective schools. The main problem was already nothing more than making sure they didn't lose their Japanese language. But then I realized one day that there had been no new posts for over a month. This was actually kind of what I'd been expecting right from the start: There were bound to be difficult times. Another post-free month later, I asked my wife if she'd heard anything from Risako. She was not as prolific a Facebook user as her husband, but she liked to talk to her friends back in Japan. But no, there had been no news from her for months now. Mails had gone unanswered too, which was very un-Japanese, un-Risako like behaviour. Something had happened... but what?

So on to Part III of the story. The part where Odie is but a fleeting background figure.

Risako finds a job in the local bakery, mostly working on the counter. It's only three days a week; it's a humble job to be sure, but it's nice. There's no denying that feeling she hasn't had for many years: Sweet freedom.

The last few months have been draining for her, what with coping with her daughter's trauma, getting the family to safety, convincing her husband that this was actually a perfect opportunity for them - wouldn't it be the best thing to give the kids the second half of their childhood in America? And it all paid off! Now things are way better than she could ever have dared to hope. They seem to be settled, the kids are enjoying school - Tomoki's already joined the local baseball team - and they've both made loads of new friends; and Risako herself has a chance to relax just a notch.

Come to think of it, even before the earthquake, she'd been working non-stop for ten years. She'd given herself over to her kids completely and was as proud of them and the way they'd turned out as any Mum could be, but in throwing herself into motherhood, while also working bloody hard to keep a constant income coming in, she had sacrificed a little more than maybe she had wanted. She was always rushing around like a demented thing, with barely a minute to stop and think.

But now for the first time in what seems like ages, she has a little time to herself. Here in the shop, it's never really that busy. She enjoys chatting to the other staff and the customers are all really friendly too. She has a chance to think about things she hasn't thought about in a while; like remembering how much she enjoyed the American lifestyle.

Her personality was made for the USA. She always loved the confidence, the swagger of the average North American. How small Japanese people seemed by comparison in almost every way; always working too hard, always worrying about tiny trivial matters. The American way of life just seemed so much more attractive. How she had enjoyed her year in Texas as a 23 year old: The Time of her Life. Had that really been her? It was so long ago that it often felt like a different person, but now, finding herself back in America, that part of her had re-awakened. It was still there, it had just been snoozing.

How she'd loved flirting with those handsome boys. Yes, she had known how to work that girlish charm all right. But what a long time ago! How many times had she felt like a woman in Japan since her eldest had been born? She could count the times she'd been out dancing with her girl-friends on one hand. All eyes on her in Kumamoto were watching Risako the mother, not Risako the sexy lady. It had been so long since she'd been the object of desire, she'd forgotten what it was like. She'd even - for a melancholy moment - wondered if her feminine powers might have vanished entirely, irrevocably.

But just maybe that was not yet quite the case. Here, working in the bakery, she notices some of the second glances the customers give her · and it's a nice feeling. She still makes heads turn. Of course; she knew Japanese were always young-looking to American eyes, so that she probably looked over a decade younger than her 44 years. Her figure was still very tidy · she'd never had any problems controlling her weight (and not to be smug, but she's only half the size of the other employees). Yes, she could see that she still had it, she was still desirable. She didn't mind a bit of flirting. At first it was just to see if she got any response. And it wasn't really flirting anyway, was it? Just good old polite Japanese customer service. Do everything with a smile. And throw in a little flutter of the eyelashes for her favourite customers.

Be careful, Risako, somebody should have told her.

You too need to reset your culture switch. It's not only Gaijin Males living in Japan; it applies to Female Foreigners in USA too. Yes, it's nice when good-looking guys notice you, when they make eyes at you. Didn't happen much in Japan lately, did it? It's just not the Japanese way. It's got to be good for your ego, but what's good for your ego is not necessarily going to be good for you. You have to watch that ego, make sure it doesn't get over-inflated. If you're not careful it can get out of control, turn into a monster. You still have a great family, they need you; don't you go and do anything stupid to ruin everything. Please, Risako.

Oh dear, there's that blindness returning. Or is it more a deafness this time, a refusal to listen to the voices of sense in her head frantically warning her she's literally flirting with danger. And there's that dude again, the friendly guy in the wheelchair. He seems to come in almost every day lately; he must love these cookies!

Risako treats him to her extra special radiant smile. "So what can I do for you today, Sir?" she asks.

Picking out the cookies he chooses from the counter and carefully wrapping them gives them a chance to talk for a few minutes.

"You're not Chinese, right? I'd say you're Japanese," he says with a charming smile.

"Nice guess, mister. That's right I'm Japanese. Or do you prefer Chinese girls? I bet you like Asian ladies don't you?"

"Well if you're a typical Japanese lady, then I guess I like Japanese ladies."

Over the weeks he's asked all kinds of questions - why does that feel like such a novelty? - and she's told him all about the horror of the earthquake, the rush to escape from Japan.

"Oh my God, I remember seeing it on TV. That's the city you're from?"

And the mother in her couldn't stop herself proudly adding a few details about her sports-mad kids.

"You have a *teenage* son?" he asks, managing to look genuinely shocked. "Get outta here! Did you get married in high school?"

She can't stop blushing.

No, don't do it Risako, please. I know your husband can be a little insensitive sometimes; I know he should probably be a little less interested in himself and try harder to ask after others, at least occasionally. Plus it would be nice if he wore superhero outfits slightly

less often and talked a little more quietly - but you've been with him
for long enough, you must be used to it by now, surely?

"Poor fellow," thinks Risako. "He can't be much older than thirty, and yet he's consigned to a wheelchair. I wonder how he manages. Does he live alone? Maybe he still lives at home with his parents?"

She puts everything one by one into a paper bag, as he continues asking questions about the earthquake, about Japan, about her family. "It's funny, but when you see somebody like that it makes you realize how lucky we all were in the earthquake, Michiko's panic attacks were bad enough, but they're over now. This guy presumably is wheelchair-bound for the rest of his life? He always seems so cheerful, though."

Order ready now, she steps out from behind the counter.

"So can I ask how you ended up in a wheelchair?" she asks as she hands him the bag filled with cookies.

"Drunk driving, Ma'am. Had a crash just a few months after I got my license. Paralyzed from the waist down. Lucky to be alive. Still just a kid, really."

"And you've been in a wheelchair since then?"

"Yes, ma'am."

"Gosh, I'm sorry. That's awful."

"You know what," he says with a piercing stare. "It's probably the best thing that ever happened to me. I was a bad kid, did lots of bad stuff, but that crash set me right. It was a long road back, some real dark times, but it really toughened me up mentally. A guy I met in rehab encouraged me to take up basketball, so I joined a team. Seem to have a knack for it. Who would've thought it? I was never a sporty kid. Now, they say I have a chance to make the US Paralympics team; that's my goal. Although I should probably cut down on these cakes!" he adds with a laugh.

Oh dear, this is going from bad to worse. The guy had a terrible accident, but refused to let it get him down for long. He made the most of a bad situation, and now he's on the verge of an Olympics appearance. Watch yourself, Risako, Yes, it is an impressive story, yes he has cute dimples, yes he is kind of young, but can't you see he's playing you. He sees your weakness. Time to step back, Risako. Risako? RISAKO!!! CAN YOU HEAR ME???

"So I was thinking; you have a day off on Friday, right? Would you like to come and watch our team play? Then maybe I can take you out for lunch. I know this beautiful spot down by the river."

"Well, OK, I'd better check with my husband first though."

"Oh, absolutely, please check with your husband."

And here is Odie's last chance.

Let's see if your radar is working, Odie. Look: Here's your wife, home again. Can't you see there's something a little different about her? Look: She's opening her mouth, she's going to ask you something, you've got to listen carefully, Odie. This is important.

"So, there's a guy who sometimes comes to the bakery. He's disabled actually, in a wheelchair. He invited me to watch his basketball team play on Friday. Do you mind if I go?"

You have to admire the way it just slips casually off the tongue. She might as well have said, "There's a nuclear war just started" and Odie wouldn't have noticed.

But this is more than a nuclear war, Odie. Come on, remember your interrogatives. I know there're in there somewhere, this is the time to use them. Ask her why he wants her to go, ask her more about him. Please believe me, there is a lot riding on this.

"Sure, have a good time."

FAIL, Odie.
You have FAILED the test, and you are OUT. GAME OVER.

Risako did go. Risako had a good time · so good that she went the next week. And the week after that. And then three times the following week. In fact it was only months later that she moved in with her new Paralympic boyfriend.

But the good news is…it didn't last.
Risako somehow managed belatedly to reset her ego switch, gradually came to realize she'd made an awful mistake and that she had to go back and correct it. Some things take a while, right? The luxury of time to ponder on the meaning of life had been something denied to her for so long that when it came, she had forgotten how to use it. She'd briefly lost sight of what was important.

That was the core of the apology she gave to Odie when she came to see him six months later, wiping the streams of tears away from her cheeks, asking to be welcomed back into the family. And a shell-shocked Odie was hardly going to refuse now, was he? He almost even - almost, mind - started to ask some of the many questions that had started spontaneously and imperfectly forming in his mind of late.

What did I do wrong? What didn't I do? Why did you...

Does he... Could he...? How did you...

Do you think we can still... Are you still... Can we go back to...?

But somehow they never got asked. There are some questions that don't need answers. Sometimes things work out without the need to ask why. The kids were doubtless confused for a while there, but compared to the horror of the earthquake it was probably nothing so bad.

When they refer to it now, if they mention it at all, they simply call it "Mama's blip." It doesn't seem to have unduly affected either the kids or Dad in any fundamental way. I haven't spoken to him since he left, but I can confirm this to be true. I opened up Facebook just the other week and there was Odie dressed up as The Mighty Thor. Yep, I nodded, struck by the aptness of this image. I remembered thinking he had no chance of surviving back in America; that starved of Japanese oxygen he would curl up and die.

But really, how could I ever have underestimated The Mighty Thor?

8) Sally: The Country Gal

OK, I hear you. You're sick of reading stories about another boring Gaijin male and the awful things that happened to him. Enough MAGMETs right? You know, Middle Aged Gaijin Male English Teachers. You want to hear about a girl for once, right? Yup, I couldn't agree more and I only wish I had more to work with, I really do. It could have been so interesting. We could have had Shantel fighting against racism in Omiya. Maybe Helen terrorizing countless Japanese middle-aged men in Kumamoto. Or Natasha finding her Japanese Jack and a reason not to return to Chicago.

But the fact is most of the ladies who've appeared in these pages simply stayed for a year or so and left. Nothing to write home about, much less write a book about.

Very simply put, it's less common for girls who arrive here with no long-term plans to end up staying long term. We've seen the trap many Gaijin males fall into, lulled into a kind of trance by the safety of the country, the ease of making a living, plus the improved chances (even for certified no-hopers!) of catching a girlfriend. While the first two obviously apply equally to females, the likelihood of a Gaijin lady finding her perfect Japanese man somehow seems to be that much lower.

But why should this be, if indeed it is at all? It would appear to boil down to two main factors. The simplest one is very mundane: Japanese men are so damn busy!

"Wow, you very beautiful. White skin. Red lips. Beautiful England girl. Like England rose. I water you. I pollinate you. Japan man very Gentleman. You come on date with me?" he asks.

"Well now, that sounds rather intriguing. How about you pick me up after work tomorrow, maybe I'll bring a bottle of rosé wine and you can cook me something? I like it juicy and just a little spicy," she breathes.

"Ah, wait a sec; actually I have to work overtime tomorrow. Every day this week in fact and probably next week too. I was wondering about next month...I'm free on the 25th?"

A nice try, but maybe slightly lacking in romantic appeal.

Secondly, the Gaijin lady instills a certain fear into many a Japanese man. The stereotype of the independent feminist foreign female resonates. She is not as easy to control, less willing to bow to the wishes of her husband. Japanese guys tend to be not only ridiculously busy but also a little shy, and the thought of not only making the effort to ask out a girl, but one who's taller, possibly stronger, louder and not constricted by the mores of Japanese politeness, is rather intimidating to many. It requires a greater demand on their limited time. Added to which there's the not unimportant assumption that she's less likely to be able to make a perfect *bento*.

So while it really is crazily easy for the male Gaijin to find himself a Japanese girlfriend and therefore a reason to extend his stay in Japan, this is relatively more unusual for girls. There are of course many female Gaijin who do land a Japanese partner, but most seem to have had their fill after a year or so, and are only too ready to go back with conflicting tales of an exotic land filled with hot springs, misty forests, exquisite seafood - and unattractive ageing Gaijin men.

But not all.

Thank God for Sally.

Sally had already been here for a while when I first met her, and she had the look of somebody quite settled, going about her business with a certain efficiency often lacking among others of my profession. This was explained very easily during one of our early conversations when she casually mentioned about her training as a teacher back in America.

"My God. You're...a...teacher?" It admittedly must sound strange to be so stunned when you ask an English conversation teacher working in Japan what she has trained as, and the answer comes back: "I'm a teacher." Cutlery stops. People stop mid-conversation and turn their heads. The camera zooms up to Sally's face, her eyes nervously moving from side to side, aware that she has just committed a major error of judgment in allowing her secret to slip out, but unsure how to go back and correct it.

"Like, you mean, not a mechanic, a failed businesswoman, a bum, a good-for-nothing, a trainee architect, budding actress, circus performer, lap dancer or rocket scientist? You are actually a teacher?"

It seemed she really was. She knew her adverbs from her adjectives, her definite articles from her indirect ones, her gerunds from her infinitives.

"My God, Sally, how to you know all this stuff?"

"I learned it during training."

Yes, folks, welcome to the wonderful world of teaching English in Japan. Is there any other occupation where so few of its practitioners have any training?

"You are a native speaker - therefore you can teach English!" This is the near universal assumption that fuels the huge racket that is the industry of teaching English. In some cases it may even be true, but it is not a given. People are not expected to give lectures about the respiratory system based on the fact that they can breathe. It takes more than being able to run to become a running coach. Yet when it comes to teaching English, a foreign passport and an absence of a criminal record will almost always suffice.

Young Sally therefore had, most unexpectedly, found herself in a position of some respect even before she started. Like the cliché of the Harvard graduate who is refused a job serving fast food because he's over-qualified, Sally probably had to convince her employer that she had forgotten all that teaching stuff before she was offered the position.

"Alright, we'll give you the job. Just don't use too many prepositions, OK?"

So, to recap: Sally trained as a teacher because she wanted to be a teacher, and now she was a teacher she was happy doing the thing she'd trained for, but a little confused at being lauded for being able to do something she assumed everyone else would be able to do because they had been hired to do it, but in fact it turned out that they hadn't been trained for it and if they hadn't been trained for it then why had they been hired to do it, and more to the point what were they actually doing?

It's a valid, if slightly long-winded, question. Sally sensibly side-stepped most of these issues, accepted that there was something a tiny bit odd about the fact that most Gaijin were doing this job in spite of knowing very little about tiresome things like teaching methods, and just got on with doing her job - teaching.

So, sticking out as a teacher even though she was a teacher probably struck her as a tad unusual, but it must have been rather helpful for her in overcoming her other difference, that of being a girl in this male-dominated occupation. As already noted, there were Gaijin ladies living happily in Japan, but it became increasingly uncommon the longer she stayed. Already after passing one year in the country, she was becoming a rare breed. And there were no signs that she was planning to leave any time soon.

The final thing that stuck out about Sally, if you'll excuse the pun, was her bottom - and more to the point, the size of it. There was no way round it, sorry again. It was huge.

Sally was in many ways an all American girl, with shoulder length mousey blond hair and blue eyes. She was naturally disposed to smile rather than frown (but without excessive cheerfulness) and inclined to be positive rather than negative (but without being too annoying); in other words she was easy company. Her proportions were, if not petite, perfectly normal until you got down to the hips and then, what can you say, it was as if the designer's pencil had slipped and suddenly you were faced with these huge hips culminating in a seriously big posterior. It was her defining feature, how could it not be?

"I know my bum's kind of big. It tends to stand out more in Japan. Everyone's way too small over here," said Sally perfectly reasonably. If it hadn't been for her bottom weighing her down, life would probably have been very simple for Sally. "One look at my ass sends them running away screaming," she said sadly, certainly not referring to her many admiring students.

She was genuinely happy to be here in Japan. Our social circles overlapped, we often found ourselves out in the same bars, and she was fun to hang out with. She was a frequent face at all the parties.

She enjoyed reading, she liked drinking and she loved dancing, all of which put her high up in my books. She wasn't shy to get on the dance floor when DJ Odie was spinning the discs on a Saturday night. Shake that bootie, Sally! You go, girl! Fair to say, we clicked pretty easily. She hailed from one of the few American States I was familiar with: Montana.

"Whereabouts in Montana?" I asked. A reflex question, this - little chance I'd have heard of her town.

"Bozeman."

"Really? That's on the corner of Yellowstone Park, right? Big Sky country. I spent two months in Jackson Hole, Wyoming, summer 1991. I drove through Bozeman one time with a friend." How about that? "Beautiful place," I added.

"Oh, sure it's a beautiful part of the world." Sally said this as if yes, it was undeniably scenically blessed, but that beauty wasn't everything when it came to choosing the perfect place to live. Other factors counted, these outweighed the idyllic environment arguments, and in fact she was on the whole rather happy not to be there anymore. I could detect this as she used almost exactly the same tone which I employed to convey my almost identical opinions on the desirability or not of Yorkshire as a place in which to settle.

"Have to say, don't think much of country music mind," I confessed.

"Oh really? That's the one thing I miss about it."

We seemed to be on a similar wavelength. It was always enjoyable talking to her because she was so enthusiastic about Japan. There was often a tendency for conversations with other Gaijin to gravitate towards all the negative things here in Japan and how stupid everything was compared to back home. This was always rather tiresome for me. I guess it was kind of like watching the news on TV. Always bad things because good happy things are rarely newsworthy. Likewise, congratulating each other on what a nice, safe place we lived in was kind of boring conversation material. Once you moved onto the bad points however, there were rich pickings to be had. It was almost endless. You could run from the Japanese tendency to work themselves literally to death, move onto the over-fussiness of taking shoes off when entering restaurants, pass by the oddness of the Japanese bus tour, herded about by flag-wielding tour guides with their ferocious attention to the ticking of the clock, and finish with the strange phenomenon of the bedroom hermits, a whole army of young males who spend years or even decades locked away permanently in their rooms - or countless other variations - and suddenly you'd spent a whole evening damning the culture of the country you'd been living so many years in. It was rare to head down this route with Sally.

"I love this country. I love the food. We went to this bar yesterday, and the octopus snacks they had were out of this world," she'd say. Or she'd be talking animatedly about a kimono lesson she'd attended, a kabuki performance, or the latest Murakami book. It was quite refreshing to focus on the positive.

Uniquely among our peers, we could actually have a conversation about teaching methods, more relevant ways to introduce second conditionals, or better ways to explain the nuances of the various future tenses. All this only when nobody else was listening, of course.

The melancholy usually came out after around five drinks.

"You're so lucky, Peter, you have a wonderful wife." Well, I certainly wasn't going to disagree there. "You know it's not the easiest thing for us American girls to get a Japanese boyfriend. Why are they all so shy?" She sighed wistfully, and I could feel huge sympathy. It really was so unfair. Plus-size male Gaijin were of course commonplace. There was 'Big Bob', at *Jake's Bar* every night, always sat at the counter, always looking like the stool might crumble beneath his huge mass. 'Boring Joe' was another regular. He was an undertaker apparently, actually a tad less boring and if anything even fatter than Big Bob, but presumably had arrived in Kumamoto when that nickname had already been taken and he loved talking and Japanese girls were always too polite to run away and instead stood there for thirty minutes painfully trying to understand what this huge boring guy was talking about and at a certain point they'd agreed to go out on a date except it wasn't really a date, they told themselves, it was just an excuse to get some free English practice, and Joe was already working out how many more dates he needed before he'd be able to get into their knickers. It's outrageous that some of these girls are able to turn a blind eye to the fact that the likes of Joe or Bob are unattractive, overweight and dull. But what can you do? And here's our sweet Sally, pretty, smart, good cook too, very romantic, wants nothing better than to find a nice boyfriend, and she has no luck at all. There was no justice. Only a humongous…

Butt one happy day, Sally was grinning from ear to ear. "I think this could be the one," she said. Suddenly gushing now, she launched into a completely unsolicited, entirely unexpected and rather eyebrow-raising history of her romantic exploits since arriving in Japan. It seemed that she had, in fact, been remarkably busy in that department in spite of previous complaints to the contrary. It was all I could do to stop blushing. So anyway, Sally, I think you were telling me about your shining prince, the new light of your life, The Chosen One?

"His name's Naoki. Oh, my God, he's gorgeous. He's six years younger than me and we've been together for almost two months now." She could obviously barely believe the longevity of their relationship. This "Naoki" seemed to be working for his Dad's construction company, so it would appear unlikely that he would be Sally's intellectual equal - as if that mattered.

"But you know what the best thing is?" she continued.

I hate it when people ask these rhetorical questions as if they really are questions, leaving a pause long enough that you feel obliged to answer. I guessed that the best thing for Sally would be if he had a Huge Ass Fetish, but thought it unlikely she would be sharing this with me even if it was true. So...erm...he has a second house in Hawaii? He has a set of perfect white teeth?

"The best thing," she went on, pausing mid-sentence as if to soak in the impossible perfection of it, "is that he likes country music." She finished with a radiant smile.

So while this clearly did absolutely nothing to endear the guy to me - anyway, I was hardly desperate to meet him - then it did make me see Sally in a somewhat different light. There she was in her suit, clutching her grammar textbooks to her bosom as she shuffled off to the classroom for her next lesson, but that smiley face, the dreamy expression just stuck in my mind. Her whole aura spoke of a country girl. As I watched her walk off, the suit faded away to be replaced by a t-shirt and blue jeans, streeeetch fit, topped off with a cowboy hat, and in my vision Sally was back in her native Bozeman, strolling along a lane on her way home from college, under the blue sky that went on forever, giving a shy wave as two young cowboys rode past, bowing their heads slightly as they said, "Howdy, Miss!" It was over in a flash, but I realized that while Sally often seemed quick to brush aside her hometown, or to find fault with the smallness of her neighbours back home, then in truth her humble Montana upbringing formed a greater part of her essence than she would usually care to admit.

One week later, I met Sally's new love for the first time. He was friendly enough, had a strong build, distinctive brown eyes, and Sally was clearly besotted. There was definitely something about him which spoke of open spaces, plains, horses. Your average Japanese salaryman would look pretty damn stupid if you were to click your fingers and magic away his suit and place him on a horse riding through a creek in the shadow of the Grand Tetons. But I could imagine Naoki galloping through the Wild West more easily than I could picture him in a dark navy suit heading down the steps to the subway entrance of Shinjuku station. Maybe she really had found her man.

It was only months after first meeting that they found a small apartment not so far from the appropriately named Country Park and moved in together. Sally's email address changed to *Naoki 4ever*. She had changed from a mildly cheerful colleague into a permanently grinning monster. She seemed ready to burst into song at any moment.

Was it just my imagination, or had Sally started to look less teacherly? It was almost as if she was starting to feel that now she'd got her man, she could give up on things like work. Instead of spending time in the classroom, she'd prefer to devote more time to sweeping the veranda, preparing a nice hearty meat broth and making sure she was all woman to her man once he came home after a long day rustling cattle.

I was probably hallucinating. Those months in Jackson had been quite a culture shock, to say the least. Everything had been so cowboyish, and meeting Sally - a real life Montana girl - had triggered a flood of memories: A blur of stars and stripes, rodeos and lassoes, saloon bars and Coors beer; Obese guys in their Stetsons swaggering down the streets with their guns visibly sticking out of their holsters. Now these flashbacks were mixed with either Sally or Naoki, sometimes both of them, line dancing or atop a trusty steed. And why did Sally's twang sound so much more country every time we greeted in the morning?

Things reached the next level when we were invited to a barbecue at Naoki's parents' house in honour of Sally's Mum and Dad who had come over to visit their daughter. There was Naoki's father - not hard to spot the resemblance, both in build and expression. And his Mum, chain-smoking - not a very common sight among older women in Japan - both of them wearing cowboy hats and, you had to admit, looking very much the part too.

"Are they dressed like that just to make your folks feel more at home?" I asked.

"Oh no," laughed Sally, "they always do. It's their style."

Well, I was taken aback. I couldn't remember ever seeing a cowboy hat in Japan before. Or England, France or anywhere I'd ever been outside Wyoming or Montana for that matter. But it was also strange how it didn't seem so out of place. The house was not in the city and could, with a little creative imagination, have been in the prairies. There was a wide open space in front of the house, and the mountains of Aso rising up in the distance just might have passed for the Rockies. But for real authenticity, there were two real-life cowboys in the shape of Sally's Mum and Dad. I remembered one of Sally's stories, how her Dad had held a gun up to scare off one of her first boyfriends. "That's the way they do it in our town," she shrugged. Yes, I had been in Jackson just long enough to be able to picture the whole thing as it must have happened.

"Nice to meet you, Sir. I've been a good friend of your daughter for a few years now," I said, stretching out a hand. He was clearly not impressed by the British accent which for some stupid reason I always liked to exaggerate whenever I talked with someone not of a British background. "I went to Montana briefly a few years back, and I think I passed through your home town. Bozeman, isn't it?" I shared a quick glance with Sally, who seemed to sigh a little, and then her Mum opened her mouth and let rip with a stunning invective against what I'd been led to believe was her hometown.

"Those folk in Bozeman they think they know it all, boy they look down on us, them all living in their fancy houses and driving their fancy cars, there's no one else as stuck up as those rednecks."

"Oh, I wasn't aware of that." It turned out that they hailed not from Bozeman itself, but from a small town a short drive away, and obviously there were some issues between the two neighbouring communities - in Sally's parents' minds in any case. I was slightly disappointed that they weren't interested in the fact that a Yorkshire boy they were talking to on a faraway island in Japan had passed very close to their house. But obviously one solitary afternoon all those years ago hadn't been enough to discover how bad those Bozeman people were.

The marriage and the news of the pregnancy seemed to happen almost at the same time. These country folk don't hang around! My wife and I had only just welcomed our first child into the world almost nine years after first dating, and Sally and Naoki were only going to miss out on trumping us by six months. We went to visit them in their apartment, one of our first outings with our newborn. I was a little disconcerted when Naoki reached down to pick Risa up. It was of course good practice for the father-to-be, and it was impressive that he wasn't afraid of such small, dainty parcels of human flesh and bones. I myself had always avoided where possible picking up other people's babies, the terror of dropping or otherwise injuring them was too strong. I'd taken the longest time to trust myself with my own daughter, but Naoki didn't seem to have any such misgivings. He held her in his strong arms, played peekaboo for a few seconds, and then suddenly and totally unexpectedly started to rock her quite violently from side to side. Nothing ginger or gentle about that.

"Erm, actually, do you mind not shaking her like that," I said quickly going over to reclaim my daughter, ever so slightly concerned that she may have sustained some brain damage from this sudden attack. She seemed fine.

"He has such a way with kids," cooed Sally, watching on with that proud wifely look, apparently with no doubts that her husband was overflowing with paternal tenderness, and barely able to wait until the baby he'd be rattling was his own. I couldn't disagree.

"I wonder if that's in the Cowboys' manual of bringing up kids?" I asked my wife on the way home, shaking my head at the memory. "Maybe that's how they prepare them for the rodeo?" We didn't go to their house very often after that. In fact that was the last time to visit them there. I still saw Sally at the school every week, watching as she got bigger, and I couldn't help thinking that she seemed to be losing a little of the infectious enthusiasm for her cowboy boyfriend-turned-husband.

Was it just me, or were there problems brewing?

The baby was born, and we went to visit Sally in the hospital. I was slightly concerned for Risa's sake, but figured Naoki would be all consumed by his own bundle of joy. Actually, I was right not to worry because when we arrived at the hospital, Sally was all alone in her room, with her baby. It's a strange moment indeed when your own little one is no longer the smallest kid in town. It suddenly hits you how much she's grown, and you don't realize that it's the first of a life-time of similar moments when you are faced with the relentlessness of the process of growing up. Was my baby really as tiny as that? No way!

But what was this slightly muted emotion coming from Sally? Well, of course in those first few days, happiness to have safely delivered a healthy child is often blunted by the exhaustion of the whole thing. But how was the father? Was he overjoyed? Was he right now decorating the cot, covering it with stickers of horses and cowboy hats? There was a slight pause. A sadness in the eyes. "He hasn't been here yet." A brief, slightly embarrassed laugh. "Maybe tomorrow."

Sally then started telling us the story of how the last few months had effectively marked the end of their previously idyllic life. It seemed that the apartment where we had visited them was paid for entirely by Sally. Naoki's work was sporadic, which was probably a polite way of saying that he did bugger all. Sally was the bread-winner, and now with her having to take time off, what with those annoying little things like giving birth and spending time adjusting to motherhood, they'd decided to save money and move in with the in-laws. Maternity leave varies considerably in Japan, but is almost always less generous than in the West, even in full-time employment. But Sally, like myself, was working a number of different part-time jobs - no insurance there - so there would be nothing coming in. Sally's salary had been the sole income for the family, and its loss would be sorely felt.

If they were hoping that worries about impending motherhood would be softened by moving in with the in-laws, boy were they to be deeply disappointed. It didn't take long for Sally to realize that Naoki's parents were not the types to benevolently cater to their pregnant daughter-in-law during her confinement. If she'd entertained notions of enjoying a safe, loving, stress free environment allowing her to concentrate exclusively on the all-important job of bringing a precious life into this world, she'd come to the wrong place. No bending over backwards to satisfy her every whim for them. They belonged to the "Not Welcome Here" school of thought. Right from the start the feeling of resentment hung heavy in the air, no mistake there. Another pair of mouths to feed: "God, you think we're made of money."

At first it was Sally who had to bend over backwards - metaphorically speaking of course - showing her gratitude, and working her considerable ass off to help with the chores around the house, frequently cooking for the whole family - not that they ever appreciated it.

"Least she could do," they said. "Not as if it tastes good or anything."

Yes, here in Sally's new surroundings she was about to learn that the curse of the mother-in-law is so much more than an over-worn cliché. And let's not forget the extra curse of the idle husband. Two for the price of one.

In a slight twist on the more traditional mother-in-law, in Naoki's family there was no sense that their son deserved a better wife. They were certainly no proud, indulgent parents. Actually they had been rather relieved when he'd finally moved out, already in his mid-twenties and showing no aptitude for any type of employment. His efforts working for his Dad's company on the building sites had been more of a hindrance than a help, and they were frankly glad to see the back of him. But now, barely six months later, he'd returned. And not only that, but with his wife. And a baby on the way! One step forward, three steps back.

Not much love was lost between them. Mother rather seemed to delight in pouring scorn upon her useless son in between drags on her omni-present cigarettes, so that he chose to avoid her as much as he could. Avoiding Mum meant not being in the house, which therefore also meant avoiding Sally. Everything seemed the opposite of how it should be. Wasn't she supposed to be taking it easy, to rest as much as possible? Weren't her husband and his family supposed to be taking care of her? That was the original plan, but if her husband was constantly slinking off without lifting a finger to help, then Sally knew that not doing anything would only set Mum-in-law off again.

Sally wanted peace more than anything - it often seemed that she was alone in this goal - and tried her best to get along with them. Her Japanese, already pretty fluent, was improving day by day; nothing like constant strife for rapid linguistic improvement. She did more than her fair share of things around the house, tried to bite her tongue whenever Naoki came back, tried not to attack him for being pretty damn near completely useless. But already only a week after moving in, she looked to the future with a certain dread.

Sure enough, slowly her mother-in-law's verbal tirades against her son turned into attacks on the both of them. It wasn't just the son who was a good-for-nothing, she was too. Probably Sally was mostly to blame for Naoki's laziness - why hadn't she forced him to do more when they were living together? Maybe "Miss Bossy" was too proud to let her son do anything, content keeping him like a pet.

The moment when Sally was admitted to the clinic didn't come a second too soon. A chance for a breather, if giving birth can really count as a breather.

And then after a lonely but quiet week in the hospital it was back into the lions' den.

As every mother knows, the first few months are the toughest. If Sally was hoping that the baby might cause a magical improvement in relations, she was flat wrong. Naomi was not the most demanding baby ever born, but she might as well have been. On top of the general stress of simply living in a place where she was so obviously unwelcome, was added that of looking after the baby, entirely on her own.

"What's wrong with these people?" she thought over and over. Wasn't every grandparent supposed to go all dotty when they set eyes on their first grandchild? Not here. If she'd sometimes been unfairly blamed for her husband's general idleness before, then now she was absolutely to blame whenever Naomi was crying.

"You know, in Japan mothers usually go to their parents' homes when the baby is born," said mother-in-law both pointedly and pointlessly one day when little Naomi couldn't stop crying.

To add insult to injury, even Naoki would chip in with a few choice words of criticism. Apparently Sally had vastly over-estimated his potential as the perfect father. He was indeed pretty much useless. Occasional violent rocks were his sole contribution to the job of child-caring, and this unsurprisingly set Naomi off in tears, requiring even more comforting from her Mum. Faced with unjust criticism from her husband, Sally couldn't help the odd sarcastic remark. In fact with the combination of his parents' continued barbed comments, and now his wife getting in on the act, accusations were continually flying around the house in all directions - and then there was that infernal screaming baby, why didn't Sally make it stop?! No wonder Naoki chose to make himself scarce even more than before. Sally knew that he was taking her money too, mumbling something about having to pay his parents some rent.

Phew, it was all a world away from this time last year. Sally realized that she had to get back to work. It really wasn't her first choice; she dearly wanted to spend more time with her daughter. How much she enjoyed escaping, going out, taking little walks around the area, just the two of them enjoying a moment's silence away from the madhouse. But seriously, where would the money come from? She was already starting to give up on her husband. She'd been the bread-winner before, she'd just have to be the bread-winner one more time. Plus there was the not-so-trivial matter of her sanity.

She started back at the school, doing a few part-time lessons. "Welcome back, Sally, how's the baby?"

"Oh, it's pretty tough," said Sally.

"Yes, I can imagine," we smiled back.

She had reverted back to full-on teacher mode; that much was clear. The idea of giving it up and becoming a full-time housewife to a cowboy husband seemed to have lost its allure somewhere along the line.

"Come to our house some time," I said, "let's get our kids playing together." Sally didn't need a second invitation. The next weekend they came round - just her and Naomi, naturally. Risa was happy to have another play-mate; Naomi seemed slightly surprised to discover that there were other little humans besides just her. We made an informal group of four or five families all with babies and toddlers, and we met up once a month or so. You could see how happy Sally was coming to these, and nothing was said about Naoki's absence. This was after all quite normal for Japanese fathers - those not working overtime probably out for a game of golf or else just sleeping, recharging for another exhausting week in the office. No explanation was sought, no explanation was given, but the gushing Sally of pre-motherhood days was such a recent memory that the contrast with now, where his name was never even mentioned, seemed extra stark.

One day a few short months later, Sally had two pieces of news. First, she was pregnant again. Well, that was good, a sign that Naoki hadn't in fact dropped off the face of the earth. Secondly · and you suspected she was actually more excited at this one · she'd got a job at this year's Country Gold. Yes, the famous country music festival that Charlie had loved so much and that I had successfully avoided going to for, ooh, almost ten years now. All the artists were apparently bona fide country stars back in the USA, and there was work to be had interpreting, which was a dream job for Sally. Of course she was happy going along as a fan · she'd been a regular attendee before Naomi was born and it was always a great event · but working there meant some extremely welcome extra dollars on top of which was the chance of coming face to face with some of her heroes.

"You should come, you'd love it," she said to me in a moment of enthusiasm which had been noticeably lacking of late.

"Erm, Sally," I said wearily, "I seem to remember you saying the same thing two years ago, and the year before that, and, unless I'm very much mistaken, the two years before that. And as I always tell you, I still absolutely cannot think of anything I'd like to do less. But thanks for asking!"

"Suit yourself," she shrugged. "Don't know what you're missing though."

And in that way that time has of constantly surprising us even though it's been ticking at exactly the same pace forever, Country Gold had passed and Sally was back in hospital one more time. We went again of course, and it was a very similar scene to 18 months before: Sally alone in the room with the one tiny baby. No husband in sight, no daughter.

"I asked them to bring Naomi as much as possible, but they haven't even been once," she said with an unmistakable air of resignation. I think she'd felt quite hurt during her first hospital stay, but this time it was more of a numb sensation, merely a confirmation of what she'd expected.

Two months later, Sally was back at work again. Her features had hardened a little more. She was ever more the teacher, ever less the simple country girl. We could see how tough things were for her. We'd stopped asking questions about if Naoki had finally managed to find a job or if the in-laws had mellowed out. We knew the answer and there was just the chance that once the dam broke, the torrent of complaints might just wash us all away.

We continued to invite her out. Little Naomi had entered her terrible twos and was turning into quite a handful, as Sally ruefully acknowledged.

"You know, when I'm working, there's nobody else to tell her what she should or shouldn't do. I think she's basically left to her own devices. It's not good."

She was still living with the in-laws, any money that she earned seemed to be instantly swallowed up, whether by Naoki - "I'm sure he has a girlfriend," confided Sally - or his parents who'd generously decided not to kick them out, as long as they - she - contributed rent. Then there was the stuff for the kids. Sally seemed to be permanently in debt. "I'm sorry, I don't have any money," she tearfully said one time, declining an invitation to a lunch out.

A few months later, she called me. "I hate to ask, you know I wouldn't if I didn't need to, but do you think I could borrow $500? I promise I'll pay you back next month." She didn't offer any further explanation, but her timing was good. I'd just finished paying off a loan and had a little cash to spare.

It was also around this time that Douglas's problems had started to worsen.

"Maybe you could try to help out at Napoleon," I suggested, "become one of Charlie's Angels?" More good timing for Sally, it turned out. She started teaching a few hours there. But it wasn't enough.

Then one day she had some big news.

"I've decided to go back to the US with the kids. I just can't take it anymore. I thought things might work out if we were able to leave the house, but now I realize that it's not going to make any difference. To be honest, I'm worried about the kids. When I'm not home they're totally neglected." She paused; it looked like she wanted to add a few more details, but decided against it. "At least my folks back in Montana would be happy to look after them while I try to find something. I can probably get some teaching post at the college I went to. I still have some contacts there. I just think I have a better chance of making something happen back in the States than here."

This was no heat-of-the-moment decision. She'd obviously been thinking things over for a while now. The youngest was already running around - two young kids who needed the kind of supervision that she was worried they were simply not getting from their Japanese grandparents. It was finally time to break out.

"OK, so what does Naoki have to say about it?" I asked. Why did I always seem to ask questions even when I really didn't want to? How good it must be to be like Odie sometimes.

A pause. "If I see him, I'll be sure to ask." Ouch.

And then another pause before the knockout blow. "And so, this year's Country Gold will be my last one. I want all my friends to be there, turn it into a kind of farewell do. You have to come." Double ouch. And that second one really hurt.

Poor Sally. I gave the news to my wife that evening. She didn't seem too surprised. We both agreed that it was pretty amazing that she had put up with things for so long. I broke the other news, as gently as I could, that we were expected to attend Country Gold. To be honest, this was the one that had really floored me. I had sensed the inevitability of Sally moving away for some time now, but why the hell did we have to go to the stupid festival?

"Sounds like fun," said Asami. *Sounds fun?!* How can a country music festival sound like fun?! Sometimes, I swear I just don't understand what goes on in her brain at all.

In a curious way, I felt now that I could understand Sally's pain. Maybe this had partly been her intention in inviting me, to bring in some stress into my usually smooth everyday existence just to give me a taste, however small, of her internal conflict. She wanted more than anything to stay in Japan · and she would had it not been for her intolerable home circumstances. And I wanted more than anything to stay home on the day of Country Gold.

Sally at least had clearly been giving thought as to how to escape from her marriage for years now, but how was I supposed to suddenly wriggle out of this dumb cowboy convention? It wasn't fair.

Driving to the tennis court with Steve a few weeks later, I complained at the injustice of it. "She refuses to come to parties, pleading poverty, borrows money from me and now she expects me to go to this festival · with the family of course. That'll be $150 not including beer."

Steve just shrugged. "She paid you back though, right?"

"Well, yes. But that's not the point. She has no idea how much I hate that crap. I mean, I really feel sorry for her. The girl has been through a lot of rough shit since she got married, but it was her own choice. Is that really an excuse to put me through this torture?"

Again, Steve didn't seem too sympathetic. "It's not that bad. Who knows, you might enjoy it. It's outside, right? And it's a festival, so there'll be beer and food, you probably won't even notice the music. Who's playing anyway?"

I pulled out my wallet, produced the ticket and read out some of the names. Steve's reaction was most unexpected.

"Did you say Charlie Daniels? You're shitting me, right?"

"No, is he famous?"

"You don't know him? He's like the God of country music."

Bloody Steve. Always trying to be optimistic, not even letting me enjoy my grumbling.

"Well if you like him so much, why don't you go," I said offering my ticket.

"I thought the whole reason of going was because it's your friend's leaving party?"

Bloody Steve. Bloody Sally. I was trapped. No escape.

As the date drew closer, I imagined Sally, packing her life into a few bags, sighing as she put down each object she knew she didn't have room for. I too took a huge sigh as I packed all the nappies, spare clothes, finger-wipes, towels, sun cream, two books and · most importantly - earplugs. I took a wistful look at my CDs: Muse, Elbow, Chili Peppers, Royksopp. *Sorry*, I whispered to them. *I'm not a traitor. You will always be my favorite music. It's just that…I have no choice. It's something that I have to do.*

What was it about country music that really irritated me so much? My British DNA? Who could say, there are no rules when it comes to what turns you on musically. But it was strange; I mean even if country music is not to be heard too often in the UK, neither is Russian classical music - which I loved. I usually prided myself on my broad musical tastes. I couldn't think of any genre I hated - except country. I tried to remember the few songs that had ever made it to the UK charts. *Islands in the Stream*. Even Dolly's astounding figure had failed to make that song any easier to listen to. *Take Me Back, Country Roads*. No, never understood why that was considered such a classic. Slightly more recently there had been that awful song, *Achy Breaky Heart*, by Billy Ray Cyrus which sent my finger to the off button every time it came on the radio. I was struggling to think of any other examples.

And don't forget, I had actually spent a whole summer in the American West - in Wyoming, "The Cowboy State", no less. I'd survived evenings of line dancing. I have lots of great memories of the place, but nostalgic ballads about guzzling booze and driving down dirt roads do not feature among them. My wonderful experiences in and around The Rockies were emphatically despite the music. It could have been the Soundtrack to a Perfect Summer, but it wasn't. I remember my friends there, Billy and Kevin, inviting me to a live show. To this day I still can't make up my mind if they were really serious or just wanted to see my reaction of horror. Obviously I didn't go, and thought I might be off the hook for the rest of my days until Sally...Sally... Seriously, why the hell was there a Country Music festival in Kumamoto anyway?

One night I had a dream. We'd changed places. Sally was standing there with a huge smile on her face watching me as I boarded the bus which would take me to the airport and then out of Japan forever. I was bawling. I didn't want to leave. Why did I have to sacrifice everything I'd worked so hard to build up? Next I arrived in Montana and there was Sally's Dad in his cowboy hat. He reached into his jacket and pulled out a revolver, pointed it at me: "Never ever talk to those Bozeman folk. You hear me, boy?" I sensed that Billy Ray Cyrus was lurking around in the background somewhere, about to break into song. It was not a nice dream.

So the day of Country Gold came. How bad can it be, I thought?

We arrived and it was horrible. It was if anything worse than I'd imagined all those years ago when Charlie Peach had tried to get me to go. Japanese people everywhere you looked, all totally ridiculous in their cowboy costumes which were way too new and shiny.

"I really don't want to do this," I thought.

But it's only a concert. It will be over. Think about Sally; she's giving up her life. Surely you can pretend to have fun for one afternoon?

On the way through to claim a place to spread our sheet and sit down, we noticed Naoki's Mum and Dad looking just as they'd looked at their barbecue four years before. She was smoking, he was drinking a Budweiser, both of course decked out in full cowboy gear, right down to their very expensive looking boots.

I wandered over to get a first beer, bumping into a couple of American friends. "Where's your hat, Pete?" one said, apparently amused to see me there. "On my way to buy one now," I replied, heading for the food stalls. Naoki was there. I hadn't seen him for a while, he looked very fetching. We had a friendly chat for a few minutes.

"And where's Sally?" I asked. He pointed to some pre-fab buildings next to the main stage. Busy translating, it appeared.

Back at the sheet with a couple of ice cold beers was a first chance to really take stock. I had to take off my hat, so to speak. It was quite a spectacle. There must have been some twenty thousand people altogether, spread out all over the mountain side, the huge stage below with the smoking volcano providing an unbeatable backdrop. Nothing like a beer to calm you down. Maybe Steve was right, maybe I could just ignore the music, enjoy the atmosphere and the beer.

The first band was bad. But I was busy talking to Sally. She was easy to find, exactly where Naoki had indicated and she wasn't so busy now the music had started. She seemed totally relaxed, and she had that big grin of old back on.

"Wow Sally, you're looking fantastic! A real life cowgirl!" I said, truthfully.

"Hey, thank you! You looking good too, cowboy!" I was at least wearing a checked shirt.

"I can't believe you're leaving Japan." Another true statement.

"Me neither, but I've had time to think it through. To be honest I'm actually just glad to get away. It really is no fun living with the in-laws. At least not these in-laws."

I wanted so badly to make a comparison with the festival, but managed to stop myself. How could I really be equating a watershed moment in Sally's life to a few hours' discomfort? *Grow up, Pete.*

"How about Naoki? I was just talking to him, he said he's going to come over next spring."

"Naoki says a lot of things. Let's just say I'll believe it when I see him touch down."

It was about this time that a most curious thing happened. The second band came on stage and they were fun. The power of beer, I said, fondling my glass. The third band was even better, even though they were doing bluegrass, which always normally sent me reaching for the metaphorical sick bucket. Not this time. I even went down with Asami and Risa to join the line-dancers right below the stage. Sally was down there with a bunch of other friends.

"Having fun?" she asked.

"Well it's not too bad, I guess," I said, not wanting to sound too won over yet. But there was some strange kind of magic at work here. I vaguely felt that I should be fighting it. It was one of those moments when I was forgetting who I was. Where was I again? This was a country music festival, right? Wasn't I supposed to be gritting my teeth? I hadn't even thought about using my earplugs. Why was I clapping and whooping like an idiot? Nothing was making any sense. The next band was simply awesome. We couldn't stop dancing...and the sky was a fiery red, with the sun already disappearing over the mountains behind us. The whole place was rocking, Naoki and Naomi had joined us, Japanese cowboys were coming up to us, showing us some moves, offering us snacks, laughing and pointing to little Risa and Naomi who themselves were grinning away, so cute as they tried to copy the dance steps they were being taught. The smell of delicious grilled steak kept wafting over. I shook my head, barely able to believe the perfection of the whole event.

And that's when the MC announced Charlie Daniels.

My God, I've been to some amazing concerts in my life, but I wasn't prepared for the next fifty minutes. The guy · surely he must have been close to 70? · was a burning ball of energy. In each song, he was manically directing his musicians around, apparently completely spontaneously. Throwing down his guitar and picking up his fiddle, he challenged them in turn to on-stage musical duels. Not duets, duels. It was astounding entertainment. I was blown away.

"Do you want to meet him?" asked Sally, inviting us to the after-show event. Of course I did! How often had I ever had a chance to come face to face with a famous person before? Who cares if I'd never heard of him until a few weeks ago?

There were very few people, lots of free snacks and cans of beer piled up on the tables, and there was Charlie chatting to an attractive lady in her 40s · his wife? I thrust my chest out and swaggered over to them. Then, speaking suddenly in the most ridiculous Queen's English accent, I grandly announced:

"Mr. Daniels, I'm from England, and you have just turned me into a country music fan." I think he just about understood me, and graciously accepted when I insisted on taking a few photos together. He made a few jokey comments to my daughter. Then we thanked him, and wandered around, enjoying the post-show atmosphere. There were a few other, younger cowboys hanging around in small groups. I couldn't recognize any of them, but presumably most of them had been performing too. I wasn't really interested in them. I had spoken to God. That was enough.

What a surreal day. It turned out of course that I hadn't become a country fan at all. I borrowed Sally's *Best of Country Music* CD the next week, and had to hit pause barely 20 seconds into the first song. What a relief. It was just the magic of live performance after all. Things were back to normal for me.

But not for Sally. She really was on her way out. The festival had been her last big day in Japan. And what a way to bow out. She really had seemed in her element at the concert among all the cow-people. In a way that I could never claim to be among the sheep farmers of Yorkshire. I was briefly jealous, wondering why the great British wool trade had never spawned a similar musical culture. Even cow farming back home merely conjured images of mud and wellies. Exactly the same as sheep farming, come to think of it. Nothing musical at all. Maybe my bias against country music was nothing more than a cultural jealousy. It didn't seem very likely, but who knew?

Anyway, apart from having had one of my most memorable days since arriving in Japan, it was great to see that Sally had been able to forget about her problems for a while, happy to get lost in the music and the atmosphere. And if there was only one day a year when she was able to do that in Kumamoto, surely there'd be plenty of opportunities once she got back to Montana. Life has a funny way of working out as long as you remain positive, and looking back at that day, I was confident that Sally would be OK. She'd suffered all kinds of things I'd never been close to. How she'd managed to stay in a good frame of mind with all that shit raining down on her was beyond me. But I knew that even as she saw that her Japanese dream was over, she could look to the future with a sense of relief. She'll be fine, I thought. It's going to be tough starting over as a single mother, but that girl is made of leather. A real cowgirl.

It's never easy to make marriages work. You hear stories of tugs of war, sometimes going on for years. You hear of people fleeing a violent home in the middle of the night. International marriages come with a whole extra bunch of potential problems. Like the horrible stories of one parent taking their kids away for a month and never coming back.

And then there's poor Sally. The overriding emotion she had to confront was simply apathy. On the day of her flight back to America, a friend came to pick them up and dropped them off at the airport. Dad never came to see them off. The grandparents never said goodbye. Sally said they weren't even home when she left. Waiting in the airport lounge, Sally looked around, taking everything in, wondering if she'd ever set foot in Japan again.

It was a long flight. She shed a few tears on the plane. Naomi asked her why she was crying and she said it was because she didn't like flying. She told Naomi that her father didn't like flying either which was why he wasn't coming. She knew that Naoki would never come over to America - he didn't. She knew that the kids would never again see their father or their Japanese grandparents. But she knew that she - they - would have a far better future in her hometown.

She made the right decision. It didn't take long before she found a job, a first foot in the door, her parents doing all the normal grand-parenting things that came so naturally to them, allowing Sally the freedom to gradually build her fledgling career. It was all that she needed. She never looked back. Last I heard, she'd taken her now teenage kids to live in Texas, still working hard.

And her parting gift to me was to confuse the hell out of me and make me think, however briefly, that I'd become a country music fan.

A post-script: Charlie Daniels, country music legend, died while I was writing this chapter, on July 6 2020, aged 83.

9) Mayu: The Japanese Gaijin

It's strange wandering around the streets near my house, reflecting on the variety of woes that have befallen so many of my friends and acquaintances. It's such a normal place, my family have such a normal life and yet so many things seem to have happened to the people close to me that would appear firmly in the realms of the abnormal. How much of that carefree 24 year old touching down in Narita Airport a quarter of a century ago remains, I wonder? I think he's still more or less intact, which is all the more remarkable when I look back at all that has gone on around me. The earthquakes, typhoons, tsunamis, floods and eruptions are to an extent part of the regular rhythm of life in Japan, which simply accepts that it will suffer more natural disasters than most other countries. But it's the crazy stuff that has gone on in the personal lives of so many people I know that really astounds me whenever I choose to dwell on it. John Lennon was right: Life really is what happens while you're busy making other plans.

And even more incredible is how I have managed to side-step all these metaphorical craters. But as I saunter down the supermarket aisles - what was I supposed to be buying again? Yoghurt, eggs, spaghetti and some chicken breasts, I think that was everything, but better pop in a six pack of Asahi Super Dry too - the apparent normality of everything just serves to reinforce the madness of it all. Life's not that complicated, is it? Find a job you like, a partner you like more. Find a good group of friends to hang out with, a few nice hobbies, and Bob's your uncle. My American friend was asking me if

British people really use that phrase. Yes, we do. Probably not the best example of how to use it, mind.

And as I walk back home - my bag slightly heavier as I couldn't resist a bottle of sake - still musing on the quirks of life, I'm reminded why I never get bored here. How can I? Look, there's *Ichi-Nose* Dental Clinic, *Take-Shit(a)* Hospital and *Fuku Sushi*, all on a five minute stretch of road I walk along almost every single day. It's good when you're as easy to please as me. I count my blessings for this, plus the fact that beyond my ridiculously juvenile sense of humour, I still derive genuine pleasure from my work. On top of that, I've been blessed with an amazing family, and I'm proud that I've never lost my hunger for travelling, both near and far from my home.

Poor Charlie - I wonder if he'd still be here if his house hadn't been burned down? Has Sam opened his own jazz club in LA? Never a day goes by without sighing when I remember the horrible ends met by Douglas and Harumi. I try hard not to think about Thomas at all, but I genuinely hope Ben, Odie and Sally are all doing well, their Japanese adventures so far behind them by now as to probably seem like another lifetime. I never catch sight of Bill or Gary these days, even though they both still live in the city. Once Ben had escaped back to Australia, the shindigs lost their equilibrium, continuing for a few months before coming to a spluttering halt. I can't speak for Bill, but I guess in Gary's case his few years of re-connecting to the Gaijin world merely confirmed what he already knew: That he wasn't missing out on anything and therefore that he should go the whole hog and become a total recluse, cutting contact with his last few friends. That's just what hermits do.

I hardly ever go out to the Gaijin haunts these days. Three or four times a year max? That's not to say that I've become a recluse too, just a fact of getting old. Those of my generation, my batch, are the same. When I go to *Jake's* now · *The Red Zed* closed its doors many years ago · all the new young faces turn to check who just walked in and then quickly turn away when they see my boring fifty year old features. How can it be that I'm now five years older than Jim when I first laid eyes on him? My respect for his restless energy never stops increasing.

I was in *Jake's* with a couple of friends last month. I saw the new young female bartender pour me my ice cold beer, and I was briefly back watching my wife working in this very place all those years ago just after it opened. I'm watching the smile on her face as we talk; how brightly she shines. And there's her co-worker, Mayu, laughing gaily as she prepares some bluish tinged cocktail whose name I'll never know. What a sexy pair they are, always talking animatedly as they work, high-spirited and full of life, going down to *The Red Zed* for some dancing later on in the evening, sure to be decked out in their sexy witch costumes at Halloween, sexy Santa costumes at Christmas. Good times, my God what fantastic, brilliant times they were. And while I can still catch the same smile every time I look at my wife · she's one of those Japanese who seem impervious to ageing · how unbelievably sad it is that Mayu is not around anymore. In many ways she, more than anyone else, was the embodiment of all the fun that our little Gaijin community had together in those Millennium years and only eight short months ago she went to an early grave, still only 48 years old.

Mayu was obviously not a Gaijin, but she is an honorary member of the club. She would be absolutely mortified not to have been included - her face, smile, slightly raspy voice and above all her laugh so familiar to every one of us who ever met her. She divided her time between *Jake's* and *Red Zed*, like she split her time between working or just partying. If you ever popped in to either bar at the turn of the Millennium, you'd have met her. She was one of those people that etch themselves in your memory. Just give a little mental search, she'll come back to you, she's there somewhere.

I clearly remember the first time I ever laid eyes on her. She was riding Charlie, piggyback. This, I hardly need to add, was not a common occurrence.

Someone had rented out a live house, there was to be a band playing and a disco. It was a place I'd never been to before, and there were plenty of people I'd never seen, a slightly different crowd, so I was happy to see a familiar face in Charlie, even if I was somewhat surprised by his style of entry.

"Charlie," I said, "you do know you have a gorgeous young lady on your back, don't you?" There was after all a serious possibility he might have been oblivious.

"Yes, I know," he shrugged, declining to offer any further explanation. It seemed that he was as surprised as me, in fact. He'd probably just served her immediate purpose of making a grand entrance. As I learned later, she wasn't one to do things quietly if she could avoid it. The band started playing, Bill squealing away on his guitar - yellow wig that night, I recall. Once Charlie had extricated himself from Mayu, we doubtless talked a little about more mundane stuff - money and the like - and I was interested to notice that Charlie

271

had nothing else to add about the girl he'd come in with. Obviously not his girlfriend, then. It did after all seem just a little too far-fetched that this might be his new catch. Interesting girl, I thought. I have no idea if she noticed me. Charlie didn't even tell me her name - did he know it? And in any case, she was off, looking for more excitement than we were offering. I would learn much more about her in due course, but for now I would just know her as "Charlie's Piggyback Girl". It was an evening full of surprises. Douglas had even made it out - was this the last time I ever saw him in a bar before he retreated into his little island?

Little did I know that Charlie's Piggyback Girl would become one of the most famous girls in the city within the Gaijin community. She became first a regular and then an omni-presence at *The Red Zed* and then the newly opened *Jake's Bar.* She graduated rapidly from simple party girl, one of many who were attracted to the Gaijin scene, to serving staff, quickly becoming the face of the bar.

"You know Mayu, right?"

"Sure, the Red Zed Girl!" See? No mistaking her.

Stories about her soon became legend. She was a little wild, had a zany sense of humour and loved to dance. But there was something about Mayu that was different from your average Japan-babe. She wasn't shy about voicing her own opinions. You didn't mess about with her. She wasn't cruel but, rather unusually for someone so young, she didn't suffer fools gladly. Somehow she seemed an essential part of the scene and at the same time curiously removed from it, as if she didn't need to be working here. This made perfect sense, because she didn't. If she had chosen to work here it was purely because she enjoyed being in the bar, meeting people and of course dancing. It certainly wasn't that she needed the money.

You see, Mayu was a rich girl. That was her curse. Or more precisely, her curse was to have a rich father who doted on his solitary daughter. She nominally worked for him, and he was naturally far too generous with her. Mayu, as I had gleaned from that introductory glimpse atop Charlie, was a free spirit.

Learning to be independent financially meant also learning from an early age that she didn't have to fawn. This essential Japanese skill didn't come naturally to Mayu, and it was one she never had to acquire. No false praise for Gaijin from Mayu when you used chopsticks or remembered the names of all five members of SMAP. And likewise, when it came to her fellow Japanese, there was no need for her to flatter, crawl, toady, or arse-lick. At all. Ever. Mayu, working in her Dad's company, was spared all that hierarchical crap all Japanese company employees usually have to suffer: Bowing to the correct degree, using the appropriate level of politeness in vocabulary when speaking. If you want to succeed in Japanese society, this is simply what you have to do. Mayu's lack of polish, for want of a better word, was a core part of her character, her charm. The Japanese are a famously polite nation, and this is embedded into the language. Japanese has different layers of politeness built into it which can be quite baffling to the uninitiated. There's the famous example of "Sit down", which in English could equally be used when talking to a child or a king. You get all the politeness you need from simply adding "please" and maybe smiling a little creepily. In Japanese, this simply doesn't work. I have never counted how many different ways there are, but believe me, it's a lot. There are entirely different verbs for *do, eat* and *go* which you are supposed to use when talking to others you want to show respect to, and a bewildering array of prefixes and suffixes which most Gaijin only scratch the surface of. It takes dotting your i's and crossing your t's to a whole new level. It's difficult to explain to English speakers, but maybe it's similar in a way to adopting a form of Shakespearian English when addressing either superiors or "treasured" customers. (In the West, the customer is king but in Japan they are nothing less than Gods.) In terms of linguistic complexity, you could liken it to declensions of Latin verbs, with the word forms changing merely to reflect levels of politeness rather than the different persons of speech. Often, assuming something similar exists in English, Japanese try to use the most flowery expressions they can, ending up sounding somewhere between quaint and idiotic: "Let's drink some sake together" becomes "Would you honour me with sharing the experience of the drinking of a glass of Japanese rice wine?"

Mayu never had to worry about all this shit. Her natural tendency, never checked, was to diss.

"Odie's a fucking crap singer," said Mayu. Spoken like a true native. It's hard to believe she would have spoken any differently to the Emperor himself. Oh yes, Mayu's swearing was of a Grade One level. Or when Jim tried to come over all sweet Grandpa, Mayu would be sure to tell him in no uncertain terms that she wasn't looking for a Sugar Daddy. Of course she wasn't: She was the recipient of enough sweetness from her own real Papa.

"Can you fucking imagine seeing him naked?" she asked me one night, face all screwed up. Fair play to Jim, this was testament to the fact that, unlikely and distasteful as it was, he was indeed perceived as being part of the younger crowd.

"Well, you don't have to imagine it, all you need to do is go to Kenny's house and you'll be able to see it for yourself. Quite big, I hear."

She stared back, trying to work out if I was making a joke.

Just to re-iterate, Mayu's reasons for choosing to work at the bar had nothing to do with money. She was in theory working for her Daddy's company, but it was unclear in what capacity. As much as I gave it any thought, I just assumed she'd maybe answer the phone when she happened to be in the office, assuming her hangover wasn't too awful.

One day I went to the City Hall to renew my Gaijin registration card. Aside from deriving a certain masochistic pleasure, it was never a fun place to visit. It was however an opportunity to remind myself how lucky I was. An affirmation of the joys of freedom.

The sheer monotony of the floor layout hit me every time. The endless rows of desk-bound clerks semi-hidden behind their computers and stacks of files. The vacant stares of the citizens as they sat clutching their number tickets awaiting their turn. The all-pervasive stuffiness of city government bureaucracy with its overwhelming lack of colour, and the strange muting effect it casts over everyone and everything.

You had to admire the staff, always unfailingly polite, never anything less than heroically patient in dealing with everyone. I'd heard how tough it was to pass the exam to get a job - these people were effectively la crème of the Kumamoto intelligentsia.

The upside, as you'd expect, was a decent salary and job for life - the prison sense of the word in this instance was glaringly obvious to me - but the real downside was even worse: The hardly inconsequential possibility that you might just die of boredom. There was the absolute certainty that the reality of working here would be every bit as dreary as appearances suggested.

I felt my heart start beating rapidly as soon as I set foot inside, picturing a parallel, Japan-born version of myself forced to live out my working days in this hell. Entering the building was the nearest I would ever get to James Bond de-wiring the bomb and saving the world. My body clock would start ticking down to some unannounced time in the very near future at which point I knew all my bodily systems would shut down. Unsure of exactly how long this was, and unwilling to discover, I would try to move swiftly between the various desks and simply finish my business before the internal alarm rang and I imploded or exploded - which way would it go? - when I was suddenly presented with a vision of beauty, all the more heavenly given its contrast with the nightmarish Kafka-esque setting. There, in front of me, was a sharp-cut, figure-hugging bubblegum pink suit with a surprisingly short skirt out of which emerged long shapely dark-stockinged legs ending in stylish sapphire blue high heels. I assume most male heads were, like mine, turned towards this startlingly glamorous figure - when I noticed something familiar in the facial features, the hair style.

"Mayu?" I asked.

"So dayo" - that's right - she said as naturally as if this was the bar.

How strange the pre-conceptions we have about people are. Did I imagine that Mayu had only two sides to her character - dolled up, cackling away while knocking back another round of tequila on the one hand, and recovering from ferocious hangovers on the other?

She laughed her trademark silly laugh, probably a much more accurate form of identification than her driver's license or passport would be. No question, it really was her. "Daddy's business," she said simply, registering my look of incredulity with amusement, before asking if I'd be at the bar that night.

"Never miss a Friday at *Red Zed*," I said, enjoying watching her leave, the colour of her character, quite aside from her fashion, rendering the whole building all the browner and duller.

That night I looked at her with slightly different eyes. I had no idea about her exact role in her Daddy's company, but she had certainly looked the part, gliding through those grim corridors with the confidence that only comes from knowing you're good at what you do. Unlike me, she hadn't been dashing in to get the business out of the way as quickly as possible. She'd been striding through at her own pace; she was doing whatever she was doing on her own terms. The suit she was wearing had Mayu written all over it. Most business women in Japan look almost as plain and drab as their male counterparts - the Western fashion allowing ladies to express themselves more freely is quite rare in Japan. Female university graduates setting out on their new careers will absolutely choose a standard business suit in either grey or black. But that wasn't Mayu's style at all. She tended in the opposite direction. She was different, she wanted to show it, and she did.

"Japanese are fucking boring."

Typical Mayu statement. No pussy-footing. No thought of exceptions, just condemn an entire nation, her nation, to the fire. When she spoke of Gaijin she at least tended to offer up more individualized insults. "She's a bitch." "He's stupid." Sentiments which were usually hard to disagree with, but you felt she should probably make more of an effort to keep her thoughts to herself.

"Handsome guy, Dave," I said, pointing to a Canadian guy sitting on the couch across from the bar.

She didn't seem to agree. "He's a fucking idiot." She stared back, and then burst into a few seconds of her dippy laugh.

"So who's your type then, Mayu?" Nothing forthcoming, I decided to delve.

"Charlie?"

"No fucking way."

"Jim?"

"Fucking old."

"Bill?"

"You fucking kidding me?"

"Gary?"

"Who the fuck's that?"

The further Mayu went from the f-word, the more likely grammatical errors were to start creeping in. At least I assumed that was why she was reluctant to utter any swear word free sentence.

Another guy had started working at *The Red Zed* a few months after Mayu. His name was Takumi and he was another native of Kumamoto whose roots ran deep within the Gaijin community. His high school English teacher had been none other than Bill. Naturally

Takumi had been sufficiently impressed by Bill in those days - a shining example of what to aspire to - to decide he wanted to be a part of the Gaijin world, which was the reason why he'd decided to start working there.

But it didn't take long for Takumi to discover what Mayu already knew: That not every Gaijin was as likeable as Bill. In fact, even Bill wasn't as likeable as Bill once he showed his less teacherly side come a certain hour of the evening. But Takumi took it in his stride and soon, doubtless partially inspired by close observation of his one-time teacher in this somewhat different environment, came to harbour few illusions as to the myth of the Noble Gaijin. He was a quick learner - Bill must have been proud - and what's more seemed to have a wider variety of swear words at his disposal than Mayu. He was always reliable for a quick character reference of those you might have just a brief acquaintance with.

"Hey, Takumi, you know Danny right? What's he like?"

"Oh, he's a little shit. Don't believe a word of what he says."

Or, "Tim's a good guy, right?"

"Tim? Well, he pretends to be but I have to keep an eye on all the younger ladies whenever he's around at closing time. He's like a...what's the word...predator?"

Takumi was more than just an observer. With his sweet face and patient disposition he was the frequent focus of female Gaijin lust and he wasn't above refusing the odd juicy morsel which came his way, whereas Mayu, at the end of the day, was just a little too scary even for Gaijin.

But it was still somewhat of a surprise when we heard that Takumi and Mayu had started dating. Takumi, with his front-row seat, surely had no illusions about the rather eccentric habits of this rich girl, and Mayu could clearly see that Takumi was Japanese. It didn't seem to make any sense – so maybe it really was love. *The Red Zed* suddenly became the Takumi and Mayu show.

Nobody could deny there was a certain harmony there. Takumi was in a kind of supporting role, never looking anything less than suave and professional despite his relatively tender years, while Mayu continued with her line of exuberant party-girl antics, backed up by her gaudy sense of fashion, her make-up seemingly heavier by the week.

Clearly Mayu was a girl who needed excitement. What she didn't need was the money from the bar, pulling in many times her serving salary from Daddy's company. She probably spent more on clothes than she earned from the bar. She would delight in explaining the cost of her various garments and accessories. She'd usually make us guess, enjoying telling us we'd under-estimated by half even when we'd come up with an already inflated figure. The girl inhabited a different world from me, from everyone else I knew. But she was endearing because she was so down-to-earth. You never got any sense of her being stuck-up or superior. When she said someone was an idiot, it was because he - usually he - really was an idiot. And she was happy to pour scorn over herself too. Her showing off the over-priced objects which made up her wardrobe usually seemed to have the slightly bizarre aim of showing us how dumb she was.

"I'm fucking stupid; I have no idea why I spent $200 on this blouse." With that slightly demented laugh. Again, it was hard to argue with her.

Yes, somewhat complicated, Mayu. Difficult to imagine her finding love of a worthwhile kind, which was why it was great to see her hooking up with Takumi, someone who seemed to have his head screwed on right. Takumi, we figured, had at least had the time to observe her over the months working together, knew her better than anyone else, had presumably worked out what made her tick and decided to take the plunge only once he'd weighed up all the potential difficulties of sharing a relationship with his unpredictable colleague. Right, Takumi?

"Well actually she just kind of jumped on me one night after work."

Oh, OK. Takumi obviously had something that drove the ladies wild, lucky bastard. And it didn't take a huge leap of imagination to picture Mayu probably quite literally jump on him. Charlie, it turned out, had had a narrow escape. But equally, you couldn't really imagine Takumi complaining about it too much. What was indisputable was that his calm influence was beneficial to Mayu, at least for as long as they remained a couple.

I don't think too many people would have bet money on them staying together for long, but in any case Mayu's life was suddenly rocked by the single most important event in her life: Her Daddy's company went bankrupt.

Mayu's monthly salary was suddenly a thing of the past. Daddy was already past retirement age. He had been working to pass the company on to his son and daughter and suddenly it was gone and the money evaporated.

When you're used to not giving money a second thought, spending freely for as long as you can remember, even taking a perverse enjoyment in paying too much for your purchases, how do you stop?

Mayu took it hard. She'd had a fond relationship with her father on a personal level too. She wasn't simply taking his money. And she saw first-hand how the shock of failure and sudden financial hardship quickly took its toll on her Dad's health. How could it not, and equally how could it not affect her? What to do? She took to partying even harder than before, the bar now taking on an infinitely more important role in her life, not simply somewhere to vent her considerable energy dancing and drinking, but now as a place to come to escape the new reality of her changed home circumstances.

Unaware as I was of the dramatic change in her fortunes, I can't say I noticed any difference in her demeanour whenever we talked.

"Hi Mayu, looking great today! Say, I like your earrings, how much were they? · no, let me guess, $300?"

"Hey, that's a fucking good guess. $500 actually. Don't know why I bought them though. I already have, like, 30 other pairs."

It was shortly after this that I heard about her family problems from other friends who were a little concerned about her. Her beloved Papa was bankrupt? Damn, that's awful. Good thing she at least had the bar salary to fall back on.

There's that bloody thing called life starting to happen again. I remembered the time I bumped into her at the City Hall. When you don't need to work, when it's just a hobby and you could care less about the wage, you work. But when your job is important to survive, when you need all those extra yennies, all the life force drains out and you don't want to show your face.

That's what happened with Mayu. Until now you'd be guaranteed to see her every time you stepped in the bar, but suddenly half the time there was no sign of her. Not there on Tuesday or Thursday, nor even Friday or Saturday. Had something happened to her?

"What did you do with Mayu?" we asked half-jokingly to Takumi. Now he was in an awkward position. Should he tell everyone that his girlfriend was choosing to stay home and hit the bottle with worrying frequency? Kind of personal stuff. And in any case it was time for him to reevaluate the relationship. For Takumi, the bar was his solitary income; no office day job for him. Maybe one of the attractions of Mayu, beyond the obvious physical ones, was the way she had taken him out, treated him on occasion - she was the rich one after all - but now she was asking to borrow some money from him, which was an unexpected shift in the dynamic of the relationship, and one which was bound to put considerable strain on it. Too much strain, it turned out.

I heard about the break-up on the grapevine. Our socializing patterns had shifted. We still enjoyed our nights at the bars downtown, but those of us who'd got married had started to gravitate inevitably over to home parties. A new group had formed. There was Kieran from Texas and his wife Takako. They'd first met at *The Red Zed*. Then there was Tracey, one of Douglas's angels, and her husband, Akira. Any guesses where they met? That's right, and it had been none other than Mayu who'd introduced them. Oh, and we already met Odie and Risako, Kumamoto's celebrity couple. Now we had kids crawling around, so to speak. There were several other families who'd join us and it was undeniably nice to be a part of a group of reassuringly normal people, not exactly clinging together even if it sometimes felt that way, but it was a calm oasis away from the relentlessly changing bar scene. And what did we have in common more than anything else? We were The Red Zed Family. Mayu and Takumi had been frequent members of the fledgling group; her laughter was one of the defining sounds of those get-togethers. But then she stopped showing up at our house parties. She was not to be seen in the bar. She'd taken indefinite leave. She seemed to have disappeared completely. What was wrong? My wife met her, said she'd started suffering from depression, no doubt triggered by her Daddy's bankruptcy. It fit in with her personality which never seemed too far from manic. Those who party too hard risk the biggest fall.

And then a year later we heard she had another boyfriend, Hiroshi. That name didn't ring any bells. When she turned up at Kieran's party that September evening with her new beau, the face was also one we'd never seen before. Quick introductions were made, and Hiroshi - a resolutely nondescript, inoffensive sort - definitely didn't appear too comfortable suddenly faced with this gaggle of Gaijin and screaming babies in the same place.

"What's the attraction then, Mayu?" we asked, as discreetly as possible. "Doesn't exactly seem your type."

"He's fucking rich."

What other answer was there going to be? We refrained from asking if she'd jump-started Hiroshi too. Maybe she had other moves up her expensive sleeves?

Hiroshi may not have been too taken with us, but he was an angel for Mayu, he was her protector. Mayu didn't seem to show the slightest affection to her new man whenever we saw them together -

this was not so often now, Hiroshi unsurprisingly usually preferring to avoid our parties.

In fact the next time we would see them was at their wedding. AFW, another fucking wedding, her phrase not mine. For her, it was basically a stage she simply had to pass through on the way to securing her financial security as Hiroshi's wife. His motives were the source of much speculation amongst us: Could you imagine being married to Mayu?

The Japanese have coined the expression *kekkon binbo* - literally "wedding poor" - referring to the fact that if you are invited to wedding then instead of sweating over a gift list, you simply have to pay the bride and groom $300. That's per person. No wonder couples rarely attend weddings together. Most people go through a wedding rush in their late twenties severely denting their spending power, giving rise to the term, and while we could hardly begrudge Mayu for getting married, there did seem something slightly odd about forking out $600 for our friend who was going down the path of wedded bliss for such cynical reasons. Or maybe I was just being unduly stingy.

In a strange kind of way, Mayu in her predictably splendid wedding dress - the exorbitant price of which she must have gleefully repeated a dozen times - actually shone less than she had done in her "business suit" at the City Hall. Some kind of spark was missing. She was showing neither the unrestrained joy of the besotted bride, nor the nerves of the couple who'd stressed themselves out to the max in meticulously planning every detail of their special day.

She'd obviously spent a lot of time and effort on her eyeliner and lipstick, which were most definitely not those of the typical young bride; but this, being Mayu, was hardly surprising. Beyond the make-up, it was a remarkably conventional affair. Everything passed off quite uneventfully. It wasn't one of the more memorable weddings I'd attended, but no complaints. Mayu was now a wife, so I could only assume it was mission safely accomplished.

We saw even less of her after that. We rarely went out, and neither did she. The generational shift in the Gaijin community was well and truly underway. Most of us were by now drowning in child-rearing duties, the occasions when we did go out to *Jake's* inevitably leading to little more than the bittersweet realization that the average age of customers was a good decade younger than ourselves. It's always with melancholy that most of us notice the signs of the passing of time, when the noisiest talking and laughing is coming from the new arrivals, and watching them merely conjures up the ghosts of our younger selves.

One sunny spring day, having dropped off my younger daughter in her brand new kindergarten, I was cycling happily around the city, suddenly even happier to chance upon a pleasingly proportioned female waiting at the traffic light. I started braking much earlier than I normally would, the better to appreciate this serendipitous moment. Then, pulling up next to her, I was aware of her turning her head toward me, which I didn't reciprocate, possibly guiltily aware that I'd already spent too much time admiring the rear part of her body.

"Peter!" said a familiar voice and I was astounded to find myself talking to Mayu.

"Oh, hi. You're looking good Mayu," I said, meaning: *Holy shit I'd forgotten how hot you were!*

"How's Hiroshi?" I asked, quickly regaining composure, and aware that I hadn't seen him at all since the wedding two years earlier. Working hard, apparently. It had probably been the best part of a year since Mayu had last been to one of our parties too.

"Never seem to see you out these days?"

"No alcohol. Doctor's orders. I'm not allowed to mix the medication with alcohol. And parties aren't much fucking fun for me without a drink." The "fucking" was merrily thrown in there without any particularly venomous meaning, just out of pure habit in fact, but I felt sorry for her. Mayu without a cocktail in hand, even there at the traffic light, didn't seem right, kind of like any party without Mayu's laughter seemed to be missing something.

Maybe not surprisingly she hadn't exactly found marital bliss. It had been pretty obvious - explicitly stated in fact - that money was the only thing that Mayu had expected from the marriage. But even if she still seemed in pretty good spirits when I bumped into her, things were definitely on a downhill trajectory and at a barbecue six months later I heard her latest news from Tracey.

"Have you seen Mayu? She's changed her medication and she's gained quite a bit of weight."

"Really? That's funny, I bumped into her back in April and she was looking great." I spared Tracey the details of the curves of her hips which deliciously popped back into my mind.

"Great" was a word that nobody could use to describe her the next time we met. True to Tracey's warnings, she had indeed ballooned considerably. She was out with us - that was a good thing - but the Mayu of old was not home. Everything about her suggested that the person inside had changed as much as she had externally. Her propensity to crack jokes and throw out outrageous insults had all but disappeared. As we talked to her, we noted that even if she was hardly dishing out compliments about Hiroshi, then at least she wasn't quite as dismissive about her husband as used to be the case. It seemed to be a more general apathy that had set in.

"Fucking boring," she said when asked about what she'd been doing of late. No hint of a laugh this time either, nor an invitation to guess the cost of her new larger clothes. Just constant drags on her menthol cigarettes and slurps of the Diet Coca-Cola that had become her most faithful companions.

"Went to England," she announced, at Tracey's birthday party six months later. Much more upbeat this time.

"What, like a honeymoon?"

She gave a rather withering look as if the whole idea of going anywhere with Hiroshi - now always referred to as "hus" - was preposterous. He was working of course. No rest for the wicked. It was unlikely that there had ever been any suggestion that he might accompany her.

She'd gone alone, presumably at least with her husband's blessing, and the trip certainly seemed to have done her some good. It was a little like the Mayu of old now that she had a story to tell - there were traces of the fun bar-girl we used to know - but in her present state her tale took on a slightly more sinister shade. She said she'd booked a room in a very "fucking" nice hotel, but apparently there was no "fucking" mini-bar. This was not good for a girl who needed her daily six pack of coke. And so, she added with a gleeful peel of laughter, she'd upgraded at considerable expense - care of hus's credit card - to a room with mini-bar, which she'd promptly filled with her favourite Diet Coke. She laughed at her foolishness, enjoying the sounds of the huge figures she was throwing around. While it was nice to see glimpses of the familiar crazy young Mayu still lurking somewhere within, our encouraging giggles couldn't mask the worrying sensation that this was not necessarily a good thing, especially once you stopped to think about how much money Hiroshi was paying for his nutty wife.

Wasn't she playing a dangerous game? What on earth would happen to her if he divorced her, and really why on earth didn't he do exactly that? When you even thought about it for a few seconds, which we frequently did, what did he actually get out of the marriage? None of us could ever come up with any answer. There were patently no love sparks flying between them and there never had been. In the absence of children - whether this was by design or by accident was unclear, but you sensed that Mayu had never really entertained the idea of being a Mama - they had acquired a pet dachshund, Ziggy, who had very much been the focus of Mayu's life for some time now. But was one dippy dog enough?

We continued seeing her occasionally. To be honest she'd become a mild embarrassment, a puffed-up caricature of her former self. Her stories now were invariably of the oversize dresses she bought monthly on internet shopping. You kind of worried what was going to come out of her mouth next; she never made any effort to reduce her swearing amid the growing army of young children. She seemed to live on an exclusive diet of anti-depressants, cigarettes and Diet Coke. How sad it was to see what Mayu had turned into as she approached her 40th birthday. If she had been getting looks most of her life for her beauty and outrageous fashion, now it was increasingly hard not to stare at her in horror. A real life warning of how things could go upside down if you weren't very, very careful. A sign that maybe it was in fact worth clinging together. Was her deterioration really so inevitable after the onset of her Dad's misfortunes, which apparently had ended in his death the previous year, but which Mayu never mentioned to us?

She needed a pet project to throw herself into, and when she found it, it caught all of us by surprise. A wedding invitation was lying in the mailbox one morning.

Mayu was going to get married again.

No, this didn't mean Hiroshi was being cast aside; it would be the two of them walking down the aisle a second time.

It appeared she had been unsatisfied by the first one. In rushing to the altar, she had in fact missed the opportunity to shine as she would have liked. Then she'd seen some story on the internet about a "wedding vow renewal ceremony" and saw that this would give her the chance to choreograph the whole event to her precise wishes, the way they should have done it the first time.

"What a load of tosh," I thought. Every day seems to throw up some bizarre new modern take on tradition, but "renewal of vows"? Getting married to the same person again? Surely that's just for people who are envious of their divorced friends having a chance to relive the joy of putting on a wedding dress. Jesus, people really do get jealous of anything. "It's not fair! I still love my partner, so I don't get the chance to walk down the aisle again. Wait - how about if there was a new-fangled ceremony which would allow me to bask in that special moment one more time?"

It was not one of humankind's greatest ideas, I felt. But at the same time, blowing aside the initial cynicism, then given the outrageously high divorce rate, just maybe the fact of being able to survive each other's company for 20 or 30 years really was worth celebrating. In Mayu's case however, how long were we talking about? Five years? Certainly you felt Hiroshi deserved a medal for having reached even this modest milestone with an increasingly demanding, not to say deranged, wife · but did they really have to involve everyone else?

Well yes, apparently they did. If the idea had started as a germ somewhere in the depths of Mayu's atypical Japanese brain, then as she worked through the idea it took on an increasingly bizarre turn.

Mayu and Hiroshi were still sufficiently rooted in reality to know that there was no way their friends · Mayu's friends that is; there was a notable lack of Hiroshi's friends, colleagues or even a single relative, come to think of it · would be willing to fork out the full price of a wedding invitation just to humour her rather outlandish idea. Hiroshi offered · was forced · to foot the bill for the entire ridiculous thing. Even knowing I didn't have to pay, I had decidedly mixed views about the whole project. But then again, who's going to say no to some free food and drink?

On the day of the wedding, we found ourselves gathered once more at the chapel. In spite of it being the exact same place they'd got married five years earlier, it felt like very unfamiliar territory. There was a foreboding that something off the wall was going to happen.

First, Mayu came in, I'd like to say resplendent in her gown, but everyone's attention was drawn to the outrageously excessive make-up. She'd really out-done herself this time, combining a touch of The Cure's Robert Smith, Lullaby-era, with, more worryingly, overtones of Beatrice Dalle's unhinged character in *Betty Blue*, the scene towards the end of the movie when she chops off her hair and smears lip-stick all over her face in reaction to losing her baby.

She was guided down the aisle by her erstwhile employer in *The Red Zed* · drawing the attention of all those present to the fact that her father was no longer alive · to be handed over to her husband upon reaching the altar. Cosmetics aside, so far, so normal. But at this point, things took a sharp turn away from tradition. And here, you just didn't know whether to laugh or just turn away, for they had chosen to act out a scene which in movie terms was exactly half way between Tarantino and Ben Stiller.

"Do you take this woman to be your lawful wedded wife?" asked the priest.

"No," said Hiroshi, very reasonably, but somewhat unexpectedly.

There was a surprised murmur among the gathered guests. Had the guy finally seen the light? Could have saved himself several thousand dollars if he'd realized a few months earlier. But no; the whole thing was scripted. The Best Man picked up the violin case which had been sitting on the floor, set it down on the altar, opened it and took out a machine gun. Picking this up and pointing it at Hiroshi's head, the priest repeated the question. This time Hiroshi, sensibly deciding that it would be better to say yes than get his brains blown out, uttered "I do," which was greeted with joy by those around the altar, in on the joke, and with considerable bemusement by those who hadn't been party to the rehearsals. Back down the aisle they walked, Mayu smiling defiantly at each of us, Hiroshi's face as inscrutable as always: Husband and Wife. Again.

"What the hell was that about?" was just too obvious a question - I could only assume that was the reason why nobody asked it, even though each and every one of us was thinking it. Why was Hiroshi willing to spend so much money on what was effectively just Mayu's big joke? What in fact were us guests doing? Where did this leave the marriage now? Would there be a similar renewal of vows ceremony every five years?

If Mayu had always seemed more at home with foreigners than "fucking boring Japanese", her screwball take on life being more readily accepted by those crazy free-thinking folk from overseas, then she had just taken things to a whole new level. Ten years earlier it might have been hilarious, but here's the thing: All our outrageous Gaijin behaviour, such as it had ever been, had long since gone south and we were now well and truly sunk knee-deep into mid-life ordinariness at least as dull as Mayu's not-so-beloved compatriots.

That might have been Mayu's final gift, to let us know - cheers for that, Mayu! - that we really were as boring as we feared. The wheels in her brain may have been turning more slowly, the words and jokes less forthcoming than before, but here she was, able to well and truly show us up. It was quite a coup that she had pulled, no less. None of which made it any more pleasant to imagine what the hell would happen from here, although you probably didn't want to think about it too much, knowing that it wouldn't be a happy ending.

I think it's true to say that actually nothing much of note happened thereafter. A few of us re-assessed our relationship with

Mayu, slightly aghast at the thought of being dragged into her next joke. But this time, she'd exhausted her ideas. There was to be no second hoorah. The wedding farce had apparently satisfied whatever had been left unfulfilled by the first one. Now she never came out with us, choosing to spend all her time at home in her 7th floor apartment, communicating with everyone - her husband too, it appeared, even though he was in the room next door - by Facebook, and even then there were only ever uploaded pictures of Ziggy, or expensive dresses. Our invitations to her - honestly speaking out of a sense of duty rather than any deep desire to meet her - went largely unreplied. My wife and other friends occasionally went round to see her for a cup of tea, helped her with things that needed doing, but invariably came back with reports of how she was getting slower and slower as her weight kept increasing. Her diet of anti-depressants was just sucking out the last traces of her zest and humour. There were no further trips to Europe - she seldom ever set foot outside her apartment - and thankfully no further wedding invitations. Once a year - seemingly that was all she had the energy for - there would be a rant on Facebook about how fucking boring life was.

It was not good. How was it possible for Mayu to get back to that place she'd inhabited before? Why was Hiroshi still with her? What would she do if Hiroshi decided to go through with the divorce which it appeared he was in fact contemplating, that is if we could believe Mayu's only vaguely coherent ramblings? These were all questions which just seemed to stay absolutely constant and which it was preferable to choose to ignore. Hadn't we been asking the very same things for years now?

The last time I saw her, at my wife's 50th birthday party, she was the same as she had been for many years now. It was like talking to Grandma. Stay on certain safe topics, try not to confuse her. Ziggy: OK. Recent clothing purchases: OK. Do your fifteen minute duty talking to her and then excuse yourself and pass her on to someone else.

Three months later she posted her declaration. Life was awful, she was sick of everything, she'd decided to jump. It was the only choice left.

"Did you see what Mayu wrote?" asked my wife.

No, I hadn't. I checked and it was pretty wild. But it wasn't the first time. She'd written similar stuff before, lashing out at the unfairness of life which had seen her - young, rich and pretty - sink to an old, bloated, unloved and hopeless object of pity.

These were entirely justified rants. Life had been cruel to Mayu, at least everybody could agree on that. Our main hope was always that she still had enough imagination to somehow conjure up another project, find some reason to view the future with an optimism which to us on the outside looked frankly unlikely.

Her comments provoked a few worried replies from her friends scattered around the world, many of them unable to understand the transformation Mayu had gone through, not having witnessed her ballooning growth first-hand and still remembering her simply as that fun, crazy barmaid. Sally back in the US posted: "Can somebody call Mayu?" She'd tried from Texas but hadn't been able to get through. My wife succeeded, managed to talk to her, said she seemed much calmer than she had in her post. I was out with a couple of friends in the morning, both of whom knew Mayu quite well. "She's just letting off steam," we said. "It's a cycle. Talk about Ziggy, complain about "Hus", threaten to kill herself." Like sun, cloud and rain, all bound to follow one another in a pattern forever.

That afternoon we happened to have planned a party, the usual crowd, the Red Zed family. The kids were all crowded into the tatami room, busy playing some video game, while the adults sat out in the garden, cracking open the beers, nattering away. What do you think about Mayu? we said. What can you do, what can anybody do, we replied. It's a shame things have turned out the way they seem to have, but at least she has Ziggy, how she loves that stupid dog. Only a couple of months ago she'd talked about taking French lessons, she used to study a few years ago. Maybe she was even planning a trip to Paris? Wow, poor Hiroshi. Hope he doesn't give her free reign on his credit card · how many millions of yen would she be able to spend in Paris? Just how much longer was he willing to put up with her eccentricities? What exactly was keeping them together?

The dog, of course. Ziggy: Mayu's pride and joy. It was always Ziggy, Ziggy-chan – "Little Ziggy". A lot riding upon that unsuspecting, gormless mutt. As long as Ziggy was around, we didn't need to worry. Ziggy was not so young any more, but he'd be good for another three or four years. Then some serious shit was going to hit the fan, that much seemed pretty certain, but luckily we didn't have to worry about all that quite yet.

Hmm, *Ziggy-chan*. Why did that name seem to harken back to an alternate unlived past? What were these odd images blowing around in my head, echoes of a bleak and hostile land shrouded in mystery and brimming with the promise of countless adventures? A place where woolly hamsters scampered among the roaark plants. And tattooed nomads battled the elements in their daily struggle for survival, while dark, shadowy beasts lurked behind every tree. Where was all this coming from? Very strange.

It was a good evening. We talked a bit about *Bohemian Rhapsody* · the movie, that is. A few of us had seen it and we put a few songs on. This was the safe crowd; I wasn't going to get an earful for singing along to *Crazy Little Thing Called Love* with these guys. It's always fun to hang out with people you know, but it's great to know when you've got a real tight set of friends, when your kids start playing with their kids and it all feels natural, and nobody's complaining about not wanting to be there and one evening is nowhere near enough to catch up on our news, our kids' news. Something about being Gaijin together in this country seems to intensify any insignificant moment into something slightly more precious in a way hard to explain to non-Gaijin. People you know you probably wouldn't hang around with in your home country suddenly end up being irreplaceable best mates and each subsequent party just goes to reinforce that feeling. Yes, it had been a very satisfying evening all round really, a bit of a shame it had been slightly spoiled by worrying unduly about Mayu, but that's just her. No, actually, it's not fair to put it all down to her, everybody has their problems and that's what groups of friends are for; it's the nature of things that some will have more than their fair share of shit to deal with, but the most important thing really is to stick together and remember why you became friends in the first place, understand that the good times are going to come with bad times. Those "stay with each other through thick and thin, through sickness and health" lines really shouldn't be limited to marriage vows, they should apply to any group of friends wanting to live up to that name, and you don't need a machine gun pointing at you at a farcical wedding to make you realize how everybody needs somebody and how the older you get, the more important it is to be there for each other and not to run away and become a recluse no matter how tempting it may feel. Getting older with a bunch of mates may just be the most important thing there is in life, whether you're in a foreign land or not.

"Thanks for hosting," I said to Kieran and Takako, waving through the car window at all the kids. My, how quickly they grow! Little Emma really isn't so little any more. High school next year for our eldest.

"You do realize that it's possible we might be grandparents in another five years," I said to Asami as we pulled away. Within our small group we'd had our upheavals. Odie's family used to make it to every one of our gatherings. It was still hard to believe that they were no longer here. "Odie: The Last Man to leave Japan," I mouthed, shaking my head. But at the end of the day, it was all part of that crazy little thing called life. Driving home that evening, I suddenly felt happier than ever in my adopted home, listening to the kids singing along to the Queen Greatest Hits CD in our car. *Play The Game* came on, always one of my favourites and in many ways my unofficial soundtrack. That's what I'd been doing for the last 25 years, playing the game of life. In Japan. It was wonderful to think about our daughters' own game, just beginning. Yes, Kumamoto had been good to me and good to my family. I wouldn't have wished for any other way.

And just as we were turning into our driveway, cursing the fact that it was almost nine o'clock already - why did it always get so late so quickly? - shooting orders off to the kids to have a quick bath and get ready for bed, another busy week ahead, Asami's phone rang.

It was Hiroshi.

He was at the hospital. Could Asami go there?

I didn't need to know anything else. Hiroshi never rang us.

Trying to suppress the rising sense of foreboding, I chose instead to marvel at how impeccable the timing was. Didn't cause us to leave the party early. Didn't wake us in the middle of the night. For that at least I was immensely grateful.

Asami headed straight off to the hospital while I made sure the kids did their bedtime routine as quickly as possible. "School tomorrow, girls!" I reminded them, even if for me school suddenly seemed to have lost its importance and maybe my habitual gruntings about them missing their bedtime yet again had lost some of their usual urgency.

Once they'd finally been put to rest, I switched on the TV and laid back on the sofa. I just couldn't get Queen songs out of my head: *Killer Queen, Don't Stop Me Now, Save Me, You're My Best Friend, Let Us Cling Together (Te o Toriatte), Somebody To Love, Another One Bites The Dust.* Damn, was there a single song that didn't seem to have some relevance? And how often do people say that about Queen? I flicked through the channels, then checked the internet sports news, tried reading a few pages of my *History of The French Revolution*, but nothing registered. I was just going through the motions, killing time. Asami finally called, but I didn't need to speak to her to confirm what

I already knew. Mayu had jumped. Nobody survives a fall from a 7th floor apartment. Mayu had looked into the future and realized it was a future where she would become less and less able to take things into her own hands. This was maybe her last opportunity to do things on her own terms, and she'd done it.

She did it! Jesus Christ, she actually did it. You could hardly say you couldn't have seen it coming, but even so...

I could see her looking down on everybody and with one last peel of her bonkers laughter announcing, "I fucking did it!"

I could hear Ziggy, tongue out, barking accusingly at us. "What the hell were you doing, guys? Kind of passing the buck big time, no? Did you really think one stupid dog could have stopped all this? That's a lot of pressure on a simple pooch."

And it's true, it's absolutely true. Hand on my heart, I'm sorry, Ziggy. Please forgive us.

But you have to realize this, Ziggy: The Mayu that you knew, the one that jumped, wasn't the real Mayu. We were just kidding ourselves when we looked at this large lady with a vague facial resemblance to the girl we once knew and assumed it was the same person.

It wasn't.

That girl may have been crazy but she would never have done anything like this.

The real tragedy was that the old Mayu was already dead, had been for years, but nobody had ever mourned her.

It was two funerals she needed, not two stupid weddings.

So fuck you Mayu for going ahead and deciding to jump. We really were all there for you: Hiroshi, your old Red Zed friends, Ziggy. You really didn't need to do it.

But at the same time, we understand. We really fucking do.

R.I.P. Mayu.